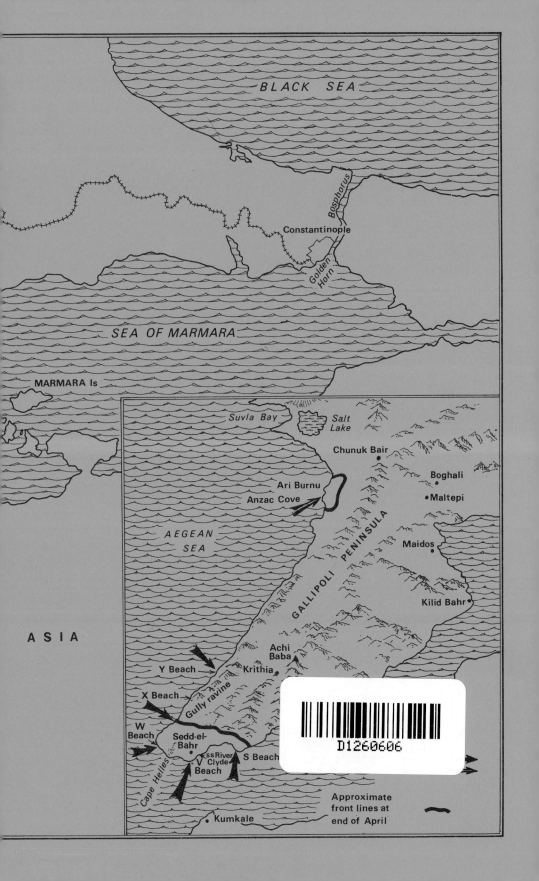

# HELL'S
# FOUNDATIONS

# HELL'S FOUNDATIONS

## A Town, its Myths and Gallipoli

Geoffrey Moorhouse

Hodder & Stoughton
LONDON SYDNEY AUCKLAND

The author and the publishers would like to thank
Mrs Nicolete Gray and The Society of Authors on
behalf of the Laurence Binyon Estate for permission to
quote from *For the Fallen (September 1914)* by
Laurence Binyon on page 157.


*British Library Cataloguing in Publication Data*

Moorhouse, Geoffrey
    Hell's foundations: A town, its myths and Gallipoli.
    I. Title
    942.7083

    ISBN 0-340-43044-3

Published by Hodder and Stoughton,
a division of Hodder and Stoughton Ltd,
Mill Road, Dunton Green, Sevenoaks, Kent TN13 2YA
Editorial Office: 47 Bedford Square, London WC1B 3DP


Photoset by Rowland Phototypesetting Ltd
Bury St Edmunds, Suffolk
Design by Tim Higgins
Printed in Great Britain by
BPCC Hazells Ltd, Member of BPCC Ltd,

In Memory of
William Enoch Hoyle
Lance-Corporal, 1st/5th Battalion
The Lancashire Fusiliers
and my Grandfather

# Contents

# Illustrations

*Sources*
[1] Bury Library
[2] Royal Regiment of Fusiliers (Lancashire HQ Museum)
[3] *Illustrated London News*
[4] British Library
[5] Bury Parish Church
[6] The author
[7] *Bury Times*

*At the sign of triumph*
*Satan's host doth flee;*
*On then, Christian soldiers,*
*On to victory.*
*Hell's foundations quiver*
*At the shout of praise;*
*Brothers, lift your voices,*
*Loud your anthems raise.*

Words by S. Baring-Gould
Tune (ST GERTRUDE) by Sir Arthur Sullivan

# PART ONE

## AUTHOR'S NOTE

The vigilant reader of this book will sooner or later come to the conclusion that the figures given for recruitment and for casualties leave a great deal to be desired. They are often manifestly incomplete and they sometimes seem to be inconsistent, though I hope they are no worse in these respects than in other books referring to the Great War. The fact is that, in the second decade of the twentieth century, the craft of statistics was crude and often slipshod. Some sources used the word "casualties" to include all who had been killed, wounded, or were missing; others referred only to the dead in this way. Both usages will be encountered in *Hell's Foundations*, and I have simply tried in each case to make the position clear. Recruiting figures, too, are sadly imperfect, so that it is impossible to say with any precision how many men from Bury went to war between 1914 and 1918. It is, however, known that by May 1915 – that is, in the first nine months of a conflict that lasted over four years – 7,000 men from the town had volunteered to serve in the Army or the Navy, most of them in the Lancashire Fusiliers. The total population was approximately 50,000 at the time, and wholesale conscription was yet to come, in 1916. A particular difficulty facing anyone who tries to log the progress of the local Territorial battalions of the Fusiliers in the First World War is that all the relevant records were destroyed in the Second, when Home Guard ammunition exploded in the Drill Hall on the penultimate night of 1942. This set the place on fire, disastrously for the regimental and any other historian.

# INTRODUCTION
# A Mythology Explored

The most haunting agony remains Gallipoli. The First World War would see even greater bloodshed before it was done; on the Somme, around Ypres, especially at Passchendaele, and elsewhere. But no other battle or campaign fought between 1914 and 1918 has ever been remembered quite as tenaciously as the ill-fated Allied expedition to the Dardanelles. No other date, with the exception of Armistice Day, has been marked quite so steadfastly in so many places as April 25, 1915, in whose dawn the first landings on the Gallipoli peninsula were made. Few military events in any war have continued to nag at posterity with their horrors, their heroisms, their pathos, their utter futility, so long after they occurred. It is more than three quarters of a century since the Gallipoli campaign was finished, and it still grips the imagination of populations at opposite ends of the earth. There may not now be a single survivor left alive and yet, in two countries at least, thousands will gather every time April 25 comes round, for a remembrance that is partly celebration and partly lament. No one who has been in Sydney or Auckland, or in the small towns of the Riverina or the South Island when the Dawn Service takes place, can ever have forgotten the experience, can ever have been in any doubt about Anzac Day's continuing potency.

There are many elements in this mythology. There is above all grief at the loss of life and for the young men who were mutilated for the rest of their days; at the scale of these losses, these disfigurements. Well over half a million were killed or wounded in just thirty-seven weeks, and although these figures were to be overshadowed later by the casualties of Flanders and France, they were appalling when measured against anything that had happened in conflicts before. In two and three quarter years of the Boer War the comparable figure is lower than 150,000 – and that includes the highest estimate for civilians who died of disease in the concentration camps. The Gallipoli legend also depends on the sheer bravery and stubbornness demonstrated by Allied troops and Turks alike in the most dreadful conditions. These changed from blistering summer heat to lethal snowstorms and floods later in the year, though the survivors swore that nothing was worse than the filth and the flies that plagued them with dysentery as the bodies began to mount in no man's land. "We were all lousy and we couldn't stop shitting," said a veteran of Gallipoli in his old age. "We wept, not because we were frightened but because we were so dirty."

And yet in these vile circumstances men endured even more terrible things, like shellfire and bayonet charges and the likelihood that if you left the shelter of a pestilential trench you would die within seconds, or at the very least be maimed by a sniper's bullet or a slash of machine-gun fire. They spent days and weeks struggling to advance up a hill, reached the top and were flung back, to begin the struggle again; and this they would do repeatedly until the humiliation of the Allies was completed with the withdrawal of the last of their forces on January 9, 1916. Somehow they managed to stay cheerful for some of this time, and they even showed great tenderness in the midst of all the brutality. They would risk their lives to rescue a comrade lying wounded between the opposing lines and they would comfort him gently until he died. They were also able to transcend enmity, to offer succour sometimes to an injured foe: there is evidence that both sides behaved honourably in this respect. But the troops shocked some of their officers by their callous indifference once a man became a corpse, when he might be regarded as a useful addition to the protective parapet, or a potential source of extra nourishment. "Did he have his rations on him, sergeant?" asked one hungry Englishman when a friend was killed. The German Colonel Kannengiesser, attached to the Turkish Army, one day saw two of his men contentedly perched on three bodies while they ate their lunch.

There was a terrible poignancy in the losses borne by the Australians and the New Zealanders in particular, for these soldiers came from young lands and the blood they shed at Gallipoli symbolised the youth of so many who were butchered there. It could be seen as more innocent blood more nobly given, too, for were not these colonials in the war only as an act of imperial deference to a Motherland that did not deserve such generosity? These troops had earlier fought for Great Britain's interests in China during the Boxer Rebellion, and in the Sudan against the Dervishes, and in South Africa against the Boers, and any gratitude that might have been felt in London on these occasions was never expressed with more than passing warmth. Rather there was a general assumption that colonial loyalty to any imperial cause was in the natural order of things, something that could be totally relied upon. Nor did this reflex die at Gallipoli. Within hours of the British declaring war on Germany in 1939, Australia and New Zealand followed suit on their own initiatives. "Where Britain stands," said Prime Minister Savage in Wellington that day, "we stand. Where she goes, we go!"* But something did change after the Dardanelles and 1915. The men of the Australian and New Zealand Army Corps won such renown there in their own right – not as Britain's auxiliaries – that they caused people at home and overseas to see the two countries in a different light. They gave the world a new word, Anzac, which would always afterwards stand for a peculiarly Antipodean form of gallantry, devoid of European rigidities but well endowed with more attractive characteristics like the ability to improvise, the willingness to try anything once, and something they called mateship which could disturbingly ignore the priorities of rank. They gave their own people a pride and a confidence they had not known before; which, before the next generation had passed, would enable them to dispense totally with London's patronage. Gallipoli was in every sense a blooding of the Anzac lands.

It was also an important step towards another nationhood. Turkey, so long regarded as the Sick Man of Europe, was still a ramshackle entity even after the Sultan Abdul Hamid was deposed by a group of young officers in 1908; "scandalous, crumbling, decrepit, penniless Turkey", in Winston Churchill's withering view. Among, Enver Pasha's Young Turks who were responsible for the overthrow, was Mustafa Kemal, an early rebel against the Sultan but not a particularly prominent one. He had been sidelined from the mainstream of the new politics by more ambitious men, and few of his compatriots had heard of him before the Great War began. He had been a military attaché in Sofia but in 1915, as a half-colonel of thirty-four, he was given command of the 19th Division, a promotion that was to change his life and eventually transform his native land. He was not thought to be much of a tactician, but he

* Michael W. Savage (1872–1940). Prime Minister of New Zealand from 1935 to his death.

was extremely brave and his particular genius was for rousing in his troops their very considerable reserves of Turkish ferocity. On one occasion he told them, "I do not expect any of us would not rather die than repeat the shameful story of the Balkan War. But if there are such men among us we should at once lay hands upon them and set them up in line to be shot." On another, his order of the day included the following sentiment, "There is no going back a single step. It is our duty to save our country, and we must acquit ourselves honourably and nobly. I must remind all of you that to seek rest or comfort now is to deprive the nation of its rest and comfort for ever." It was by threatening them with execution if they would not be patriotic that he kindled the fighting spirit even the Anzacs could not subdue, the stubbornness the invaders could scarcely even budge. It was Kemal's command that held up the Allied advance time and time again and finally brought it to a halt. He had left the peninsula for other duties before the campaign was over, but he was already known throughout the land as Saviour of Gallipoli. With this reputation he acquired a more vital authority after the Allies had finished picking over the remains of the Ottoman Empire at the end of the war. He it was who raised the standard of revolt against the Greeks, who had been awarded Smyrna in the disbursement of loot, and he it was who drove them out. On that triumph he proceeded to build his uniquely secular Islamic state, for which his people hailed him as Father of the Turks, Kemal Ataturk.

For them, Gallipoli was a deliverance at least as great as the one the British experienced in the next war when their army was rescued from the beaches of Dunkirk. It achieved the status of myth for Anatolian peasants and boatmen round the Golden Horn, just as much as for any of the invaders who fought over it. Here was yet another legend in an already mythical place, for this campaign was waged beside the Dardanelles, which was the ancient Hellespont. The sun rose each morning over Troy, whose ruins were visible across the straits to anyone looking through field glasses from the foot of the Gallipoli peninsula. Bright young men in the Royal Naval Division went to this war with copies of the *Iliad* in their knapsacks, itching to see where Homer's epic was set. As the great Allied expeditionary force sailed towards its awful destiny, officers who had been schooled in Latin and Greek could be heard trying to fire their men with enthusiasm for the old tales, which were shortly to be given the added attraction of an identifiable topography. Not only had the Trojan legends occurred just over there, they pointed out, but many other tremendous happenings had taken place hereabouts. Xerxes had built his bridge of boats across the Hellespont in 480 BC, when he came out of Persia to invade Europe; and Alexander the Great had crossed this water in the other direction, on his way to conquests as far afield as India. This was where Leander swam from one shore to the other to be with the priestess Hero, and where he was finally drowned in a storm. It was where Lord Byron had celebrated the old love story by imitating Leander's swim in 1810. There was no end to the heroic and literary associations of the Dardanelles. There would be something grotesquely appropriate in Sub-Lieutenant Rupert Brooke's death on his way to this war, two days before the landings began; the romantic poet, looking forward to it all, randomly killed by something as improbable as a mosquito bite.

The writer Compton Mackenzie, who was to survive Gallipoli, was as susceptible as anyone to the Classical tradition, and his imagination transposed it most strikingly into the present, after watching some Anzacs bathing in the sea one day. "Much has been written of the splendid appearance of those Australian troops; but a splendid appearance seems to introduce somehow an atmosphere of the parade-ground. Such litheness and powerful grace did not want the parade-ground; that was to take it from the jungle to the circus. Their beauty, for it really was heroic, should have been celebrated in hexameters, not headlines. As a child I used to pore for hours over those illustrations of Flaxman for Homer and Virgil which simulated the effect of ancient pottery. There was not one of those glorious young men I saw that day who might not himself have been Ajax or Diomed, Hector or Achilles. Their almost complete nudity, their tallness and majestic simplicity of line, their rose-brown flesh burnt by the sun and purged of all grossness by the ordeal through which they were passing, all these united to create something as near to absolute beauty as I shall ever hope to see in this world . . ."

This was more eloquent than most eyewitness observations on Gallipoli that were destined to find their way into print. But Mackenzie was far from being the only European favourably impressed by the physique, by the vigour, by the bearing of the Australians and New Zealanders. Apart from a number of Regular Army officers who patronised them – as they patronised everybody in sight except their superiors – most of the British admired the colonial troops, for qualities other than, as well as, their fighting ability. The renown of the Anzacs was spread by their comrades and their enemies much more than it was by themselves. The British had shown a decent respect for such men long before the Great War – were they not "sons of Empire" after all? – but after it, respect was heightened into admiration, though often cautiously expressed. There is little evidence that similar feelings were ever entertained by the Anzacs for them, either during or after the war.

Instead, downright hostility was the response as soon as the scale of the Gallipoli disaster became apparent. The Anzacs had rushed to the colours enthusiastically when war was declared and had been transported across the world in expectation of an easy success. This was to have been an imperial victory they would gladly have shared provided the cost was not too high; but the failure was seen as a catastrophe for which the British were wholly responsible at the colonial expense. It is impossible to refute the essence of that complaint. The plan to take Turkey out of the war by forcing a naval passage of the Dardanelles and then to send troops up the peninsula until Constantinople surrendered, was conceived in London, and its bungling was entirely the responsibility of British warlords. Churchill was to take much of the blame, not only because the great vision was his in the first place, pressed upon the rest of Herbert Asquith's War Council by force of character. As First Lord of the Admiralty he also had the overconfidence of supreme arrogance: "a good army of 50,000 and seapower; that's the end of the Turkish menace," he wrote in September 1914. But there were others who shared his dangerous optimism. At the War Office, where Lord Kitchener was in charge, they were estimating the total casualties in landing troops on the peninsula and then in capturing it, to be no more than 5,000; an assessment made in early April 1915. There were other weaknesses in the imperial planning long before battle was joined. While the First Lord of the Admiralty was obsessed with this adventure in the eastern Mediterranean, Kitchener was much more interested in gaining successes on the Western Front. Meanwhile, the Secretary of State for India was preoccupied with the campaign in Mesopotamia, which affected the Suez Canal and lines of communication to Bombay and Delhi; and the Colonial Secretary's energies were focused on the German threat in East and West Africa.

Muddle and even worse continued in the Dardanelles itself. The combined operation between sailors and soldiers was left to the respective commanders to arrange, but the views of General Sir Ian Hamilton, Commander-in-Chief of the Mediterranean Expeditionary Force, and Vice-Admiral Sir John de Robeck, C.-in-C. of the Eastern Mediterranean Fleet, did not always coincide. Hamilton operated under the additional handicap of being supplied with intelligence about local Turkish dispositions which had not been revised since 1903, though much later information was available but had simply not been passed on. There was an early naval disaster when one French and two British battleships were sunk in a minefield on March 18, though picket boats had been out the previous night looking for mines. That could be counted a typical misfortune of war. But incompetence is the only reason why the troops were not landed at Gallipoli until sixty-five days after the naval bombardment of Turkish positions began. The shelling had long ceased to be effective when the soldiers waded ashore, and the Turks had been given ample time to refortify and prepare for the amphibious assaults. The next eight and a half months were to be studded with failures like that, so glaring that almost at once a Royal Commission was appointed to investigate them. By 1919 it had produced two reports, after interviewing every individual with some political or military responsibility for these events; with the exception of Lord Kitchener, who had been drowned when HMS *Hampshire* was sunk off Orkney in June 1916. The commissioners decided that the Gallipoli campaign should never have happened and that, on top of this, it was poorly directed in the field. They were impressed by only two things. One was the heroism of the troops. The other was the acumen and conduct of General Sir Charles Monro, who was brought from France to succeed Hamilton at the end of October, took the decision to evacuate the peninsula, and had it carried out with quite remarkable success.

No one, therefore, should be surprised at the bitterness of Australians and New Zealanders who suffered so much, so needlessly, from the inadequacy of men who conveyed to them a powerful impression of self-satisfied superiority. The bitterest comment, in fact, would be made by an Englishman, E. M. Forster, between the two world wars, when imagining a conversation between two graves on Gallipoli. If they go to war again, says one, there will be more graves, but where will they dig them? The other replies; "There is still room over in Chanak. Also, it is well for a nation that would be great to scatter its graves all over the world. Graves in Ireland, graves in Irak, Russia, Persia, India, each with its inscription from the Bible or Rupert Brooke. When England thinks fit, she can launch an expedition to protect the sanctity of her graves, and can follow that by another expedition to protect the sanctity of the additional graves. That is what Lloyd George, prudent in counsels, and lion-hearted Churchill have planned. Churchill planned this expedition to Gallipoli, where I was killed. He planned the expedition to Antwerp, where my brother was killed. Then he said that Labour is not fit to govern. Rolling his eyes for fresh worlds, he saw Egypt, and fearing that peace might be established there, he intervened and prevented it. Whatever he undertakes is a success. He is Churchill the Fortunate, ever in office, and clouds of dead heroes attend him. Nothing for schools, nothing for the life of the body, nothing for the spirit. England cannot spare a penny for anything except her heroes' graves."

Less understandable than the colonial bitterness directed at British war leaders and generals, was something close to contempt that the Anzacs appear often to have felt for ordinary British soldiers – for the privates, the corporals and the sergeants who fought and suffered on the peninsula, too; men who did not patronise the colonials, but who tended to look up to them as improved and emancipated versions of themselves. There was a very capable Australian war correspondent at Gallipoli, Charles Bean, who on August 29, 1915, made the following entry in his diary: "Our men have tremendous admiration for the little Gurkhas – they say they don't mind getting up against the NZs or Gurkhas – but they (and the NZ men, too) do not trust the Tommy – they all except the regular army, but they do not have the slightest confidence in Kitchener's army – nor have our officers – nor have I. The truth is that after 100 years of breeding in slums, the British race is not the same, and can't be expected to be the same, as in the days of Waterloo. It is breeding one fine class at the expense of all the rest. The only hope is that those puny narrow-chested little men may, if they come out to Australia or NZ or Canada, within two generations breed men again. England herself, unless she does something heroic, cannot hope to . . ."

A couple of weeks later, Bean returned to this theme: "Well, the problem of Gallipoli reduces itself to – why can't the British fight? Take one of these slum kids and turn him into a different man by nine or ten years of hard training, or even less – and put in a set of

NCOs over him who have will enough to make the *stickers* of the army – the percentage who go into action with their minds made up to stick, and who really make up the minds of the other ninety per cent who are simply going in to do what somebody else does; give him that training and those NCOs and he can fight like the 29th Division did. But in a year's training he can't be turned into a soldier because to tell the truth he's a very poor feeble specimen of a man – and it seems to be the British social formula to make sure that he sticks there. In a nation with only one class, it's in nobody's interest to keep anyone else in 'his place' – and his place is, from his birth, the best place he can get and keep. To my mind this war, as far as I have seen it, is just Britain's tomahawks coming home to roost ... They have neither the nerve, the physique, nor the spirit and self-control to fit them for soldiers ..."

On the day Bean was admiring the Gurkhas and despising the Tommies, Sergeant Francis Hardey was writing a letter home to New Zealand after an engagement up the Monash Gully. "We got pushed right off and had to retire, getting an awful gruelling going back. The stunt had been horribly bungled. What between mis-understandings, bad guides, and the reinforcements, we had a real good scare. The reinforcements were English – RMLI – and they let us down in a most disappointing way. We have had reason now, on several occasions, to be bitterly disappointed in our brothers from England. We ask ourselves 'Where is the Army for which England for generations had such pride?' To France and mostly under the sod, and these volunteers from rural England and from the huge mill towns are a disappointment to us Colonials who have had the Army held up to us as an example and pattern incomparable." Those English reinforcements were the Royal Marine Light Infan-try, whose initials the New Zealanders were wont to translate as Run My Lads Imshi, a clear imputation of cowardice. This was an impression that many Anzac survivors of Gallipoli would carry for the rest of their lives, to be passed on in extreme old age to anyone wishing to hear how things had been on the peninsula in 1915. It is relevant to note that the New Zealand war historian who quotes Sergeant Hardey's letter remarks that "The Royal Marines should not have been committed, and became scapegoats for a failure that was due to inadequate planning." He places the blame for the failed action on three officers commanding the Dominion's troops. Two of these were New Zealanders: the third was General Godley, the

Divisional Commander, an Anglo-Irishman who had been GOC in New Zealand from 1910 until the outbreak of war. The point is, however, that the rank and file of the Anzacs believed that the British soldiers were inferior.

"I still think about Gallipoli quite a bit," said a ninety-year-old from Invercargill to a man with a tape recorder one day. "It accomplished nothing. I remember the New Zealanders were taken from Anzac down to Cape Helles and ordered to charge across the Daisy Patch. That was just like going to commit suicide and that's what they did. Actually committed suicide by doing that. They were ordered to do it and they did it. But it was the silliest thing that ever was thought of. New Zealanders thought more of themselves after that. They didn't think so much of the British. The British let them down." Pity for the inadequate Tommies was about the most generous emotion such old men seemed capable of. Of that same action at the Daisy Patch, an octogenarian said: "What I most remember about the Cape Helles end of the peninsula is leaving our trenches. We were relieved in the middle of the night to go back to Anzac. A Lancashire battalion took over from us. Little kids, they seemed, about sixteen. And they were blubbering, crying their eyes out. Terrified. We tried to help them by saying those trenches were safe. They weren't, of course. We were just trying to soothe those kids. That was a fairly disillusioning experience." Yet another veteran had an almost identical recollection. "We were there two or three days until relieved by a very amateur lot of young British territorials in the middle of the night – a pig of a night, with rain lashing down. They were just boys, most of them, seventeen or eighteen years old, and physically most unimpressive compared to the Australians and New Zealanders on the peninsula. Their sergeant-major came along dumping these poor young chaps in our trench to hold it against the Turk. Relieved as we were to be getting out of that position, we couldn't help feeling sorry for them. Our commanding officer or perhaps junior officers or NCOs should have remained in the trenches to settle them in. These boys had seen no front-line action and were hopelessly up against it in that position. They were bound to suffer pretty fair casualties. I don't know what happened to them; that was the last we heard of that particular unit. To this day I remain sorry for those poor young fellows."

A great deal of popular antipathy to "Pommie bastards" and "bloody Poms" across the last two generations Down Under could probably be traced to the soldiers' lore of the First World War, and especially to that of Gallipoli. In the case of Australia it would obviously be mixed up with a much older hostility, deriving from the country's penal origins, as well as from the ancient resentment of Roman Catholic Irish, who provided significant numbers of the early population there. Certainly no Englishman who finds himself in either Australia or New Zealand on the occasion of some big sporting contest between his country and the locals – typically in cricket or in Rugby – can ever be in any doubt that a proportion of the spectators have no great regard for him or his kind. Often enough this is transmitted humorously, though with a distinct cutting edge; but sometimes the aversion can be unpleasantly aggressive. It is quite likely that the more disagreeable forms of barracking to be heard at Test matches on Sydney Cricket Ground or Lancaster Park, Christchurch, derive from a painful folk memory of what happened all that time ago along the Dardanelles. A suspicion of having failed one's friends through cowardice in war is the most disgraceful contradiction of what mateship stands for. The mythology of Anzac has always insisted that a man would rather die than be accused of that.

Unfortunately, a mythology of craven behaviour at Gallipoli by inferior British troops has never been seriously challenged in Australia and New Zealand, where it is generally assumed to be an accurate account of what happened in 1915. The myth has even been revived in recent years, as the 75th anniversary of the campaign approached: both Charles Bean's diary and the tape-recorded interviews with New Zealand veterans were published for popular readerships in the past decade. A little before them came Peter Weir's moving film *Gallipoli*, which told a great deal of truth about the Australian tragedy there. It did, however, contain one flaw which may be thought disreputable. There had already been a couple of stock thrusts which can be dismissed as sharp scripting with an eye to the box office rather than to art: one of the principal characters says straight out that "It's an English war" and reveals that his grandfather was an Irishman – "the English murdered him, hung him up by his own belt at the crossroads." A much more serious objection can be made to an incident later in the film, when the Australians are being swept by Turkish fire, taking heavy casualties, quite obviously going through hell. The field telephone rings in the dug-out, the radio operator listens to someone at the other end of the line, and calls out to his officer:

"Sir, the British are ashore at Suvla."

"Are they meeting heavy opposition?"

"None, sir. Apparently, they're just sitting on the beach drinking cups of tea."

In this fashion a new generation of people in the English-speaking world, in an age which prefers to be instructed and entertained by something watched, rather than by something read, is led to believe that while gallant Anzacs fought and died in misplaced loyalty to the imperial cause, the imperialists themselves sat on their butts and did nothing to help. There must now be millions who, whenever the word Gallipoli is mentioned, understand that to have been the case. There are doubtless tens of thousands in the Antipodes who are under the impression that while Anzac blood was shed copiously in the Dardanelles, such British troops as even saw battle there got off very lightly indeed. In this they are misinformed, though a visit to the Australian War Memorial in Canberra provides a suitable corrective. Set amid parkland on the outskirts of the federal capital, its grey stone buildings are both a monument to Australian valour and loss, and a museum which explains and illuminates these things. An arcade almost encloses a pool of water and on its walls are engraved the names of every Australian killed on active service during the First World War and since. This is as terrible, as distressing, as unforgettable as the Vietnam Wall in Washington DC. The museum inside is divided into sections which are self-contained and which each illustrates some theatre of war in which Australians have seen action over the years, from the nineteenth century on. Nothing is more dramatic than the Gallipoli Gallery, with its model showing the terrain of the peninsula, its dummy soldiers dressed in the equipment of 1915, its photographs taken during the campaign, its collection of artefacts. In front of these things stands an easel with a blackboard on which the casualty figures, the lives lost at Gallipoli, are carefully set down: Australia 8,709; New Zealand 2,701; India 7,594; France 9,874; Britain 21,255; Turkey 86,692.*

* It will be noticed that those Allied figures total 50,133; but in his definitive study of the campaign, Robert Rhodes James puts Allied deaths at 46,000. In doing so he explains that it is difficult to arrive at casualty figures for Gallipoli with any precision, and suggests that the Turkish assessment of 86,692 dead was a considerable underestimate. He believes they had 300,000 men killed and wounded, the Allies something in the region of 265,000.

## INTRODUCTION A Mythology Explored

It is not the purpose of the following pages to reassess responsibility and performance at Gallipoli in an attempt to defend some part of British national honour. Enough ink has been spent on the Dardanelles campaign itself and anyone wishing to read a balanced account of what happened there, and how it came to pass, can do so without difficulty, for reliable texts already exist, together with much that is unreliable. There is, however, a wider topic that has so far been unexplored, related to Gallipoli and including the development of its mythology. What lasting effect did the campaign have on its surviving participants, and how did they fare in later years? What influence did it have on the subsequent history of places that were affected by the events of 1915; on the peninsula itself and on communities in half a dozen countries which supplied the men who fought over the territory? How has the memory of those appalling months been kept so vividly alive for so long, and to what end? What uses, if any, have been made of the mythology, what lessons have been learnt from it; or not? These, and other such questions, might be asked of any campaign, any great battle, in any of the wars that man has ever fought. The most important question of all perhaps is this: how do we use our legends of heroism in the years that follow the courageous acts? What are our purposes in keeping them alive? Military history has always been abundant, and in recent years it has been one of the conspicuously flourishing points in an otherwise unsteady publishing industry. But, as John Keegan once suggested, there are many areas of social history which lie adjacent to military events, that seem almost wilfully to have been ignored, and have manifestly suffered from neglect.

The American Civil War, for example, would be fruitful ground for such enquiry. When the news reached Washington in March 1861 that the Rebels had seized Fort Sumter, the regular army of the United States numbered 17,000 men, and most of them were stationed out West. Abraham Lincoln immediately called upon state governors to supply 75,000 militiamen for short-term reinforcement, and the response was overwhelming wherever the recruiters went. Ohio was asked for thirteen regiments, but so many men volunteered that the state produced twenty almost at once. In every part of the Union, similar enthusiasm was rampant and it was not at all uncommon for whole towns to sign up. The 10th Michigan Volunteers consisted of nothing but the eligible manhood of Flint, under the command of their mayor, while the regimental doctor had been acquainted with many of the soldiers from the moment they were born, having delivered them with his own hands. The 9th New York Volunteers consisted of colleagues from the metropolitan fire department and were popularly known as the Fire Zouaves. Similar patterns emerged in the raising of the Confederate Army, with the 1st Virginia Militia recruited from Richmond, the Maury Grays proud of belonging to Nashville, Tennessee.

These local affiliations doubtless did much for the morale of the troops, but there was a devastating price to be paid for mass recruitments if things went ill for such units in battle, which inevitably happened as the war dragged on. At Shiloh, in April 1862, the 6th Mississippi Regiment rushed up a hill to attack the Ohioans and, of 425 who started at the bottom, only one hundred made it to the top. What did those casualties mean, in the long and short term, to the relatively small area of the South from which the stricken company had come? For that matter, what was the effect of the war on one of the states remote from the battlefields, which also sent its youth to be blooded and to die? The 20th Maine Regiment consisted of farmers, lumbermen, seamen, storekeepers, trappers and the like from a thinly populated area, and they were commanded by a college professor of rhetoric and modern languages, Joshua L. Chamberlain. They fought at Fredericksburg in 1862, which was a disaster for the North; then at Gettysburg six months later, a bad place to be whichever side you were on; then at Petersburg in 1864, another bloodbath. Chamberlain survived all these actions, and skirmishes in between, to return home and to become President of Bowdoin College, eventually Governor of Maine. To what extent did these promotions depend on his celebrity in war? How did his military experience thereafter influence his politics, or even his rhetoric? And what of the families considerably less fortunate than his? In how many clapboard dwellings along that superbly rugged coast, or amid those endless forests of pine, is some sad genuflection made even today to a photograph in sepia, framed on a wall, of the staring young man who might have made a great-great-grandfather if only he'd returned?

Since 1915, although so much has been written about Gallipoli, much more has been virtually unremarked. In Europe, in the Antipodes and elsewhere outside Turkey, most people think of the peninsula as a barren, arid place devoid of anything but rock and sand and scrub. This impression has been formed because all the pictures taken during the campaign were photographs from sea-level of beaches with gaunt cliffs split by ravines and gullies immediately behind; and indeed, the topography in the hinterland of Anzac Cove and Suvla Bay, up the western side of the peninsula, was almost completely as bleak as that, with bushes and trees growing wildly on the higher, less precipitous ground. But the southern end of the peninsula, also fiercely fought over, was quite different above the sand-cliffs by the sea. It had been farmed for two thousand years or more, as it still is today, when crops of wheat and corn and barley and sesame are extensively cultivated, together with groves of olive trees, figs and pomegranates. There are villages and small towns dotted around the south of the peninsula and along the side which comes down to the Dardanelles. The lives of those Turkish families must have been hugely disrupted by the events of 1915, but no one has yet described to us how. Was their economy totally devastated during those eight and a half months? Did they lose many people? How long did it take them to rebuild, replant and harvest again? What profit was there in scavenging for abandoned military things, which tides and storms and stumblings in the undergrowth are still liable to turn up?

Many questions might profitably be asked in the North Island of New Zealand, in order to complete our understanding of what happened as a result of three days in August 1915 at Chunuk Bair. That is a ridge almost 1,000 feet above the Aegean Sea, to the north-east of Anzac Cove, and the New Zealand Infantry Brigade was required to attack the heavily fortified Turkish positions that ran along the top. The Auckland Battalion made the first assault in broad daylight and was massacred. Next day the Wellington Battalion was sent up and actually captured the ridge after the most frightful hand-to-hand fighting, which left one trench so choked with New Zealand dead that a second one had to be hastily dug for the protection of the living. The remnants of the battalion were then withdrawn and two units of Englishmen, the Loyals and the Wiltshires, were sent up to hold the line, which they did for twenty-four hours. After that a massive counter-attack threw them off the ridge, where they left hundreds of their own corpses beside the colonial dead. This action resulted, more than half a century later, in an angry stage play by Maurice Shadbolt, who wasn't born till 1932. But how, in those years between, had it more pressingly affected life on the North Shore and up the Hutt Valley, in Pukekohe and Palmerston North, some of the places from which the New Zealand troops had volunteered for this war?

Someone ought also to trace the terrible consequences, in all its ramifications, of a simple failure to synchronise watches on August 7, which was the day the Aucklanders were struggling to get up Chunuk Bair. As a feint, to draw attention away from their assault, the 8th Australian Light Horse Regiment were ordered to make a dawn attack at the Nek, another ridge some distance away. There was to be a preliminary bombardment of the Turkish positions which would not end until the Australians began to charge; but the shelling stopped seven minutes before the troops expected it to and the Light Horsemen, operating as infantry, were cut down the moment they went over the top. So were a second line of the 8th, which set off a couple of minutes later. They were followed by a wave of the 10th Light Horse Regiment and they, too, were slaughtered *en masse*. This was the incident which became the climax of Peter Weir's film, and it is also the subject of a celebrated oil painting by George Lambert.* Out of 600 men who went over the top that day, 234 were killed and 138 were wounded. We know more than enough of this by now, and of what went wrong to cause such casualties. But what was the result in small towns and homesteads, separated by great distances, throughout the immensity of Western Australia in the desolate years that followed? Referring to the 10th Light Horse in particular, someone said afterwards that "with that regiment went the flower of the youth of Western Australia." Many of the state's pioneering families lost sons and brothers at the Nek. The losses to people in the state of Victoria were also grievous that day; but Melbourne's hinterland was not nearly as thinly populated as was that of Perth. How did those isolated Westralians cope with their damaged, their blinded, their amputated boys, who had decades ahead of them dominated by physical handicap? How did the rural properties carry on when sons did not return to inherit and manage them?

These are the sort of enquiries we should make if we are to learn anything new about the Dardanelles campaign: this is the sole area

---

* *The Charge of the 3rd Light Horse at the Nek* by G. W. Lambert (1883–1948), which hangs in the Australian War Memorial in Canberra. It refers to the 3rd Light Horse Brigade, which included the 8th Victoria and the 10th Western Australia Light Horse Regiments.

of further enlightenment, the only useful point of historical investigation now. Investigation of the Anzac legacy, the Indian, the French and the Turkish experience I leave to others. In this book the questions have been asked, a trace has been made, in that part of England from which the Lancashire Fusiliers went forth to the Great War. This was but one of eighty-four British regiments which fought and sustained losses at Gallipoli in 1915.

# I

# A Regimental Town

The regimental home of the Lancashire Fusiliers was the town of Bury, which sprawls at the foot of Rossendale on the edge of the Pennine hills. These have sometimes been referred to as the back bone of England, and they do indeed run like a spine up the middle of the country, more or less half-way between the Irish Sea and the North Sea. Starting in Derbyshire they continue northwards for some 160 miles, until they merge with the Cheviots on the Scottish border. Just short of 3,000 feet at their highest point, the Pennines are about half that height as they traverse the eastern side of Lancashire, where they form a natural boundary which separates the county from Yorkshire; but this trifling altitude can be deceptive to the unwary traveller. Winter can be dangerously bleak on those hills, even at their lowest, even without snow, when rain is liable to sweep across them torrentially; and in any of the blizzards that frequently occur between December and March they can be lethal to those who, all too easily, become lost in the ensuing whiteout. At other times of the year they have a wild grandeur in spite of the fact that their carboniferous rocks are usually visible only in occasional outcrops and crags. The most characteristic view in the Pennines is one of sweeping moorland devoid of trees, broken by uncemented dry-stone walls which have marked out the sheep pastures since the proprietary enclosures of higher ground in the eighteenth century. The high pasture is fit for nothing but sheep, and parts of the Pennines will not even sustain any animal, where coarse tussocks grow amid expanses of barren peat. Cotton grass dapples the boggier tracts in spring and, when autumn comes, heather empurples the hills. Streams tipple out of these uplands to merge amid the bracken and the cow pastures lower down, and to become rivers which form along the bottom ground. The most memorable sounds of the high Pennines are those made by rushing water, and by the wind sweeping across the tops. These mingle with the plaintive bleat of sheep throughout the year, and with the bubbling trill of the curlew, which means that spring has come again.

Typical of the small rivers running out of these hills is the Irwell, which flows down the length of Rossendale, one of the valleys formed in the Ice Age between the main Pennine range and its numerous spurs. Some distance before the river joins the Mersey and goes into the sea at Liverpool, it reaches Bury, the biggest of several communities it has passed through since its source, and not much more than a dozen miles away in the hills to the north. Places like Bacup and Rawtenstall, Helmshore and Ramsbottom, clinging to the hillsides and spread along the river's banks, all drew most of their sustenance from the textile trade at the time of the First World War. Bury, also lying in the lee of the hills, but a bit further away, had a much bigger share of industry than any of the townships further upstream.

It had no ancient history, though a couple of Roman roads ran not far from its boundaries. One of these, to the north-west, was an extension of Watling Street, which subsequent civil engineering had kept so up to date that none of the original roadworks were visible. But the other relic of those times, which crossed the Pennines into Yorkshire over Blackstone Edge, still revealed one of the finest Roman pavements in the country for several hundred yards before being subsumed in a wilderness of turf and bog. In Bury, however, there was nothing before the Middle Ages, when a licence to crenellate – effectively, to build a castle – was granted in 1465. The Wars of the Roses were at their height between the Houses of York and Lancaster, not to be settled (in distant Leicestershire) for another twenty years; the fortification was a sign of troubled times, but it had already fallen into ruin by Henry VIII's day. Nothing of it survived into the twentieth century apart from the word, which appeared in Castle Street, Castlehill Road and one or two other thoroughfares.

The Middle Ages also saw the start of textile manufacturing, at first on a modest scale and exclusively in wool. The sheep was the very basis of the national economy, bred chiefly for its fleece, from which English weavers produced the finest broadcloth in Europe. The small communities of East Lancashire obtained their wool from the Pennine flocks and for ages the weaving was done in the upper rooms of farmhouses and other dwellings by people operating handlooms. On these they produced varieties of cloth for the markets in London and even further afield, each fabric known by a distinctively evocative name; sackcloth and fustian, stammel and russet, yellow buffine and red durant – and perpetuana, which the Puritans liked, because it was close-woven and its colouring was chaste. The dampness of the Lancashire climate was a help in this manufacturing, because it reduced the risk of thread breaking while it was being spun: it would be even more beneficial when Lancashire turned from wool and established its cotton industry.

Cotton was first imported about 1600 from the eastern Mediterranean; from, among other places, the Smyrna that Mustafa Kemal would liberate from the Greeks in 1922. But this fibre was never more than an occasional additive in predominantly woollen or linen cloth until well into the eighteenth century. By then the handloom was beginning to be displaced by the power loom, driven by the rivers and streams running out of the Pennines. A number of Lancashire inventions were steadily advancing the technology of the industry. First came the flying-shuttle, devised in 1733 by John Kay, who was a Bury man. Some thirty-two years later James Hargreaves of Blackburn produced his spinning jenny, a hand-operated machine for domestic use, but an improvement on what had gone before. Four years after that, Richard Arkwright of Preston came up with his water frame, and in 1779 Samuel Crompton of Bolton at last made large-scale power spinning possible with his invention of the spinning mule. These appliances were not popular with the Lancashire workers. As each one appeared, mobs rioted in protest, because the operatives could perceive that such machinery would not only undercut anything a handloom weaver might produce, but would inevitably lead to mass production in the miserably overcrowded conditions of a mill. First Kay and then Hargreaves saw their inventions smashed by angry workers, and Arkwright was so apprehensive at the prospect of similar damage to his water frame that he encouraged a rumour which reckoned he was designing a machine to measure longitude.

The rioters were trying to beat back history and they were doomed before they even began. The port of Liverpool, which had sent its first ship across the Atlantic in 1667, was expanding annually on a trade in West Indian sugar and everything that the plantations of Virginia were willing to sell of their tobacco and cotton crops. That was where the raw material for Lancashire's textiles would chiefly come from in the years ahead, until the supply was cut off during the American Civil War. But two other things in the last quarter of the eighteenth century were principally responsible for the industry being utterly transformed. One was the halving of the tax on pure cotton goods, which was ordered in 1774. The other was the perfecting of the steam engine the following year. Within a decade it had been adapted to drive machines that would spin and weave cotton, and these no longer needed running water to power them. They required only coal, which had been mined in Lancashire since Tudor times, though the deep shafts driven vertically underground didn't come until the steam engine propelled winding gear at the pithead. Most of the collieries ran across a belt of south Lancashire to the west of Manchester; but one or two small pits were worked on the outskirts of Bury and round towns to the north. And with coal-fired power for cotton and other manufacturing, the Industrial Revolution began in this part of northern England. One measurement of its progress was a swift rise in the population of Bury itself. In 1773 no more than 2,090 people lived there: by 1801 there were 7,000 and sixty years later some 30,000 were in the town. When the Great War began, its population was 50,000 or so.

The textile towns developed their own specialities in cotton manufacturing, in much the same way that the handloom weavers had with fustian, perpetuana and their other cloths. Broadly speaking, spinning was the dominant process in Manchester, Bolton, Oldham and elsewhere in south-east Lancashire, weaving the major business in Blackburn, Nelson, Colne, Chorley and other towns to the north, including the communities up Rossendale. But there were several exceptions to this pattern. Proud Preston (as it liked to be known) had a leading role in both operations, while Bolton bleached and dyed cotton yarns as well as spinning them; and Rochdale, in the midst of the spinning area, preferred to weave. So did Bury, which also printed its cloth. One of the leading calico printers in this period was Robert Peel, whose business prospered enough for him to donate £10,000 for the defence of the realm when a Napoleonic invasion was expected. His grandson would be remembered as Bury's most famous native when, as Sir Robert Peel, repealer of the Corn Laws and inventor of the Metropolitan Police, he became the first British Prime Minister to come from a commercial family rather than a landed one.

Many and great were the fortunes made in the Lancashire cotton industry, once it got into its Victorian stride. Its heyday was from the middle of the nineteenth century until the First World War. By then, with more than half a million people working the local textile machinery, the Lancashire mills were exporting 6,600 million yards of cloth a year, which was fifty-eight per cent of the world's entire manufacture of cotton goods. The country was generally bursting with confidence, expressed as arrogantly as anywhere in the epigram "What Lancashire does today, England thinks tomorrow!" (although this was occasionally varied to "What *Manchester* does ... *London* thinks ..."). The prosperity was most visible at the Royal Exchange in Manchester, where trade was transacted in a huge chamber that could accommodate several thousand members at one time: the floor covered three quarters of an acre and Mancunians boasted that it was the largest business room in the world. At first the great day of the week was on Tuesday, when High 'Change began at noon and beautifully dressed men in tall silk hats gathered there, American visitors being conspicuous because their voices did not utter the flat vowels of this region and because they almost invariably wore superb boots. Later in the nineteenth century High 'Change occurred on Fridays as well, when the manufacturers and the merchants, the importers of raw cotton and the yarn agents, the finishers, the cotton-waste dealers, the shippers, the bankers and the insurance men – all the people who had a finger in this rich and substantial pie – congregated beneath the trading board high on the wall, that told them how the market was in Liverpool and New York, what was the going rate for raw cotton in Madras and Rangoon, Shanghai and Khartoum.

The trade did, however, have its ups and downs and one reason for this was that it depended ultimately on a harvested crop which, like any other, was at the mercy of weather and disease. But the biggest disturbance the industry faced in those years was when the Southern States broke away from the Union in 1861 and could not export their cotton because the Union blockaded the Southern ports. Within a year there were more than 56,000 Lancashire operatives receiving charitable assistance to stay alive, and the gravity of the situation was conveyed in a letter to *The Times*: "Sir; I am living in the centre of a vast district where are many cotton mills, which in ordinary times afford employment to many thousands of hands, and food to many thousands of mouths. With very rare exceptions, quietness reigns in all these mills. Hard times have come; and we have had them sufficiently long to know what they mean. We have fathers sitting in their houses at midday, silent and glum, while children look wistfully about, and sometimes whimper for bread which they cannot have . . ."

It was during the quietness of those mills that Samuel Laycock began to compose his *Lyrics of the Cotton Famine* in Lancashire dialect, the most famous of them being written while he was awaiting the birth of another child he could ill afford to support. Here are the beginning and the end of "Welcome Bonny Brid":

> Th'art welcome little bonny brid,
> But shouldn't ha' come just when tha did;
> Toimes are bad.
> We're short o' pobbies for eawr Joe,
> But that, of course, tha' didn't know,
> Did ta, lad?
>
> . . . Thi feyther's noan been wed so long,
> An' yet tha' sees he's middlin' throng
> Wi' yo' o.
> Besides thi little brother Ted,
> We've one upsteers, asleep i' bed,
> Wi eawr Joe.
>
> But tho' we've childer two or three,
> We'll mak' a bit o' reawm for thee,
> Bless thee, lad!
> Th'art prattiest brid we have i' th' nest,
> So hutch up closer to mi breast;
> Aw'm thi dad.

The American Civil War was also to have an influence on the British relationship with India, and one that would ultimately bring about the end of the Lancashire cotton industry. From the moment the manufacture of textiles in north-west England was revolutionised by steam-driven machinery, a large part of Lancashire's prosperity was gained at the expense of hand weavers on the subcontinent, who simply could not compete with mass-production. Between 1814 and 1832 the export of Lancashire cotton goods to India rose by no less than 7,500 per cent, and the muslin industry in Dacca was virtually destroyed as a result. In exchange, Lancashire took no more than thirteen per cent of its raw cotton requirements from India, where the staple was neither as strong nor as clean as the variety grown in America. But when a disastrous harvest across the Atlantic in 1846 resulted in massive unemployment in the British textile towns, the Manchester Chamber of Commerce lobbied the imperial Government of India to increase Indian cotton production and, with some difficulty, this was achieved. By the time the Civil War broke out, the growing of this crop had again become an important part of the Indian economy to the extent that, between 1863 and 1865, raw cotton worth £36.5 million was exported to England, to rescue Manchester and the other towns from their slump. When the supplies from America were restored, the Indian quota was again cut back; but this was to have a totally unforeseen result in the long run. Faced with a huge surplus of home-grown cotton, having ample funds at their disposal as a result of the recent boom, enjoying certain preconditions for an Industrial Revolution of their own (like the discovery and mining of coal in Bengal, and the availability of the new technology) the Indians began to build cotton mills, too, chiefly in Bombay and its hinterland. By 1874 there were nineteen of them at work. By 1914 there were 264 and the figure was growing annually. Lancashire had a serious competitor for the first time, and one that paid even lower wages than were customary in Proud Preston and the neighbouring towns. This time, eventually, it was Lancashire that was unable to compete.

That day, however, was still two generations away as Bury flourished in the years leading up to the Great War. Not only was it fairly prosperous for the moment, but it had attained that size which is not too small for individual privacy and not so big that it is possible to feel lost in a community. It had some decent and quite ambitious public buildings, one of which was its Parish Church in the very centre of the town. The church stood on the site of a medieval predecessor and was designed in the manner of the thirteenth century, though most of it was started in 1871. Just across the street was a group of buildings which the well-connected Sydney Smirke – architect of several London clubs, including the Carlton and the Conservative – had composed in the Classical style. Among these was the Derby Hotel, which had recently been the scene of a sensational tragedy. One Saturday in January 1899, a man and a woman – he clearly a gentleman of about forty, she much younger and fashionably dressed – had registered with false names and taken a room. Next day they were found dead in bed, poisoned with prussic acid. A letter addressed to the local coroner contained enough money for funeral expenses but no clue to their identities, which might never have been established if the man had not forgotten that his tailor habitually stitched a client's name into the lining of his trousers. He was John Knight, a bachelor from a wealthy family in the Netherlands, and she was Marie-Louise Rousseau, described in the press as "a beautiful queen of Rotterdam's underworld". Marriage had clearly been out of the question and so they had conceived this desperate alternative. But what no one ever worked out was why they had chosen Bury for the climax of their suicide pact, unless it was because its name seemed in tune with their unhappiness.*

This was, at any rate, an improbably romantic thing to have happened in such a thoroughly workaday mill town. The industrial events of the previous century had transformed Bury's nature as well as its size, so that although it still retained many of its traditional stone-built cottages, with stone slab roofs and mullioned windows, a majority of homes were now constructed more cheaply with mass-produced bricks. They were ranged in terraces in every part of the town, with sometimes as many as fifty in one line. Some terraces had little gardens in front, but more commonly nothing but a door separated the interior of a house from the pavement and the cobblestoned street. These were where the millworkers dwelt, the worst of them known as back-to-backs because that is how they were built, without intervening space. In an improved version of such dwellings, each house (usually called a "two-up, two-down" because that was the number of rooms on each floor) had an enclosed yard of flagstones at the back, which terminated in an earth closet. Once a week the night-cart would come up the narrow lane separating the two rows of backyards, removing the excrement from the cubby holes to left and right. During the day, the housewives were wont to hang their washing on lines which stretched

---

* Bury's name, in fact, originated in the Old English *Burh* which, in turn, was derived from a Germanic root meaning protection or shelter. It is more common as a suffix (eg Shrewsbury) and is related to the English "borough" and the Scottish "burgh".

across the full width of the lane; and children would play their games of hide and seek amid endless lines of billowing sheets, trousers, shirts, petticoats and pillow slips. Wash-day was an urgent occasion in the prevailing conditions of industrial Lancashire, and women were severely judged on how clean they managed to keep their homes and families. Most of them extended hygiene to scouring the front doorstep, often the window sill as well, with a white or yellow donkeystone obtained from an itinerant rag and bone man, who toured the poorer parts of the town with his cart and offered these things in exchange for worn-out clothing. The cart was pulled by a donkey, hence the name given to the sandstone block.

Keeping clean was hard work after decades of the Industrial Revolution. The brick that made the cheap housing usually came from Accrington and was harshly pink when it emerged from the kiln. Within a year or two it had been blackened by soot, and so had the older cottages and the grander buildings constructed with stone. The air had become so polluted that visibility was rarely greater than two or three miles, which meant that the main ridge of the Pennines could no longer be seen from Bury. Even the nearer outlying hills were often indistinct unless the weather was especially good, as scores of factory chimneys plumed smoke into the air, adding to the natural overcast. Occasionally, the combination of winter cloud and smog produced in the town a darkness at noon which was almost as complete as that at midnight. Worst of all was the transformation of the Irwell, which was no longer recognisable as a river flowing down from the wild Pennine heights. In 1870 it had been reported that in the first two and a half miles from its source it received the effluent from nineteen Rossendale cotton factories, two dyeworks, two flour mills, a sawmill and a printing works; it then passed through the town of Bacup, which added the whole of its untreated sewage. "After that," a later commentator remarked, "what happened at Ramsbottom, Bury and further downstream was almost irrelevant . . ." By the time the river passed under Bury Bridge, the most noticeable thing about it was the thick white scum, which strangers mistook for soapsuds, floating on the top; and the smell of putrefaction and chemicals. Although an Irwell and Mersey River Authority had been formed in 1891 to deal with such matters, nothing at all had been done by the time of the First World War. Too many vested interests had too much to lose in restoring the river to its original purity.

The greatest culprits in all the pollution hemmed in the dwellings of the workers at Bury as they did in all the industrial towns. The factories were everywhere: rearing above an embankment, forming one side of an entire street, creating a cul de sac across the end of two terraces, sloping up the side of a hill, shutting off much natural light from anything else built nearby. The most characteristic of the factories were the cotton mills, which were also easier to identify than the buildings for any other form of manufacture. Whether they were made of stone or brick they rose several floors above the ground – up to six storeys sometimes – and they were unique in the number and size of the windows on every floor so that, when darkness fell, light blazed from them and the imaginative observer could see some resemblance to great liners at sea. Their chimneys sometimes rose as much as 250 feet into the air and the name of the mill would often appear on these totems in glazed and coloured letters, set one above the other, which could be read from some distance – Pilot, Egyptian, Eagle, India, California, or whatever the millowner's fancy had been. They throbbed with energy during cotton booms, when the workers would operate round the clock in shifts. If you walked down a street beside a mill you could hear the muted clash of the looms inside, on one floor above another, and if you placed your head against the wall you could feel it vibrate. Enter those weaving sheds and you were deafened by the din as hundreds of machines flung their beams back and forth, while a shuttle flew across each frame from side to side. So great was the noise that no one ever tried to make himself heard: instead the operatives exaggerated the movements of their mouths silently – they called this "mee-mawing" – and lip-read each other's conversations perfectly. They retained the exaggerated movements when speaking normally outside the cotton mill. It was one of their most noticeable caste marks.

The work force in the mills was always mixed. No skill was more highly regarded than that of a six-loom weaver (someone who could tend six looms at once, which required much nonstop dexterity) and such an expert was liable to come in either sex. In each district of the town there was a character known as the knocker-up, paid a small weekly sum by the operatives to waken them each morning with a tap on the windowpane, and he had as many female customers as men. Shortly afterwards the street would echo to the sound of people heading for the great iron gates of the nearest mill.

They all wore clogs, whose curved wooden soles gave them a curiously bobbing gait; and the clog irons nailed on to the alder sole would clatter on the cobbles and sometimes strike sparks. Going home again at the end of the shift, the women would often have cotton fluff sticking to their hair. The men were pale and did not often give the impression of great physical strength. They were heading for an evening whose main purpose was to replenish with enough sustenance to see them through another day. They mostly ate things that filled them at small expense, relying heavily on the potato above all. Such meat as came their way except on special occasions were the inferior cuts and the offal that the millowning families would not themselves have consumed. The local speciality was the black pudding of dried pig's blood, stuffed into an intestinal membrane and then tied in a kidney shape, which the people of Bury believed to have been invented in the town by a family who sold these things from a little shop in Union Square.

It was, on the whole, a frugal existence, with little to spare for luxuries. Poverty and the fear of poverty, the likelihood of unemployment before long, was always there. This was the reason the Army had settled on the town. Men would rather take the Queen's shilling than starve because they could not find work.

One of the most substantial buildings in Bury lay on its western outskirts, beside the road to Bolton. Like everything else that wasn't new, the Wellington Barracks had suffered from the industrial climate, and its stonework was blackened with more than half a century of grime. Its long dormitory blocks enclosed a square, on which soldiers could sometimes be spotted at their parade-ground drill by people passing the arched entrance, where a sentry always stood guard. On the open land behind, used for target practice, the crackle of musketry could often be heard. The Barracks had been built before the Crimean War, though the Lancashire Fusiliers had only been there since 1873, when they weren't yet known by that name. They did, however, already have a long history, which began when William of Orange landed at Brixham in Devon and marched to Exeter in 1688, to begin the so-called Glorious Revolution which brought constitutional monarchy to the land and ended for ever the Stuart succession to the throne. At Brixham, William granted commissions for the raising of two foot regiments and a regiment of horse, one of which was awarded to Sir Robert Peyton, a gentleman of fortune who had been described as "a topping anti-courtier" in Charles II's last years, and had already served under William in the Netherlands. Thus commissioned, Peyton mustered six independent companies of infantry in Exeter, to serve as the Twentieth Regiment of Foot. It was customary at this period for troops to be identified by their commander's name; and what had initially been Colonel Sir Robert Peyton's Regiment of Foot in later years was successively known as Hamilton's, then Bligh's, then Kingsley's and so on, as gentlemen tired of their military responsibility, and money changed hands profitably . . . which was also a custom of the day. But in time the convention died away and this body of troops was generally recognised as the XXth Foot; sometimes as the East Devonshire Regiment.

William may have brought peace to England by accepting the invitation to rule from seven of its great aristocratic families, but in Ireland he only made existing divisions worse. On July 1, 1690, the new regiment had its baptism of fire in the valley of the Boyne, where the Irish Jacobite forces were heavily defeated by the Orange troops, in an engagement that still had wretched repercussions three hundred years later. The regiment later took part in the storming of Athlone and acquired its third battle honour in routing the Jacobites at Aughrim, further west. It remained in Ireland on garrison duty for the next decade and for much of its early history it would return there repeatedly, rather than to England, after service abroad. Its first foreign service saw it in the West Indies, its second in Gibraltar, where one soldier of the regiment is said to have distinguished himself by receiving 30,000 lashes in a series of punishments during his fourteen years of duty on the Rock: the Army of the eighteenth century was a brutal refuge from the uncertainties of civilian life, even when it was not fighting wars. The XXth did, in fact, take part in fighting at Gibraltar, when it defended the fortress against a siege of Spanish troops. But its first major campaign did not occur until the War of the Austrian Succession broke out in 1741. It fought at Dettingen, in the last battle to see a British army commanded in the field by its monarch (George II); and at Fontenoy, which is still recognised as one of the great infantry engagements in the history of war.

Then it was hurried back to Britain, where Bonnie Prince Charlie was attempting to revive the Stuart cause, and it took part in the bloody end of his aspirations in the heather at Culloden. From that butchery, however, one of the King's men emerged with his honour intact. With dead and dying Scots all over the battlefield, the infamous Duke of Cumberland, the victorious commander, noticed a young Highlander staring at him angrily. He turned to a young officer by his side and ordered him to shoot the man. The officer replied: "My commission is at your Highness's disposal, but I can never consent to become an executioner." His name was James Wolfe, and three years later he joined the XXth as its second in command at the age of twenty-two. He saw no fighting with it, however, and seems in the regimental histories to have been a rather solemn young man, anxious to discourage his soldiers from excessive pleasures of the flesh. To his fellow officers he deplored "the shameful drunkness of the men" and further remarked that "the worst and idlest soldiers are those that are most venereal in disorders . . . they should suffer for their intemperance; and orders that 6s be paid for the cure of the pox, and 4s for the clap." These were significant sums of money for private soldiers to find in the middle of the eighteenth century; more than a man's weekly wage, out of which he had to victual himself, pay for his uniform and keep his weapons in repair.

Wolfe had left the regiment, for the campaign that would see him win posthumous glory at the Heights of Abraham, when the XXth next went into action. Once again, as at Fontenoy and Dettingen, the British were fighting the French, this time in the Seven Years War, and in alliance with Frederick of Prussia. In August 1759, 51,000 Frenchmen, supported by artillery, marched from the town of Minden, on the River Weser, to confront a force of British and Prussians smaller by 10,000 or so. There was some misunderstanding about the orders of engagement on the allied side and the upshot was that 6,000 British infantrymen, including the XXth Foot, found themselves marching steadily across fields towards three lines of French cavalry which were supported by heavy guns. Tradition insists – and this was to become an important piece of regimental lore in future – that the British passed through some gardens on their way and there plucked roses which they stuck in their caps. Decorated in this fashion, the army of redcoats pressed on, in spite of being badly mauled in the crossfire from sixty artillery pieces. Then eleven squadrons of French horse attacked them but were beaten back by British musket fire. Again they were enfiladed and again cavalry charged them from the front with the same result; and this sequence was repeated yet again, before the French acknowledged that they had lost the fight. The XXth, like the other five British regiments at Minden, took heavy casualties that day, but were saluted by Marshal Contades, who had commanded the French, in the following terms: "I never thought to see a single line of infantry break through three lines of cavalry ranked in order of battle, and tumble them to ruin."

The pattern of their soldiering was by now well established, and when the regiment's second century arrived it continued in the same manner as the first. There would not be a decade until the end of the Napoleonic Wars in which the XXth Foot did not engage in combat somewhere overseas, and while most of their battles were fought in various corners of Europe, they were often enough despatched further afield. Twice they took part in campaigns in North America. On the first occasion they were incorporated in General Burgoyne's army which was charged with preventing American independence, and with the rest of his troops they surrendered at Saratoga; where, according to a tradition disputed by some, they burned their colours rather than yield them to the victors. There is no debate about their second excursion to the United States, however, when they were among the British troops who took part in the burning of the White House during the war of 1812. Of this, their commanding general, Robert Ross, wrote: "So unexpected was our entry and capture of Washington, and so confident was Madison of the defeat of our troops, that he had prepared a supper for the expected conquerors; and when our advance party entered the President's house they found a table with forty covers. The fare, however, which was intended for Jonathan was voraciously devoured by John Bull, and the health of the Prince Regent, and success to His Majesty's arms by sea and land, was drunk in the best wines . . ."

The XXth fought against Napoleon on the Peninsula and in the Pyrenees and, though they missed Waterloo, they were the regiment charged with guarding him during his exile on St Helena. It was their regimental surgeon, Dr Arnott, who tended the Emperor during his last illness and, as a token of his respect, Bonaparte presented the doctor with Coxe's *Life of Marlborough*, which was to become a regimental treasure; as was the lock of Napoleon's hair which someone thoughtfully secured before twelve soldiers of the XXth carried his coffin to the grave. No other event of any significance occurred to the regiment until the Crimean War broke out more than thirty years later, when they distinguished themselves in several battles, but nowhere more than at Inkerman in 1854. This was the most savage engagement of the entire war, which cost the Russians 12,000 men and in which the XXth lost more than any other British unit except the Guards. Of one particularly awful moment in the battle, Alexander Kinglake wrote, in his eight-volume history of the campaign: "And at the thought of the bayonet these men of the Twentieth seemed to have but one will ... they were glowing with that sense of power which is scarce other than power itself. To men of their corps and to none other had been committed the charge of a sacred historic tradition; and if they were to use the enchantment they must not, they knew, ensure that, in their time, its spell should be broken. The air was rent with a sound which – unless they be men of the initiated regiment – people speak of as strange and "unearthly". After nearly a century from the day when their cry became famous, and forty years after the time when it last resounded in battle, these men of the Twentieth once more had delivered their old 'Minden Yell'."

One other episode stands out from this period of the regimental history, and it followed swiftly on the end of hostilities in the Crimea. British soldiering in India so far had been left to the private army of the East India Company, but when the sepoys mutinied at Meerut in 1857, soldiers of the Queen at once set sail to assist the loyal Company troops on the sub-continent. By the time the XXth reached Calcutta, after a voyage of over three months, much of the lost ground had been recovered, but they were in Sir Colin Campbell's army which finally settled things at Lucknow, and they were therefore involved in the dreadful revenge which British troops took when the Mutiny was finally put down and punishment was exacted for atrocities committed by the sepoys. Scarcely any-one emerged from the Mutiny with credit, but a healing did begin surprisingly soon afterwards, largely because Victoria put her own weight behind her Viceroy's insistence that reconciliation must be the watchword on all sides, not retribution. The new order which followed made a big difference to British soldiering, for the Company army was disbanded. In its place an Indian Army of native troops with British officers was established, supplemented by soldiers from England, whose infantry regiments in turn provided battalions for Indian service, each one spending five years at a time on the sub-continent to reinforce – to keep an eye on, the cynics said – the Indian Army. The XXth, both before and after becoming the Lancashire Fusiliers, were to be well acquainted with the brightest jewel in the imperial crown under this arrangement.

All of this was Kinglake's "sacred historic tradition", the oxygen of all soldiering, which the regiment brought to Bury in 1873. This wasn't the first time it had been quartered in the English North. Its connection with Devon had always been rather tenuous after the first enthusiasm. In its first hundred years it had only once been stationed in Exeter, its birthplace, and Devon had not proved a successful recruiting ground. One reason for this was the relatively low level of population in a chiefly agricultural area, another the fact that in eighteenth-century Exeter there was a prosperous woollen industry which paid high wages. From time to time the XXth had ventured to the less comfortable North in search of fresh man-power, and in 1838–39 it had been quartered variously in Stockport, Ashton-under-Lyne and Rochdale in the course of suppressing Chartist disturbances, for which at least one Lancashire civic authority gave it an official vote of thanks. When it wasn't serving overseas it was, as often as not, on garrison duty in Dublin. It was a massive reorganisation of the entire Army, however, which caused the regiment to make its home permanently in the cotton-mill town on the rapidly deteriorating River Irwell.

The British Army had become atrophied ever since Wellington's great successes against Napoleon, largely because the Duke was still a powerful presence until his death in the middle of the nineteenth century, and would countenance no change in the military machine that had given him so many resounding victories. But both the Crimean War and the Indian Mutiny had exposed woeful failures of one sort and another in British soldiering, and the man who decided that the old order must at last go was a new Secretary of State for War, Edward Cardwell, who was appointed in 1868. His most important stroke was to abolish the traditional method of obtaining an officer's commission – by buying it from the colonel of a regiment. He made the Commander-in-Chief subordinate to the Secretary of State, instead of leaving him as a potentially dangerous freelance. He stopped the brutal discipline which had produced 30,000 lashes on Gibraltar, and he introduced the twelve-year engagement divided equally between time with the colours and service in the reserve. But his most considered blow at the existing

A Volunteer Battalion of the Lancashire Fusiliers marches towards Bury Parish Church for a service of dedication before sailing for South Africa and the Boer War. The engagement on Spion Kop was to be a disaster for the regiment.

In 1905, a memorial to the Fusiliers killed in South Africa was unveiled in Bury Market Place, near the existing statue to Sir Robert Peel, in front of the Parish Church. This surprisingly exuberant military figure – designed by George Frampton, who later sculpted

Peter Pan for Kensington Gardens in London – was subsequently moved to another site in Bury, to make way for a tram shelter. Note the four men with placards urging the crowd to be silent.

A drawing of the Bury Drill Hall – headquarters of the local Territorial battalions of the Fusiliers – when an extension was opened in 1907. The original structure was built in 1868 on the site of medieval fortifications, which caused it to be known alternatively as the Castle Armoury.

BELOW Physical jerks at the Wellington Barracks, Bury, as a preliminary to the slaughter of the Western Front. These are very new recruits who volunteered for the 17th Battalion of the Lancashire Fusiliers in March 1915, just before the landing on Gallipoli. The regiment raised a total of thirty battalions in the Great War.

system was to reorganise the administration of line regiments in the standing army (such as the XXth Foot), together with their auxiliary forces, into sixty-six districts which coincided as closely as possible with the county boundaries of Great Britain. One of the auxiliaries, the Militia, had already been associated with the counties in some shape or form since Tudor times, a reserve of trained men who could at short notice be drummed up for service within the realm at the behest of the county's Lord Lieutenant, or even the magistrates if troops were needed to quell a civil disorder. Volunteers existed only when war threatened or had broken out, and were even more localised than the Militia: the calico-printing Peel who donated £10,000 for the national defence when a Napoleonic invasion seemed imminent also mobilised the Loyal Bury Volunteer Association at his own expense; and this voluntary surge to arms happened throughout the land during that crisis.

In each of the new districts established by Cardwell's reforms there were to be two Regular battalions, two Militia battalions, and the Volunteers.* At least one of the two Regular units would be serving away from home at any time and increasingly, more often than not, this meant in India; but the point was that it would have a settled home to which it could always return, and that a bond would be established between each regiment, in its various forms, and a particular part of England, Scotland, Wales or Ireland. To emphasise this intention there was a great renaming of units over the next few years in which, for example, the 13th Foot became the Somerset Light Infantry, the 23rd Foot became the Royal Welch Fusiliers, the 25th Foot became the King's Own Scottish Borderers, the 27th Foot became the Royal Inniskilling Fusiliers, the 36th Foot became The Worcestershire Regiment, and the 44th Foot became The Essex Regiment. In 1881, the XXth Foot became The Lancashire Fusiliers.

It was as Fusiliers that the regiment went to war again, this time in the Sudan. The 2nd Battalion had been on station at Quetta in

---

* The battalion was the basic unit of infantry and it became standardised by the time of the Great War at approximately 1,000 men, normally commanded by a Lieutenant-Colonel. This was subdivided into four companies, commanded by a major or a captain. In each company there were four platoons of sixty men, commanded by junior officers. It took four battalions to make an infantry brigade, and there were three brigades in each division.

northern India when it was ordered to Egypt to join Kitchener's army, which was to avenge Charles Gordon's death at the hands of the Mahdi in Khartoum. For the first time in the regiment's history its soldiers would not be fighting in the traditional red tunic and blue trousers, and the spiked helmet had also been discarded. Instead, khaki was the uniform and each man wore a pith helmet in the belief that this was the best protection from sunstroke. At Omdurman in 1898 these Fusiliers were part of the force which destroyed the dervishes in one of the most unequal engagements ever fought. The British troops were armed with the new breech-loading Lee Metford, which allowed them to mow down the enemy long before he himself had come close enough to inflict much damage. They also had artillery on their side, even more devastating. More than 11,000 of the Mahdi's army were killed that day, compared with but forty-eight of the Anglo-Egyptian force.

In little more than a year, however, the Battalion was to be heavily punished itself. The Boer War had broken out and within three days of landing in South Africa the Fusiliers were marching to relieve Ladysmith, which was encircled by Piet Joubert's army. In their path lay Spion Kop, a hill of Pennine proportions but made of sun-baked rock, not sodden turf. The British took it without much difficulty because it was thinly defended; but they reached the summit, and began to entrench, with a thick mist covering the entire kop. When this cleared, they realised they had blundered into a death trap; that there were knolls some distance from the peak where Boers were perfectly placed to enfilade the British trenches with rifle and artillery fire. Of all the British troops, the Fusiliers were the hardest hit by the Boer snipers, losing one third of their men. Some of the survivors surrendered. Even according to one of the regiment's own historians, this had been ". . . one of the worst stories of gross mismanagement and unsoldierly conduct in the Army's history". Not even the Saratoga humiliation had been condemned as bitingly as that.

And yet in the wake of this debacle the new King, Edward VII, chose to bestow on the regiment public marks of his respect. Its soldiers were henceforth to wear on the left side of their head-dress a primrose hackle, a small plume of feathers. The red rose of Lancaster was to be incorporated into the design of the Regimental Colour, the banner which already bore a rose that was supposed to have been embroidered by Queen Charlotte, wife of George III. Finally, there was now to be a motto, *Omnia Audax* – Daring in all things! Thus was more sacred tradition added to the regiment that would always refer to itself – whatever truncated form the Army might officially authorise – as XX The Lancashire Fusiliers; and they were mighty particular about retaining the Roman numerals. Such idiosyncrasy was intended, of course, to rouse that *esprit de corps* without which a military unit was under some handicap when required to get its courage up for battle. Regiments cultivated these things most carefully, often to the point of eccentricity, like the Royal Welch Fusiliers, who still wore a black pleated cloth behind the neck, though it was a long time since such a thing had been necessary to prevent oiled pigtails from staining a red uniform, and whose spelling of the second word in their name was another individual touch. A peculiarity of the Lancashire Fusiliers was not to stand to attention when "The British Grenadiers" was played: this had been a regimental march for twenty years, and in any other regiment such casual behaviour would have warranted a man being put on a charge at least.

Nowhere were these nuances cherished more than in the officers' mess at Bury Barracks. The regimental band was often in attendance before dinner, to entertain the gentlemen in their ante-room. When dinner was announced and they moved next door, the band would strike up "The Roast Beef of Old England" and play it until the officers had sat down. Toasts were to be drunk in wine or in water and nothing else, and when the President called on the Mess Sergeant to produce coffee the gentlemen could begin to smoke – but they had to use the silver table lighters, and nothing of their own. There then took place a ceremony that was meticulously codified in the regimental customary. The Mess Sergeant asked the Commanding Officer if he was ready to receive the Bandmaster and, on being given the nod, placed a chair "on the right of, and slightly behind" the CO. When the Bandmaster entered he was invited to sit down, given a glass of port, and after a few minutes returned to his band. Snuff – "the taking of which is optional" – was then offered to the gentlemen in a ritual that allowed for no deviation. It was handed round counter-clockwise by the Mess Sergeant, beginning with the officer or guest on the Vice-President's right. The instructions then went on: "The loosely clenched fist of the left hand is held out slightly behind the chair for the Mess Sergeant to place the snuff in the hollow between the base of the thumb and the knuckle of the first finger, when it is 'tamped' and 'raked' before being inhaled. After inhaling of the snuff, the hand is returned for brushing with the hare's pad." In one of the auxiliary battalions of the regiment, each gentleman was also expected to tap the lid of the snuff box twice before passing it on to his neighbour.

The auxiliary battalions were to be the most affected by yet another military reorganisation which occurred between 1907 and 1910, instigated by Richard Haldane, Cardwell's latest successor at the War Office. The Militia was abolished and in its place was created a Special Reserve, on which the Regular Army could draw for reinforcements when fighting overseas. At the same time, the Volunteers and the Yeomanry (the rural and cavalry equivalent of the urban Volunteers) were refashioned as the Territorial Force, whose obligations were somewhat different from those of the Reservists. The Territorials – Terriers, as they would shortly become known throughout northern England – were not obliged to serve overseas, though they might make a commitment to do so in emergency. They signed on for four years of spare-time training which meant doing ten to twenty drills a year, plus two weeks of continuous training in camp, plus a musketry course. In return for this, each man received a modest payment, scarcely more than an honorarium. Haldane was a philosopher as well as a politician, an idealist who believed in a popular national army, and he saw the Territorials as the great nexus between the military establishment and the civilians. How the civilians saw it may be deduced to some extent from the size of the Territorial Force in July 1914, just before war broke out again. It then numbered 268,777 officers and men. But only 18,683 had taken the Imperial Service obligation which signified a willingness to go overseas.

Cardwell in the first place and Haldane after him had been necessarily influenced in all their reorganisation by the availability of recruits, by the better response the recruiting officers obtained in one part of the country rather than in another: that was why a regiment which started life in Devon had fetched up 300 miles away in Lancashire. This policy, however, did not mean that the Fusiliers had the entire County Palatine to themselves: they shared it with the East Lancashire Regiment, the South Lancashire Regiment, the Manchester Regiment, the Loyal North Lancashire Regiment, the York and Lancaster Regiment – and that was to take no account of Liverpool, which had two regiments of its own. There was a certain amount of overlap in the designated Regimental Area of the Fusiliers, whose boundary was everywhere within ten miles of Wellington Barracks in the depot town. Most notably, this area included Salford, which was jealous of its separate civic identity even though, in the spreading conurbation of southeast Lancashire, no one but a native could have told where it finished and where Manchester began. All these Lancashire regiments were competing for recruits in one of the most densely populated areas of Europe, and the degree of overlap in this competition is suggested by the enlistments to the Regular battalions of the Fusiliers in a single year before the Great War broke out. In 1900 the regiment acquired 518 new soldiers, not all of whom stayed to complete the full term of their engagement: some subsequently bought themselves out of the Army on payment of £18, while some deserted, several were ejected because they had lied about their age, and a few memorable characters were discharged as "incorrigible and worthless" when even NCOs had come to the conclusion that there was nothing more to be done with them. Of the 518 who originally signed on, no more than 347 came from Lancashire, the rest of them a medley of fellows from almost every part of the country, including twenty-one men from different London suburbs who joined on the same day and all described themselves as "musicians". Strangely, no more than seventeen new recruits came from Bury itself and its closest neighbours, Tottington and Radcliffe – eight labourers, two carters, a printer, a piecer, a dyer, a miner, a wheelwright, a cleaner and a painter. Things were not too bad in the cotton mills that year. That was one recruit fewer than the number of newly enlisted Irishmen.

Here was a famous regiment which was held in high regard throughout the Army. In the precedence of infantry it came behind the Guards and the Rifle Brigade, and it was probably a little lower than the Highlanders as well. It was somewhere on a par with the Light Infantry regiments and the other Fusiliers; was itself a cut above the southern English county regiments and the Lowland Scots; quite lofty when compared with the Irish, Welsh, Midland and other northern regiments. So it might be thought strange that the people who were being invited to regard it as "their" regiment had seemed so studiously to ignore it. But, since coming to Bury in 1873, the Lancashire Fusiliers had not yet covered themselves with glory: Omdurman didn't count, because that was a walkover. Nor had the regiment been involved in anything that deeply affected the heart of the community: Spion Kop had been a disgrace as well as a relatively small disaster in the total catalogue of military setbacks. The Great War, and especially Gallipoli, was to change all that.

# 2

# "The Natives Here Are
# Very Funny"

At Bury Barracks the 3rd and 4th Battalions of the Lancashire
Fusiliers were celebrating Minden Day that Saturday, in accord-
ance with the regiment's proudest tradition. The great victory
against the French had been won on the first day of August and so,
in 1914, the Fusiliers remembered the battle with elaborate ritual,
as they had done on every anniversary for well over a hundred
and fifty years. The morning had begun as usual with Reveille, but
from that moment the day took on a character that was all its own,
unlike any other in the year. As soon as the bugle call had died
away across the fields on that edge of the town, martial music was
heard as the regimental band trooped round the Barracks, playing
"The Minden March", whose origins no one was quite sure of,
though for many years it had invariably been played immediately
after "The British Grenadiers" on all ceremonial occasions and was
therefore regarded as a uniquely regimental tune. At the same time,
to emphasise that this was a most abnormal day, the sergeants were
taking early-morning tea round the barrack rooms, and serving it
to the rank and file of the soldiery, who received it while still in
their beds. At every meal that day, the privates and the corporals
were treated as officers usually are; with, on this occasion, the
officers and senior NCOs waiting on them. The Barracks was generally a relaxed place on Minden Day, but there were moments of
highly imperative procedure at regular intervals.

From the regimental headquarters that dawn, greetings were telegraphed to those other parts of the Army that had been at Minden
with the old XXth Foot – the Suffolk Regiment, the Royal Welch
Fusiliers, the King's Own Scottish Borderers, the Hampshire Regiment, the King's Own Yorkshire Light Infantry and the Royal Artillery. They had also been transmitted to the 1st Battalion of the

Fusiliers, doing time in India once again; and to the 2nd Battalion which, for the moment, was stationed in Dover as part of the 12th Infantry Brigade. A special order of the day was promulgated, informing all ranks of what had happened, in all its tactical detail, in 1759. Half-way through the morning a number of civilian guests arrived at the Barracks – retired officers and their families, local dignitaries and the like – to join the families of the serving gentlemen and soldiers who were to watch Trooping the Colour, one of the big set pieces of military display. On the vast parade ground, surrounded by the sooty black barrack blocks, the Regimental Colour, intricately embroidered with crest and motto and battle honours, was solemnly borne at the slow march up and down each file of troops, braced and motionless in all their pressed and burnished discipline. The civilians agreed that the Trooping was a splendid show, as it was every time they saw it. The Fusiliers were as extremely smart and well drilled as ever. And the roses looked wonderfully fresh this year; you could catch their scent across the massed ranks.

Roses played an important part in Minden Day. Every Fusilier, from private to Commanding Officer, wore two in his cap from Reveille to Lights Out; one yellow and one red, which approximated to the regimental colours. There was a wreath of them attached to the Colour, festoons of them were entwined in the ropework of all the drums, and they decorated the Drum-Major's staff. Another rose wreath hung all day over the portrait of Lieutenant-General William Kingsley, who had been Colonel of the Regiment and in command at the battle itself. But the most curious celebration of the legend about the soldiers picking roses on their way to fight the French occurred that evening in the officers' mess. Every gentleman wore two roses on his best uniform and the dinner table was decorated with them as well. The meal then proceeded and, when the food had been eaten, the loyal toast was drunk, followed by another "to those who fell at Minden". The Bandmaster was entertained as usual but, after he had departed, the evening took a singular turn. Yet more roses were brought in, all carefully stripped of stems and thorns. One was then placed in front of every new subaltern and any other officer who had not taken part in the ritual before, every flower floating in a glass of champagne. When all had been served, each officer got up, glass in hand, stood on his chair, ate his rose, and washed it down with his wine. The initiates then sat down to applause, thankful that never again would they be required to perform that particular party trick.

Everyone at the Barracks and elsewhere in Bury had been expecting trouble long before that Minden Saturday in 1914, but they had not been anticipating the war that would, in fact, break out the following Tuesday. Matters were coming to a head in Ireland at last and the Lancashire Fusiliers were very probably going to find themselves over there in the middle of a nasty civil war. The House of Commons two years earlier had at long last passed a bill that would give the nationalists the home rule for which they had endlessly campaigned, the changed circumstances which all sane men believed would end the bitterness that had existed since the times of Cromwell and Queen Elizabeth, that had been horribly exacerbated at the Battle of the Boyne. Even though there was a notable lack of enthusiasm for this measure in the upper house of Parliament, the Lords were not in a position to delay its enactment beyond 1914. Helpless to prevent home rule becoming a reality if they stayed within the law, therefore, the Protestant Ulster Unionists led by Sir Edward Carson had decided to fight it by force of arms. They had obtained nearly 20,000 rifles with two million rounds of ammunition from Hamburg, smuggled them ashore at Larne and other places from the steamer *Clydevalley*, and started drilling with them. A provisional Ulster government was to be set up the moment the home rule bill became legal, and its decisions would be backed by this newly armed Ulster Volunteer Force. The likelihood was that these would shortly be locked in mortal combat not only with the National Volunteers raised by Catholic Irishmen, but with a British Army instructed to enforce the democratic will of Westminster.

The Irish Question was a matter of some moment in Bury, quite apart from the probability that its local regiment would soon be over there again.* Like every other town in industrial Lancashire, it included many families of Irish origin who had crossed the water in search of work during the nineteenth century and since. They were without exception Catholics and they sympathised with the nationalist cause. Towards the end of July there had been a mass

---

* By chance, the 2nd Battalion of the Fusiliers was commanded by an Irishman, Major J. C. Griffin, who had been badly wounded at Spion Kop where, among other injuries, he had lost an eye. In spite of this, he was "possessed of a genial and optimistic temperament".

meeting on the Fairground, an expanse of open land in the middle
of Bury. Scores of Irish attended and passed a resolution drafted by
their chairman, Mr O'Reilly, supporting John Redmond, the nationalist leader, and the Irish National Volunteers, and declaring their
belief that "the rule of England in Ireland as it has been carried out
in the past is forever dead and buried". Four days later three people
were killed just outside Dublin, when the military opened fire on
a crowd that had been collecting smuggled guns (again from Hamburg) for the INV. At once the Bury Irish gathered in their Davitt
Club to express their sympathy on "another sad day of atrocious
massacre". [Michael Davitt was from a Mayo family who found
work in the cotton mills of Rossendale. At the age of ten he lost an
arm in an industrial accident, but acquired an education through
the good offices of the local schoolmaster, and became a spokesman
for the home rule movement.] The outbreak of the Great War, in
fact, remarkably caused Redmond and Carson to call a truce in their
dispute and to support the British Government until the war's end,
while the home rule bill was suspended for the duration. "Little
Catholic Belgium" was an early victim of the Kaiser's aggression
and therefore an object of southern Irish sympathy, which explains
why, in many parts of Ulster, the National Volunteers improbably
settled their differences with their Protestant counterparts, so that
these antagonists actually went to war as comrades in arms. There
has always been a tendency to emphasise the part played by the
mainly Protestant Ulster regiments in the Great War – especially
on the catastrophic first day of the Somme offensive – but Irish
regiments that were predominantly Catholic and from the south
also fought gallantly and lost heavily in the hostilities. Two of these
were at Gallipoli. Yet the fact remains that when the bare order to
mobilise reached Bury on August 4, without specifying the purpose,
the headquarters of the Fusiliers were so prepared for civil war in
Ireland that billeting parties were at once despatched to Limerick,
on the assumption that the troops would be ordered to follow them
within hours.

Minden Day was the first time a conflict anywhere else in Europe
had been acknowledged publicly in the town, though a month had
passed since the assassination at Sarajevo, and the international
crisis had been growing steadily ever since. When, that Saturday,
news came of the Austro-Hungarian declaration of war on Serbia,
a leading article in a local newspaper struck a note of alarm at this

unexpected turn of events, but entertained the hope that it would not affect Bury very much: "A week ago Europe was concerned over the threatened rupture between Austria and Serbia, but at the time few people imagined that anything more serious than one of those nine-day scares which periodically disturb the sensitive barometer of the Continent was astir. Today it is realised that we are nearer a great European war than at any time since the seventies . . . We trust that our people will keep their heads and not suffer themselves to be led away by Jingo arguments. We have been assured by the Prime Minister and Sir Edward Grey that there is nothing in any unpublished obligation to foreign powers that would fetter our free choice of action in the event of a European war. And if there is nothing in our obligations to involve our national honour we are quite sure that the people of this country will look to His Majesty's advisers with full confidence to keep the Empire outside the quarrel."

The mood of the town changed abruptly that week. The Minden Day weekend was, coincidentally, a public holiday, and people from all over Lancashire as usual rushed to the coast for a few days. Between Saturday and Sunday morning no fewer than twenty-seven steamers arrived in the Isle of Man from Liverpool, Fleetwood and Heysham, and disembarked nearly 40,000 holidaymakers. Record crowds also took themselves off to Morecambe and Llandudno that weekend. For Bury people there should then have been a brief return to work before their annual Wakes Week began, when every factory closed and the town emptied itself completely, and made for Black-pool and the other coastal resorts. This was the one time in the year when visibility was doubled in Bury itself, and the nearest hills could be seen with clarity, because the chimneys of mill and householder were no longer putting out clouds of smoke. But in 1914, war was declared the day after people returned from the Bank Holiday weekend, and Wakes Week became the slackest the holi-day resorts had ever known. On the first day of the annual break, six special trains from Bury to the Lancashire and Yorkshire coasts were cancelled, followed by another three intended for Blackpool a couple of days later. Instead of making for the beaches, the promen-ades, the variety shows and the boarding houses of the seaside, the millworkers of Bury made the best of things by taking day trips to the Belle Vue pleasure gardens in Manchester, or to the city's less expensive Heaton Park. Hard times had suddenly come to the community again, and a population well accustomed to periodic hardship reacted with customary thrift. The Mayor had no need to advise his fellow townsmen and women to husband their resources, as he did the day war broke out. Some of them had started to do so the moment they heard rumour of hostilities in continental Europe. Not only did they cancel their holiday bookings at the coast, in anticipation of the worst, but they started to queue outside food-shops before they even opened, in order to stock their larders before the prices went up.

Before that week was out, the most familiar hardship of all was upon them. One or two mills and workshops closed down in the first few days, not because their work forces had been called up by the military, or because the orders had just stopped, or because raw materials had been cut off; but because private transport in many cases had been commandeered and the firms in question were unable to deliver their cloth and other products to customers. The millowners were a thrifty lot, too, keeping ahead of their employees in this as in other respects. By mid-September several of the Bury mills were working only alternate weeks, and others were employing people on short time. No fewer than 19,000 looms were affected in the town, operated by 5,000 weavers. Of these, 1,300 were out of work completely; the rest were on short time. But some firms would soon prosper in the war. The town contained the biggest maker of ambulances in England, destined to take the lead in a growth industry once the blood began to flow. A local slipper works quickly obtained government orders for endless quantities of hospital footwear.

Refugees began to arrive from Belgium very soon after Britain went to war. Some were billeted on a local convent, while another group was quartered in some cottages on a strip of land between the Irwell and the canal. Yet at the same time as taking these unfortunate strangers in, and collecting large amounts of clothing for the Relief Fund organised by Belgium's London embassy, the town became intensely suspicious of any strangers who might con-ceivably be German spies. A man "of slightly foreign appearance" was arrested near a temporary camp of soldiers one day, but turned out to be a Mancunian who had simply been trying to sell firewood, and was released after questioning. A similar experience befell a surveyor employed by a neighbouring local authority, who imprud-ently began to make sketches of a road junction at the bottom of

Rossendale, unaware that he was under observation by a police constable who happened to be guarding a nearby railway tunnel. The bobby took some convincing that the drawings were authorised in connection with wartime relief work that might be needed to assist unemployed men too old to go and fight.

Among those not yet quite old enough were the boys of the local grammar school, some of whom were preparing, and being prepared, for war long before it actually broke out. The most important source of leaders for the auxiliary forces of the Army was the Officers' Training Corps, which had existed for many years in the British universities and public schools. By 1914 there were 25,000 of these young men, and a lot of them were destined to die before 1918. Bury Grammar School was extremely proud of its OTC, which was a conspicuous fact of life among its older pupils. Twice a week, half an afternoon was set aside from lessons so that they might drill in the school yard, learn to fire rifles, acquire the rudiments of field craft, and discover how to read maps. They were dressed in the khaki uniforms of rank and file troops on these occasions, but what they were really being taught were ways and means of leading an adult rank and file on the battlefield. From time to time they demonstrated their prowess in public, and such an event took place early that July on the school playing fields in front of the headmaster, various military figures, a parson or two, and an assortment of admiring parents. They watched the cadets go through their paces, which included tent-pitching, a boat race on the adjacent Irwell, a shooting contest, and bayonet drill.

Towards the end of July the school's contingent went south to the garrison town of Aldershot for their annual camp. Similar groups of uniformed youths from all over the country converged on the base where, for ten days each year, they took part in a programme that mixed military activities with adolescent fun and games, which marked them for what they really were; not yet men and no longer little boys. The massed OTC paraded for prayers each day before breakfast and then embarked on a series of manoeuvres and other exercises. On the first night there was horseplay and stifled laughter in the encampment of tents, but after the first day's work they were too tired to do anything but sleep when they got to bed. An eleven-mile march was undertaken and, after five had been completed, one of the adult officers in charge suggested that anyone not feeling up to any more was permitted to fall out; but no Bury lad did, "which reflects great credit on the smaller boys of the corps". They were looking forward, after the first few days, to playing a football match against a rival school from Hereford, and the only casualties they had so far sustained were a sprained ankle and a couple of bloody noses. On the last day of July they practised battalion attacks, and during the Minden weekend they enjoyed themselves with football and cricket matches, "followed by leap frog and kindred games". There should still have been several days of the camp ahead, but on Monday it was suddenly called off. The camp staff were Guardsmen, real soldiers, and they had just received the order to mobilise. There was nothing for the budding leaders of the Bury OTC to do but pack up and go home, and this they did after one last night under canvas, "in our clothes and two blankets each, with rifles by our side". They arrived back in Lancashire the very moment war was declared.

The Territorials, too, had been in camp that summer, beside the sea at Prestatyn, whose citizens were pleasantly surprised by the behaviour of "4,000 khaki-clad warriors" because they included fewer rowdies than the North Welsh had expected, though they patronised the itinerant tattoo-artist much more enthusiastically than any local chapelgoer would have done. The Bury contingent of these part-time soldiers, the 5th Battalion of the Fusiliers, had been home for several weeks by the time the war began and many of them had been looking forward to the annual holiday like everybody else. Instead, they were among the great crowds which gathered at various places round town that Tuesday evening, reading the mobilisation notices posted on the walls of Corporation offices, police stations and elsewhere; so many people massing outside the Barracks in drizzling rain that they stopped the traffic and had to be moved along by the police. Wherever they assembled, the crowds were very subdued; there was none of the exuberance that marked the start of the Boer War. Next morning the Territorials began to report for duty at the Drill Hall in the centre of the town, which was the 5th Battalion's own rallying point, a significant mile and a half from the Barracks, where the Regular soldiers and the men of the Special Reserve Battalions were installed in the regimental HQ.*

---

* The Drill Hall stood on the site of Bury's medieval fortification and was otherwise known as the Castle Armoury. Originally built in 1868, it was substantially extended in 1907 as a result of the Haldane reforms that produced the Territorial Force.

Bury was full of men, some in uniform and others still in civilian clothes, hurrying to both the Barracks and the Drill Hall to sign themselves in, nearly three thousand of them all told. Many were accompanied by their wives, and the Terriers carried small parcels containing a number of items they were expected to provide for themselves as they embarked on full-time military service at last. These ("not necessarily to be of Army pattern, but sufficiently serviceable to last three months") included a pair of ankle boots, a pair of braces, shaving brush, toothbrush, comb, fork and spoon, a hold-all and a "housewife" (with buttons, needles and thread), a clasp-knife with an attached tin-opener, a pair of bootlaces, a razor, two flannel shirts, two pairs of worsted socks and two towels. On reporting to the Drill Hall they were given identity discs and rifles, and were examined by a doctor. The 5th Battalion consisted of 1,020 men and by the Wednesday night, 850 of them had reported for duty, been passed fit for service and fully equipped. Every man who lived within the borough boundary was allowed to go home after that, but had to report at the Drill Hall three times a day until further notice. Anyone living more than a mile and a half away was billeted in town.

The Reservists of the 3rd and 4th Battalions, fully trained soldiers, most of whom had fought in South Africa, were the first to leave Bury for this latest passage of arms. On Thursday night two companies, who were followed by the rest over the next couple of days, swung out of the Barracks gate and marched down into town behind a local concertina band, which played "Scotch Airs" and "Tipperary" among other tunes. When they reached the railway station they boarded a waiting train and, as this pulled out, the band struck up "Auld Lang Syne" until the last carriage disappeared round the bend towards Manchester. Then it played the National Anthem for the benefit of the crowds who had seen the troops off. These had cheered as the train began to move; but the people who had lined the route from the Barracks had watched more reticently as the khaki files passed by. A thoughtful onlooker said later: "The general feeling that the men were in for serious work and that there was to be serious work, too, for those they were leaving behind, contributed to an outward calm and soberness of demeanour altogether different from anything that the past generation has seen. In all previous wars that the England of today remembers, there have been too many people left behind whose stake in the affairs at issue has been too light to give them real ballast. And so when they left for these wars, they cheered and hurrahed and waved the flag with a joyousness that expelled all deeper feelings and even in the face of ordeal gave elation that could only be possible with the absence of all sense of responsibility. Today the tide that is flowing is too full for sound or foam. And this is evident in the departure of the Reservists. There is no lack of sympathy with the men or for the cause for which they are about to fight: there is rather an abundance of that sympathy that is so deep it seemed to find difficulty in audible expression . . ."

The Territorials of the 5th Battalion remained in limbo for another ten days, though some were pressed into sentry duty at a field on the outskirts of town, where many horses, requisitioned by the Army, grazed. Most of the soldiers were put through company and section drills in the grounds of Chamber Hall, where Sir Robert Peel had been born, and where a field kitchen was now set up. This was a preliminary to exercises on a larger scale. On August 22 the men were marched out of Bury to make camp on the edge of the moors above the village of Turton, eight miles away, a long column of khaki snaking gradually uphill and into open country, followed by packhorses and vehicles carrying their heavy equipment. They were not the only troops heading in that direction. By nightfall, the 5th from Bury had been joined in the encampment by the 6th Battalion from Rochdale, together with the 7th and 8th Battalions from Salford. These four units formed the Lancashire Fusiliers Brigade. On the hillside there, where the bracken was beginning to turn from green to brown, and where the curlews had almost finished rearing their young, the soldiers engaged in lustier versions of the activities the boys of the OTC had just finished with. In particular, they had to accustom themselves to the .303 Lee Enfield rifle, which had superseded the Lee Metford used in the Boer War. From 5 a.m. onwards they were at it, on route marches and operational exercises, with rifle inspections and foot inspections at regular intervals. "When not engaged in drilling, their animal spirits are so high that they cannot settle down to rest, but must engage in football and other vigorous games." For two of the Terriers, the war ended right there, within sight of home. Below the hillside the vehicles were parked beside the big Wayoh reservoir, which supplied nearby Bolton with its tapwater. The soldiers had taken their horses down its steep, sloping sides to drink, but fell in and were drowned.

At the weekend, parents and wives and sweethearts made for the encampment to be with their men. Tramcars and trains which ran out of Bury in that direction were packed, and so were the waggonettes and charabancs waiting to convey people the last mile or two. Turton had never known anything like it, with the village street as busy as Blackpool Promenade in Wakes Week. Sarah Scowcroft was one of the women who made the journey, to spend a few more hours with her James, though she left their two children behind in the care of neighbours. James was one of the older privates in the 5th Battalion at the age of thirty-four, a diligent husband and father who had kept his family respectably well fed and clothed only by working extra hours after finishing his main job painting lamp posts for the Corporation. He used to shift scenery for evening productions at the Theatre Royal, and both he and Sarah were caretakers at their local Methodist chapel and Sunday school, which meant more evening work. He had never in his life been further than the Isle of Man, and was quite hoping that the Battalion might see service overseas, so long as it wasn't too dangerous.

No one went to see George Horridge in Turton but, then, he didn't expect them to. He was, after all, an officer in the 5th Battalion and as such he was fully occupied making sure that his men were well fed, working and playing hard, keeping fit, and maintaining high morale. So was his elder brother Walter, also an officer in the 5th. The Horridges belonged to one of Bury's leading textile families, which owned a print works and a bleach works, and a cotton merchanting business in Manchester, where George was learning the trade in the counting house until the day the war began. They also had a herd of Friesian cattle on their estate in North Wales, and their yacht was moored close by in the lee of Anglesey. Like Walter and their younger brother Leslie, George had been educated at Uppingham, where one of his form-mates was a lad named Pratt, whom the world subsequently knew better as Boris Karloff. Although George had never joined the OTC at his public school, he had sought a commission in the Territorials as soon as he was able to, in 1913, when he was nineteen years old, following where Walter had led. The family connection helped, of course, because there was a waiting list of those wanting to join and you were commissioned only by invitation of the commanding officer, not as a result of direct application. Like many aspects of getting on in England, much depended on knowing the right person, who might have a word on your behalf in the influential ear. Leslie too would have a commission before the war was much older, but his was to be in the Royal Flying Corps. It had even been within the bounds of possibility that their father, John Horridge, would serve in the conflict, too. Among his hobbies he included pigeon-fancying and at the outbreak offered his birds to the Army's Pigeon Corps, which was a slow but generally reliable part of military communications. In return, he had been invited to accompany them with the rank of corporal; but this invitation, at the age of fifty-three, he had declined.

Preparations for war went ahead in Bury itself, where a band played patriotic tunes in the Market Place on the Saturday night, while many people were visiting the Turton camp. Pickets paraded the streets and mounted patrols came by at intervals, with carbines slung across their backs. The Mayor who had advised his citizens to tighten their belts the day war was declared had now put his name to a recruiting handbill which placarded the streets. "Wake up Bury!" it exclaimed. "Men are urgently wanted for all branches of the Regular Army. Height 5ft 9ins and over; Chest 36½ inches." According to the poster, the Army was looking for ex-Regular soldiers aged between nineteen and forty-five, ex-NCOs up to the age of fifty, and untrained men aged from nineteen to thirty-five. Every man was offered pay of one shilling a day, with another 1s 1d for his wife and 2d for each child under the age of fourteen (4d if they were motherless).* Recruiting had been brisk as soon as it started and some men joined up as privates when they found that there was no room for them as officers. It was announced that extra battalions of the Lancashire Fusiliers were to be formed, part of the New Army called for by Lord Kitchener, the old warrior who had become Secretary of State for War the moment hostilities began. Many optimistic people talked of the war being over by Christmas, but Kitchener believed it would last a full three years and from the outset determined to increase the British ground forces from the existing six Regular and fourteen Territorial divisions, to a total of seventy divisions. This had a profound effect on the Lancashire Fusiliers, as it did on every other regiment.

At the outbreak of war the Fusiliers amounted to the two Regular

* One shilling (12d) in the coinage of the time was the equivalent of 5p in sterling's much later decimal currency.

battalions, the 1st and 2nd; two Special Reserve battalions, 3rd and 4th; and four Territorial battalions, 5th, 6th, 7th and 8th. By the end of the war the regiment would have raised thirty full battalions and, although Bury was the regimental headquarters for all of them, the 5th Battalion was always the one closest to its heart, consisting as it did exclusively of men from Bury itself, and its immediately adjacent villages and townships. Under Kitchener's scheme there were, in fact, very soon *three* 5th Battalions, as the original 5th reached its establishment figure and could accommodate no more; it thereafter assumed the style 1st/5th Battalion, and its successors became the 2nd/5th and 3rd/5th Battalions. Similar multiples occurred among the other Territorial units, which had parochial allegiances to Rochdale and Salford initially. Gradually, however, as the battalions expanded and the war proceeded, with recruitment trying to keep up with losses and the need for new blood, men from a number of Lancashire towns found themselves serving in the same battalion of the Fusiliers; and sometimes battalions consisted of men from particular trades. The 2nd/7th, for example, were mostly employees of Salford Corporation, many of them tram drivers and conductors. The 9th were miners and millworkers from Bury and Bolton; the 10th miners and railwaymen from Bury, Wigan and Preston; the 11th miners and weavers from Burnley, Oldham, Bolton, Wigan, Preston and Blackburn; the 12th almost wholly miners and millworkers from Bury. From the outset there were anomalies. Young Bob Spencer lived just up the road from the Bury Barracks, was an apprentice turner in the nearby iron foundry, and went with his workmate Billy Schofield to join the 5th Battalion a day or two after war was declared. By then it was full and recruiting for the 2nd/5th hadn't yet begun, so Spencer and Schofield found themselves in the 7th Battalion instead, starting their Army life in the barracks at Cross Lane, Salford, instead of at Bury Drill Hall.

But with the rest of the Territorials they were at the Turton camp when the Fusiliers were told that almost the whole of the East Lancashire Brigade of other Territorial regiments, similarly encamped on the other side of Bury, had offered themselves for foreign service, though the terms of their engagements did not enforce this. The Fusiliers Brigade at Turton were invited to do likewise, after being given to understand that they would not be going to the front but would probably be sent to some colonial station with a healthy climate. Anyone who couldn't make his mind up was offered a twelve-hour leave pass so that he might go home to consult his parents or other relatives. Few men of the rank and file, in fact, with such a tempting prospect dangled before them, felt the need for consultation. James Scowcroft volunteered without hesitation, as did Bob Spencer and Billy Schofield. But Second-Lieutenant George Horridge's education at an English public school had taught him that easy blandishments were not often to be trusted; so he consulted his company commander, who happened to be his mother's cousin. He was persuaded that duty bound him to volunteer for foreign service, whatever this might entail. That, too, was a lesson taught at Uppingham. Yet three members of the mess did duck out, deciding that they would continue to make themselves available for home defence only. Two of these were medical officers with the 5th Battalion. The other was a Lieutenant Garth Stonestreet; and George Horridge was not the only man to suspect that the fellow was more fearful of upsetting his wife than he was of being thought faint-hearted by the regiment.

The weather had been exceptionally fine for most of the time at Turton: the men remarked on the spectacular views they enjoyed of the main Pennine range from the hill on which they were encamped. But it was raining heavily when the Fusiliers Brigade finished their training there on September 9. In a continuous downpour the khaki column wound its way back to Bury, followed by the packhorses and the vehicles with the heavy gear, steam rising from the animals and, after a mile or two, from the sodden greatcoats as the men inside them began to warm up. But the soldiers sang and whistled tunes as they swung along through the village of Harwood and down to the Bolton road, eventually marching past the Barracks, their boots slapping rhythmically on the cobblestones, rifles slung over their shoulders, down beside the gas works and across Bury Bridge, then uphill once more to reach the railway station. In spite of the rain, people gathered to cheer them as they passed through the villages, and again once they reached the outskirts of the town. Coming in from the opposite side were the Terriers of the East Lancashire Brigade – two battalions of the East Lancashire Regiment and more of the Manchesters – with whom they were to be joined in the 42nd (East Lancashire) Division. In the station yard huge preparations had been made to receive these troops, nearly 14,000 officers and men in all. Every man was given a ration of biscuits, corned beef and cheese to keep him going for the next day or so, and in relays they were sent to fill their water bottles from the supply at the abattoir beyond the station yard. Someone had thought to procure ice to cool the soldiers down after the miles they had slogged in greatcoats while carrying rifles and full packs. When all was ready they began to move out of Bury; and for too many of them it was the last they would see of the town. It took twenty-four hours and thirty special trains to get the Division away: the 13,675 human beings, the 5,680 horses, the thirty-six 15-pounder guns, the twelve howitzers, the twenty-four heavy machine guns, and the 239 carts, bound for a destination not more than half a dozen people could even guess at.

The first Lancashire Fusiliers to take part in the Great War, the 2nd Battalion of Regulars, had already seen action and received their first casualties at Cambrai earlier that week. The 3rd and 4th Battalions which had left Bury a few days after war was declared, did not travel nearly so far before reaching their destinations. The first of them was posted to the Yorkshire coast for defence against an invading force, the second despatched to Barrow-in-Furness to protect its shipbuilding yards; but throughout the war both sent regular drafts to join the fighting men, and plenty of Fusiliers who started the war in the 3rd or 4th died in battle with some other unit of the regiment. Meanwhile, the 1st Battalion was still in India, and would not leave Karachi for another month. It then sailed for Aden, where it stayed for some weeks to relieve the existing garrison, before proceeding to England. It reached Bristol on Christmas Day, still dressed in the old-fashioned red tunics and blue trousers, to the astonishment of local people, who had seen nothing but khaki for many months. The troops were given leave before reassembling, not in the depot town but at Nuneaton in Warwickshire, where they were refitted and re-equipped and drilled in the use of all their new gear with other regiments of the 29th Division. Spring was imminent before the 1st Battalion embarked again, after being inspected by King George V, and it was March 28, 1915 before these most professional Lancashire Fusiliers had sailed the length of the Mediterranean to arrive at Alexandria.

Their Territorial battalions were awaiting them in Egypt, the "colonial station with a healthy climate" that the authorities had promised the unproven soldiery in order to lure them out of Britain. The Fusiliers Brigade and the other Terriers of the East Lancashire Division had moved very slowly across England from Bury in their great convoy of railway trains at the beginning of autumn. It had been fifteen hours before they reached Southampton docks, where their troopship was getting up steam, and they were glad to stretch their legs on deck as the vessel moved down the Solent and into the Channel. Apart from the officers, virtually none of the passengers had been to sea before except on day trips to the Isle of Man, such as James Scowcroft had experienced. They were pleased to discover that the food aboard the troopship was a distinct improvement on what the field kitchens had been able to cook at Turton, and they were intrigued by the novelty of sleeping in hammocks, once they had acquired the knack of getting into them without tumbling straight out of the other side. Only the senior sergeants and their superiors were allowed the benefit of cabins and bunks. As a sort of compensation, however, everyone below the rank of sergeant was allowed to move around the ship in bare feet, and they could even wear football jerseys if they had them, instead of uniform. It was a relaxed voyage for the most part, except for a spell of rough weather when they were crossing the Bay of Biscay, and the band – which normally played for one hour in the morning and another in the afternoon – was silent for a couple of days. Some of the men were fearfully ill during the worst of it: so were some of the officers, in spite of trying a concoction called Bismarck which the medical officer recommended as a sovereign remedy – a mixture of champagne and stout in about equal parts. And yet, even when the vessel had passed Gibraltar and was sailing through the warm and lenient waters of the Med, there was a wistfulness on the troop decks that in the evenings expressed itself in a refrain the men would sing as they lounged in the open air under the brilliant North African sky:

> Homeland, homeland, when shall I see you again?
> Land of my birth, dearest land on earth.
> Homeland, homeland, when shall I see you again?
> It may be a year or it may be forever, dear Homeland.

Egypt roused them from their nostalgia, for a little while at least, as they absorbed its strangeness, inspected it critically, enjoyed some of its exotic attractions, and measured everything against the familiar things at home. They weren't much impressed by the train on which they travelled from Alexandria to Cairo, which was a bit like riding in a cattle van compared with the carriages provided by the London and North Western Railway Company. The rolling stock here was open-ended, to allow air to cool things down inside, and it looked dangerous to the Englishmen, as indeed it could be if the passengers did not take care: two soldiers were to be killed before long, after falling out when trains were travelling at speed. At the end of the journey from home, the Fusiliers were installed in Abbassia Barracks, Cairo, and this was a great eye-opener to them, an enormous white building, completely different from the grim Wellington Barracks they knew so well. "It's like a palace," Private Goodwin wrote to his mother in Bury. "There are plunge baths, shower baths and washing places, all white tiles . . ." Some of them thought it more like a hospital than anything else, about twenty times the size of the regimental headquarters at home, with massive dormitories and balconies running round the outside, on which they were allowed to sleep when it became really hot. They were very easily, very touchingly pleased by this improvement in their living standards.

As the troopship approached Alexandria it passed a convoy of vessels full of Indian soldiers, on their way to France, and there were still some Bengal Lancers and other Indians awaiting transport to Europe when the Fusiliers got ashore. "We try and talk to the Indians," wrote Private Hart, "but can only tell what they say about war. They say 'We go and cut damned German throats. We show them how to fight.' They wear turbans round their heads and very light clothing, with their puttees wrapped round their legs. They have very short pants." The young Lancastrians treated the Egyptians more cautiously and had even less conversation with them than with the Bengalis and the other brown men they came across. "The people are mostly coloured," wrote Private Smethurst, "with an odd Frenchman here and there. They came rushing to meet us with all kinds of fancy articles including such things as silks, rings, postcards, beads, watches and chains and heaps of other things, and the best of it is that we cannot understand a word they say. Mother and Florrie would feel rather strange walking down Rock Street [one of Bury's main streets, later renamed The Rock] surrounded by coloured men and women, shaking their fists and pulling all kinds of funny faces. But they are quite harmless if left alone and I think it more their fun than anything else, as they laugh heartily at every white man as he walks down the street. Still, we have been

warned to keep in the main street and leave them alone." Private
Seal also saw them benignly. "The natives here are very funny," he
wrote to his parents. "Their trousers would make us two suits."
He told how they would wash the Englishmen's clothes for almost
nothing, how you could travel for three or four miles on a tramcar
much more cheaply than in Bury, how Cairo had a White City, just
like the one in Manchester . . .

Some of the Terriers went forth to see the Cairene sights that
were not remotely duplicated in Manchester. Private Moores, who
had been a schoolmaster before joining up, explained how, after
getting off the tram in the suburb of Heliopolis, "an expert swindler
– guide I believe is his title – attached himself to us and after some
haggling (an Arab's delight) we agreed on the first cost, which we
found out was but a tithe of the total, and made for the Sphinx first,
which is in a hollow and invisible from road level. Photos have to
be taken from a certain position to include the Sphinx and the
Pyramids, and are deceptive. Those who expect to see the Sphinx
towering to half the height of the Pyramid of Cheops as in the
photos must be disappointed at first glance. The body is sadly worn
away and shapeless . . . and yet on closer inspection and appreci-
ation it is still a wonderful object and worth seeing." Inside the
Pyramid, where the guide lit a magnesium flare for illumination,
"it was very hot inside the passages but the tombs have small
airholes in or it would be awful. We were almost as glad to get out
and breathe fresh air again as we were anxious to get in."

But most men made their own amusements or enjoyed the
strange vitality of the bazaar once they had finished work for the
day. The heat meant that they did most of their parade-ground drill
either very early in the morning or in the evening, when things had
cooled off. They put in a lot of shooting on the ranges as well.
Young Second-Lieutenant Horridge, who had been a fine soccer
player at Uppingham, formed a football team at Abbassia and kitted
it out with red-and-white quartered shirts. It played only Egyptian
sides and never lost a match. On his twenty-first birthday he
gathered up all the NCOs in his company and took them out to
dinner, including a couple who were almost old enough to be his
father. Even the other ranks entertained themselves in this way
from time to time. Shepheard's was out of bounds to all but officers
and gentlemen, but there were plenty of other hotels where the
Egyptians would give you a great spread. James Scowcroft and some

of his mates in A Company had a fine meal at the Grand Continental in Cairo, and he sent the menu home to Sarah with his scribble at the foot: "This was where we dined on Christmas Eve – swank!" He bought his Christmas present to her in one of the hotel's shops: an enamelled pendant mummy case with a tiny mummy inside. He sent the children, Alice and Joseph James, Cairo tram tickets as souvenirs. Both their birthdays fell in February and he did not forget the dates or the Lancashire ritual for juvenile anniversaries, when the hair was pulled once for each year. One card arrived with "6 lugs" written beneath a kiss, the other with "10 lugs" for Joseph James.

Some of them never took to this curiously thrilling experience at all; like Bob Spencer, who thought Cairo a dirty place and in its perpetual heat dreamed only of the mineral water sold at the corner shop near his home on Bolton Road. Some had rotten accidents, like the two Fusiliers who fell out of the train, and some merely got ill; like Corporal Evans, who refused to be vaccinated on principle – his brother was a well-known herbalist in Union Square at home and probably responsible for the aversion – and was laid low with smallpox as a result. But as their weeks in Egypt dragged on into months, even the ones who had savoured the newness and the strangeness of everything with enthusiasm at first, began to wilt in the enervating heat, where one day increasingly seemed no different from the rest, and they began to wonder what on earth they were doing there, in idleness, when so much was happening in France. Their spirits rose near the end of March, when the 1st Battalion of the Fusiliers at last arrived, though maybe not quite so much as is implied by the official historian of the regiment, writing in an heroic mode: "The men looked at each other with mutual approval, for the Territorials had trained hard during the short period of embodiment, while the seasoned Regulars seemed to them the ideal of military manhood."

Private Chadwick of the 1st/5th Battalion was nearer the mark in his last letter home: "All the boys are looking as well as can be expected, but we are all fed up with this monotonous life." The monotony – and, for some, life itself – was about to end most terribly.

# 3

# Lancashire Landing

Everyone remembered, long after it was all over, the serenity just before it began. The Aegean weather had been poor that April, with high winds and squalls of rain almost every day, as the great Allied armada gathered at Lemnos, forty miles across the sea to the west of Gallipoli. Well over two hundred vessels were anchored in the bay there by the morning of Friday the 23rd, waiting for the order to go, and the weather had changed marvellously. The sun had come up hot, the early morning haze had burned away, the day was clear and utterly still. When the ships weighed anchor one after another and slipped out of the bay, their bows scarcely disturbed the motionless sea as they headed for the lee of islands closer to the Turkish shore – warships and transports and coal boats and trawlers and all the other craft that had been accumulated to bear the invaders to the peninsula. They were the only things moving in this tranquillity, which continued through that night, and the next day, and beyond. On Saturday evening, as a young Lancashire Fusilier was to recall in later years, "Nature was so peaceful. A dead flat calm, an oily sea, a silent, beautiful rock-crowned island with its replica in the bay beneath, no sound or movement in water or in air . . ." Everyone who survived the next few hours was to remember this perfection of Nature at peace for as long as he lived.

As the armada approached the coast it began to fan out, for the grand design was for simultaneous dawn landings on Sunday the 25th, to be made at many points in order to confuse the Turks and stretch their resources, as well as for strategic considerations. The French, in fact, were not to be landed on Gallipoli itself but on the opposite side of the Dardanelles, at Kum Kale, only a few miles from Troy, where Turkish artillery – in spite of naval bombardment – still commanded the straits and threatened Cape Helles, the tip of the peninsula across the water. On Gallipoli there were to be two great thrusts at the defenders. The Australians and New Zealanders were to be put ashore in the vicinity of Ari Burnu, a point of land a dozen miles or so above Cape Helles, where the Aegean coastline was indented in a series of shallow coves. It was intended that the colonial troops would swiftly move inland, take the high ground behind the beaches and sit astride the peninsula, isolating Turkish troops to the south from those to the north and cutting them off from the road to Constantinople. Meanwhile, British forces would have landed in an arc at five different places round the foot of Gallipoli, codenamed S, V, W, X and Y Beaches. S Beach faced Kum Kale across the Dardanelles. X and Y Beaches were on the Aegean shore. V and W Beaches were separated by the headland of Cape Helles itself. The plan was for the British to push the Turks north until they found the Anzacs at their back and, it was hoped, surrendered. The Allies would then roll on together up the peninsula and beyond it until they reached the Turkish capital.

There were many reasons why not one of these objectives was achieved, and abysmal staff work was the fault with the most far-reaching effects. It resulted, for example, in the armada sailing from Lemnos with only one of eight floating piers which had been specifically designed to make landings on Gallipoli easier than wading ashore on to a beach; and it was responsible for the Australians being landed beneath a scrub-covered cliff when they were expecting to be put on to a low sand dune a mile to the south. The preliminary naval bombardment had not devastated the Turkish positions, as planned, and this also contributed to the ultimate debacle. The tenacity of the Turkish soldiers, moreover, had been seriously underestimated by Allied commanders, who had expected resistance everywhere to crumble almost at once. On S, X and Y Beaches, it is true, British troops found no serious impediments, but the Turkish defence was extremely fierce against the two Cape Helles landings and where the Anzacs went ashore.

The worst carnage of all was at V Beach, where men of two Irish regiments – the Royal Dublin Fusiliers and the Royal Munster Fusiliers – together with soldiers of the Hampshire Regiment, were put on to Gallipoli in a 1915 version of the Trojan Horse. A naval commander had come up with the idea of packing an old collier, the *River Clyde*, with 2,000 troops and running it ashore: the troops would then rush out of sally ports cut into the ship's sides and

down gangplanks before crossing a bridge of lighters to step on to
dry land. The Munsters and the Hampshires were given this task,
while the Dublins were to be landed from naval cutters, wooden
boats propelled by oars, further along the beach. The Turks, waiting
for the invaders in an old castle standing on the shore, did nothing
until the cutters and the collier grounded; then they put down a
hail of machine-gun fire, a mixture of lead and incendiary shells.
The men in the cutters were almost wiped out, and so were the
first troops to emerge from the *River Clyde*, mown down as they
ran along the gangways, body falling over body and tumbling into
the water, where wounded Dublins had already sunk under the
weight of their packs and been drowned. So many men were so
quickly lost in trying to get off the collier that a halt was called to
this stratagem until nightfall, when what was left of the Munsters
and Hampshires got ashore under cover of darkness. Few men from
either the cutters or the steamship reached the overhanging shelter
of the cliff during the day. A British airman who flew overhead
shortly after this disaster began, reported that the sea for fifty yards
from the shore was "absolutely red with blood". A Turk, looking
down from the castle, likened the bodies in the water and along the
sand to a stranded shoal of fish.

V Beach, then, was a massacre; and W Beach was nearly as bad.
It had been decided that the 1st Battalion of the Lancashire Fusiliers
should be the first of the invading army to go ashore there; and they
had been primed for this responsibility by a special order of the day
issued at Lemnos to themselves, the Dublins, the Munsters and the
Royal Fusiliers (assigned to a landing at X Beach) who together
constituted the 86th Infantry Brigade. "Fusiliers – our Brigade is to
have the honour to be the first to land and to cover the disem-
barkment of the rest of the (29th) Division. Our task will be no
easy one. Let us carry it through in a way worthy of the traditions
of the distinguished regiments of which the Fusilier Brigade is
composed; in such a way that the men of Albuhera and Minden, of
Delhi and Lucknow, may hail us as their equals in valour and
military achievement, and that future historians may say of us, as
Napier said of the Fusilier Brigade at Albuhera [a battle against the
French in the Peninsular War in 1811]: 'Nothing could stop this
astonishing infantry!'" Thus charged, the 1st Battalion sailed out
of Lemnos that peaceful Saturday evening aboard the troopship
*Caledonia* – on which they had come from Egypt – and when they

reached the offshore island of Tenedos after dark they were trans-
ferred to the warship HMS *Euryalus*, although one company of the
battalion, which could not be accommodated in *Euryalus*, sailed
aboard HMS *Implacable*. Just before dawn the cruiser took them to
within 2,000 yards of their destination and there the Lancashire
soldiers were put into cutters, identical to the ones the Irishmen
were using further round the Cape, which were towed in flotillas
of six by steam picket boats commanded by young midshipmen.
The tows stood off from *Euryalus* while she bombarded the Turkish
positions, but the moment the naval gunnery ceased, the flotillas
began to make way for the shore.

W Beach, ahead of them, consisted of white sand some 350 yards
wide, with cliffs about 100 feet high on either side and a gully rising
to a low hill in the middle. The Turkish trenches lined the high
ground above the shore, and although the bombardment had been
heavy it had not destroyed them, while the barbed wire entanglements stretched across the length of the beach were almost un-
damaged. Nor had the surviving defenders been broken by the ordeal
of lying low under the intense shellfire. Having survived in deep dugouts excavated especially for that purpose, they were grimly ready to
repulse the invasion, and they had retained their discipline. They had
been ordered not to open fire until the last minute, to surprise the
invaders and do maximum damage. Not a sound was heard from
those trenches as the picket boats steamed inshore and cast off the
cutters to row the remaining short distance to the beach.

"Not a sign of life was to be seen on the peninsula in front of
us," was the subsequent recollection of Captain Willis, sitting with
men of C Company while the sailors pulled them the last few yards.
"It might have been a deserted land we were nearing in our little
boats. Then, crack! The stroke oar of my boat fell forward to the
angry astonishment of his mates, and pandemonium broke out as
soldiers and sailors struggled to get out of the sudden hail of bullets
that was sweeping the beach and the cutters from end to end. Men
leapt out of the boats into deep water, encumbered with their rifles
and their 70 lb of kit, and some of them died right there, while
others reached the land only to be cut down on the barbed wire."

Major Shaw described the horror facing A Company. "About 100
yards from the beach the enemy opened fire and bullets came thick
all round, splashing up the water. I didn't see anyone actually hit
in the boats, though several were; eg my Quartermaster-Sergeant

and Sergeant-Major sitting next to me; but we were so jammed together that you couldn't have moved, so that they must have been sitting there, dead. As soon as I felt the boat touch, I dashed over the side into three feet of water and rushed for the barbed wire entanglement on the beach; it must have been three feet high or so, because I got over it amidst a perfect storm of lead and made for cover, sand dunes on the other side, and got good cover. I then found Maunsell and only two men had followed me. On the right of me on the cliff was a line of Turks in a trench taking pot shots at us, ditto on the left. I looked back. There was one soldier between me and the wire, and a whole line in a row on the edge of the sands. The sea behind was absolutely crimson, and you could hear the groans through the rattle of musketry. A few were firing. I signalled to them to advance. I shouted to the soldier behind me to signal, but he shouted back, 'I am shot through the chest.' I then perceived they were all hit."

Captain Clayton, of D Company, discovered that the wire was unusually strong. "I got up to my waist in water, tripped over a rock and went under, got up and made for the shore and lay down by the barbed wire. There was a man before me shouting for wire cutters. I got mine out but could not make the slightest impression. The front of the wire by now was a thick mass of men, the majority of whom never moved again ... The noise was ghastly and the sights horrible. I eventually crawled through the wire with great difficulty, as my pack kept catching on the wire, and got under a small mound which actually gave us protection. The weight of our packs tired us, so that we could only gasp for breath. After a little time we fixed bayonets and started up the cliffs right and left. On the right several were blown up by a mine. When we started up the cliff the enemy went, but when we got to the top they were ready and poured shots on us."

The worst of the casualties occurred in the middle and on the right of W Beach, but the gallantry was everywhere as the Fusiliers struggled with the wire, often falling dead while they did so, but always with a comrade coming from behind to take their place; and eventually gaps were torn out of it where luckier men than they could dash through. On the left side of the beach, Willis's company and Clayton's – what was left of them – managed after a struggle to take Hill 114, and with it one of the Turkish posts that had been doing so much damage on the shore. It was becoming vital to get the naval gunners to raise their sights, but the artillery observation officer and his corporal were both killed going up the hill and the remaining signaller had to wave a large flag while lying on his back. He was never seen again. The capture of the Turkish trench was the crucial stroke in securing some sort of bridgehead on this stretch of Helles, and it enabled reinforcements from the Worcestershire and the Essex regiments to get ashore later that morning without facing the terrible barrage of fire that had greeted the Lancastrians. These were soon to be joined by men from the Royal Fusiliers, who had landed on X Beach unopposed by anything more than a dozen unfortunate Turks, who prudently surrendered on the spot. The British newcomers were dismayed by what they found round the tidemark on W Beach. One of their chaplains recorded that "One hundred corpses lay in rows upon the sand, some of them so badly mauled as to be beyond recognition. All over the strip of sand, and on ledges of rock, wherever any cover could be got, men lay about wounded, cut, bleeding and dying. Some of the Lancashires lay dead half-way up the cliffs, still holding their rifles in their cold, clenched hands. Dead and wounded lay about, mixed up together."

And such a small force of Turks it was, no more than three platoons of determined men holding the high ground, that had caused the havoc this day. By nightfall they were outflanked and outnumbered by about ten to one, but the cost to the Lancashire Fusiliers had been high in obtaining the initial advantage. At the end of March, 1,029 officers and men of the 1st Battalion had left England for Egypt and Gallipoli. When April 25 was done, they were down to 410.* Only the Royal Dublin Fusiliers had suffered more grievously than that.

The primary objective of the British forces, once they had obtained a foothold at Cape Helles, was to reach and take Achi Baba without delay. This wasn't a hill so much as a hump on the skyline to anyone looking from the cliff-top above W Beach, though it rose some 700 feet above sea level and to that extent it dominated the surrounding landscape. The best part of four miles separated it from

---

* The figures are from the official history of the regiment and somewhat at variance with those offered by Rhodes James. Remarking that 950 men disembarked from *Euryalus* that morning (but another company came ashore from *Implacable*) he reckons that the Fusiliers had 6 officers and 183 men killed, 61 men missing, 4 officers and 279 men wounded; a total of 533 casualties.

the Lancashire Fusiliers when they first saw it across gently rising ground. Just in front of the hump was the village of Krithia, which the invaders would have to go through or round if they were to reach the summit. Though the feeble Allied intelligence was unaware of it, the Turks were heavily outnumbered at the end of the peninsula and had suffered heavily in the landings, too. A determined march on Achi Baba would very probably have taken the high ground there, and its capture so soon after the invasion might have changed the subsequent course of the campaign. But the Allies were in some disarray by nightfall on April 25. "Confidently expecting a walk-over, the Army was numbed by the reality." The casualties sustained by both the British and Anzacs in getting ashore had never been remotely anticipated by the authorities; and W Beach, among others, was a desperate place for wounded men to be when the facilities there were inadequate for the numbers needing treatment. "It was difficult to select the most urgent cases," a medical orderly noted. "Men had lost arms and legs, brains oozed out of shattered skulls, and lungs protruded from riven chests; many had lost their faces and were, I should think, unrecognisable to their friends . . . One poor chap had lost his nose and most of his face, and we were obliged to take off an arm, the other hand, and extract two bullets like shark's teeth from his thigh, besides minor operations. It was really a precious hour or more wasted, for I saw him next morning being carried to the mortuary."

A march on Achi Baba started on the evening of April 27, in spite of the fact that few guns or transport animals had yet come off the ships, so that the infantrymen had to carry ammunition and other supplies themselves, as well as their own gear. At first there was almost no opposition, and a bombardment by naval guns led the troops to believe that there might be no hard fighting in this advance; but then, as they reached Krithia early on April 28, all sorts of things began to go wrong. Orders were misunderstood or never came, Turks who had been retreating to the upper slopes of Achi Baba, there regrouped and counter-attacked, and the British began to take heavy losses again. They had put 14,000 men into this assault and by nightfall that Wednesday they had sustained 3,000 casualties. The survivors were pulled back, the First Battle of Krithia came to an end, and Achi Baba remained inviolate. It never would be captured. In the manner of all soldiers, the Allied troops gave it affectionate nicknames – Archie Barber or Archibald – but the truth was that, as the campaign proceeded and it always loomed above them, wherever they were, they felt threatened by it. Increasingly, they sensed that an extremely determined enemy was up there, watching them through binoculars, taking note of every slightest move they made.

After three days on Gallipoli, and two searing fights, the surviving Lancashire Fusiliers were close to dropping with exhaustion. So were the other men who had taken part in the first landings. Their condition, and especially their losses, together with the unexpected determination of the Turks, persuaded the Allied Commander-in-Chief, Sir Ian Hamilton, that he needed reinforcements with some urgency. These came initially in the shape of the 29th Indian Division, consisting of Gurkhas and Sikhs, and the British 42nd Division, which included those four battalions of Lancashire Territorials who had been finding life in Cairo a bit monotonous. Most of them were glad to be away from Egypt at last, and their general mood was expressed when their convoy approached Lemnos at the beginning of May. A couple of transports bearing wounded were steaming out of the harbour, *en route* to Alexandria, and as the ships passed, the soldiers from Lancashire shouted across the water "Are we downhearted? Nooooooh!" Normally, this exuberance would have been saluted with an answering cheer. On this occasion the response was low-key and sardonic: "But you bloody soon will be!"

Not all the newcomers were itching to spill Turkish blood in order to break the tedium of their recent routine. Private Haslam, of the 1st/5th Battalion, a young father and Methodist who had joined up in Bury the day war broke out, wrote to his wife: "All the lads seem to be in good spirits because they are going today to meet the foe. I only hope we shall come back safe and sound, but we do not know how we shall go when we get into the field. We are not coming home, so I don't know when I shall see you again. I don't want you to upset yourselves. I am sure God will watch over me and bring me back safe to you both . . . Tell Mother I shall come back safe and don't upset yourself. Remember me to all I know and tell them I shall see them all some day, if not in this world it will be in the next." He was dead long before that letter reached Bury at the end of the month.

The 1st/5th, the 1st/6th, the 1st/7th and the 1st/8th Lancashire Fusiliers came ashore on W Beach eleven days after their illustrious predecessors of the 1st Battalion had landed there. They arrived in darkness and they lay down in shallow sandholes, shrammed with cold, until the night had passed. The beach had been cleaned up somewhat since the slaughter of April 25, but the fighting was not far away and the Terriers were in the thick of it within a few hours. Private Round described their first engagement to his parents: "We landed here last Wednesday night, marched inland early on Thursday and bivouacked near the firing line in holes and trenches. There was plenty of shrapnel bursting all around. One man was hit within a few yards of me. Had many escapes from being riddled. There were stray bullets flying all over the place long before we reached the firing line. After walking along the trenches a mile or two a party of us made a dash and reached the top of the ravine or gully. Before we had been there many minutes a maxim gun began firing at us. We stayed there some time. It simply rained bullets. At last we managed to crawl back to the trenches and afterwards tried to get away, but the maxim guns spotted us and the same thing happened again. After falling back a second time we were shelled with shrapnel but finally managed to get away, returning to base at night fagged out . . ." Second-Lieutenant Horridge was never to forget the moment the bullets began to fly, either, and a mixture of terror and common sense flung him flat upon the ground, with his entrenching tool and his rifle butt held in front of his face while he squirmed his way to more substantial cover. A less agile officer named Hudson was hit and fell on top of him, but his wound was not serious and he survived Gallipoli. Two years later the very same thing was to happen again at Passchendaele, but when Hudson fell on Horridge the second time he had been shot in the head and was dead.

In their first two days ashore the Lancashire Territorials suffered 673 casualties, many of them caused by shellfire as the Turks brought up artillery in their efforts to dislodge the invaders. Much of May was spent by the newcomers digging more trenchworks in the ground they held above the beaches and the cliffs. The Helles area was soon networked with these defences, which traversed fields and barren land in a series of sandbagged, parapeted dog-legs running across the width of the peninsula. The troops gave them familiar names from home to mark out their particular regimental territory: Holborn Circus, Clapham Junction, Sauchiehall Street, Great North Road, and so on. The Lancashire soldiers could eventually be found where the signposts said Ardwick Green, Oldham Road, Nelson Avenue, Wigan Lane and the like. And in these deep and narrow ditches – for that is all they were – the men made themselves as comfortable as possible but were never allowed to forget the purpose for which they had been dug. The best description of sheltering from bombardment on Gallipoli comes, as it happens, from Chief Petty Officer Johnston, of the Royal Naval Division, who was there: "For quite an hour the huge guns blazed away, whilst we in the trenches lay full length on the ground or stuffed ourselves into small holes cut in the trench side. It was good if two fellows could get together in one of these holes – it meant company. Your feet and legs stuck well out in the trench, but your back and head were safely protected by perhaps two feet of earth which any ordinary size of shell would cut a way through in the hundredth part of a second. You are both squeezed together, you don't dare think how easily a piece of shell would penetrate your shelter. You light a cigarette, look at each other and wait . . . You press your back harder against the wall and your head harder into the roof. You know you are not safe, but you press harder and that seems to help a bit. You can only see in front of you the opposite side of the sandy trench, at which you gaze in a vacant stare. The shells scream louder and more often, the screeches, whistles and bangs are hopelessly intermingled, and the ground beneath and around is rocking and trembling."

That first engagement of the Territorials was the Second Battle of Krithia. The Third Battle started on June 4 and all five battalions of the Lancashire Fusiliers were in it together, as well as other British regiments, a naval brigade, two French units and the Indians. It boiled down to 30,000 Allied troops fighting maybe 28,000 Turks for a full week without a break. June 4 dawned exactly as April 25 had done, and a perfect summer's day was again defiled by the noise and the eruptions of a massive naval bombardment. At 11.20 a.m. the shelling stopped and every British soldier poked his fixed bayonet above the trench parapet, as if about to go over the top in a classic infantry charge. This was a ruse to get the Turks out of their deep dugouts and into their open trenches, where they would be a better target for the naval gunners, who opened fire again ten minutes later. But at noon the barrage did come to an end and the charge followed immediately.

What was left of the 1st Battalion of the Fusiliers was in the middle of the front line and had already suffered that morning from a counter-bombardment by the Turks, which had done more damage than the British naval guns. Nevertheless, over the top with fixed bayonets the survivors went, straight into a hail of rifle and machine-gun fire at a range of no more than one hundred yards. Before the remnant of A Company had covered even half that distance Major Shaw, leading as he had done on W Beach, was killed. The commander of D Company, Captain Clayton, who had found the Turkish wire so tough on the day of the landing, actually got as far as the entanglements in front of the enemy trenches before he, too, was cut down. His body would still be visible to the Fusiliers, hanging as it had fallen on the wire, a couple of months later. Many men in the 1st Battalion died the moment they climbed over their own parapets, others were shot before they could scramble into the shelter of a nullah beside the line of advance. By nightfall the survivors were back in their own trenches and under heavy machine-gun and artillery fire. Early on June 6, the few men who were still unscathed after this second mauling of the Battalion on Gallipoli, were pulled out of the front line. They would not see action again for another three weeks: by then some of the wounded had recovered enough to return to the trenches, and fresh men – trained Reservists of the 3rd and 4th Battalions – had arrived from England.

The Territorial Fusiliers had also been having a rough time, but they distinguished themselves by forcing a gap through the Turkish wire and reaching the trenches beyond, only to be thrown back when no reinforcements arrived to back them up. The cost for them, too, was high. Corporal Evans, brother of the Bury herbalist and lately a victim of smallpox in Egypt, rejoined the 1st/5th Battalion at Gallipoli on June 3, only to be killed the moment he went over the top on June 4. There were, in fact, parents and children as well as brothers fighting together in these Territorial ranks, and in some cases one would survive the Third Battle of Krithia while the other did not. Private Jim Scotson was standing alongside his father in a trench on the second day of the battle when he became briefly visible to a Turkish sniper, who shot him dead. The elder Scotson fainted with the shock of it and was taken out of the line with a nervous breakdown, to be sent back to Egypt on a hospital ship. Also in the 1st/5th were the Tennant brothers. The elder boy, Harry, had been a tram driver in Bury, while young Fred worked in a local dyeworks. It was Harry who died that morning in June and Fred who wrote home to their mother: "I was just near Harry at the time, and I am sure it will be some consolation to know that his death was instantaneous and painless. He fell with his face to the enemy, and I am sure no man could wish for a more glorious death. I am sure, dear Mother, you and I understand each other's feelings, and we must pray to God to give us strength to bear the great loss we have sustained." Before the month was out, someone else was writing in the language of patriotism and stilted emotion to Mrs Tennant: Fred was badly wounded only a few days after his brother was hit, and later died of his injuries.* Someone also wrote such a letter to Sarah Scowcroft after James – father of Alice and Joseph James – was killed early on the morning of June 6, when A Company of the 1st/5th were in a trench enfiladed by a Turkish machine-gun, which hit virtually every man in it.

Second-Lieutenant Horridge was luckier. On the first day of the battle, the Manchester Regiment had left the trenches ahead of the 1st/5th, immediately after the naval bombardment, and Horridge had peeped over the parapet to watch them charge the Turks. He saw a man lying face down about thirty yards away in no man's land, with his hand raised as though asking for help. The young officer instantly recognised with frightful clarity that a turning point had come in his own life. Although the wounded soldier was not one of his own men he had to try to rescue him, and he might not survive the attempt. He would not be censured by anyone if he looked the other way, because he was duty bound to remain with the soldiers he was personally responsible for. But he knew that he would be morally damaged, that he would have failed his own deepest need for self-respect, if he left the Manchester to die out there without having at least tried to bring him in. So he asked one of his company, a lad named Parks, if he'd come, too. The Terrier simply looked over the top, then climbed straight out without a word, leaving his officer to struggle after him. Horridge had run no more than a dozen yards when he felt as though a hammer had struck his left side. He promptly turned and staggered back to the trench, bleeding heavily from the bullet that had hit him in the ribs

---

* Mrs Tennant was cursed with recurring tragedy. Her eldest boy Arthur had died in the Boer War, as a result of black fever; then, inside three years, she lost her remaining sons and her husband.

then gone through his arm and out again. He was semi-conscious with a medical orderly bending over him, when Parks returned with the Manchester soldier slung over his shoulder; but the man died shortly afterwards. Horridge was taken down to the nearest field dressing station, then aboard a hospital ship which sailed for Alexandria. On the way it stopped periodically, for the burial at sea of soldiers whose wounds had been too shocking for the body to tolerate.

By June 10 the Allied assault had petered out and Achi Baba had once again resisted all efforts to capture it. The cost on both sides had been terrible, the invaders suffering 6,500 casualties, the defenders faring even worse with 9,000 killed, missing or wounded. By the time the Third Battle of Krithia was called off the Turks were at the end of their tether, and subsequently admitted that one more heave by the British might have seen the great objective gained. Yet it was the Turks who were strongly counter-attacking at the finish, and only great stubbornness by the Lancashire Territorials held the British line and prevented the defenders pushing their adversaries back beyond their starting point of June 4, towards the beaches of Helles and the sea. When all was done the 1st/5th had lost 130 men in the battle and the 1st/7th were even harder hit with 179 casualties. Bob Spencer, who joined the second of these battalions when the first was oversubscribed, was fortunate enough to get away with a leg wound, which put him on the hospital ship for Egypt with George Horridge. But his pal from the Bury ironworks, Billy Schofield, was one of the bodies left in heaps below the walls of Krithia.

It took days for those dead to be buried, and as the thousands of corpses lay in the sun with their guts and their shattered limbs and their stove-in heads disgustingly exposed, the stench of death sickened the living for miles around. Someone said of Helles at the time that it looked like a midden and smelled like an opened cemetery. So much raw meat was scattered around this part of the peninsula in the mounting heat of summer that the flies multiplied with Biblical abundance and more. They were a species of greenbottle, but smaller than the ones the English were familiar with, and they were everywhere in their millions, becoming more bloated by the hour. The soldiers knew them as corpse flies, because that was where they swarmed and lay their eggs, which became maggots and caused burial parties to throw up with revulsion and nausea.

They also swarmed round the latrines, which were nothing more than open pits, with a cross-pole to hang on to so that you wouldn't fall in. They swarmed and crawled all over food the moment it was broken out of tins or packets, or came out of a field kitchen's oven. They caused the dysentery that reached epidemic proportions from one end of the Allied battlefront to the other during July: someone worked out that eighty per cent of the men were affected. No one on Gallipoli had ever seen such a plague of insects before; and no one would ever forget the utter and wholesale humiliation and misery they created. After a few weeks of these conditions all the Allied troops were visibly declining, as one of the Lancashire Territorials remarked: "It is impossible to describe how these men were living. Tall men slouched, thin, round-shouldered, bandaged over their septic sores, dirty, unshaven, unwashed. Men were living like swine, or worse than swine. About those crowded trenches there hung the smells of latrines and the dead. Flies and lice tormented men who had hardly enough strength left to scratch or fan the flies off for a few seconds . . ."

The men were still required to fight, though. On June 28 the 1st Battalion returned to the campaign and were told to advance up Gully Ravine, which ran at an acute angle from the west coast of the peninsula to a point well behind Krithia on the flank of Achi Baba. The action began with the customary bombardment, and when the Turkish artillery replied in kind they inflicted heavy casualties before the Fusiliers had even moved off the beach and into the ravine. But throughout that day and into the next, the soldiers plugged away towards its top, even taking some prisoners, until they were forced to withdraw by one counter-attack after another, which cost them 166 dead and 25 wounded. Those casualties exposed a fatuous idea that someone in authority had come up with: for every man to wear a triangular piece of biscuit tin between his shoulders so that, by reflecting the sun, these would indicate to the British gunners how far up the gully the leading Fusiliers had advanced. It hadn't occurred to anyone that when a dead man fell forward his piece of tin would continue to glint and thoroughly confuse the British artillery, especially when his comrades were in retreat and needed a barrage creeping downhill immediately behind them.

On August 6 came the disastrous enterprise at Suvla Bay, which occupied most of the month and effectively buried the Allied ambition to conquer Gallipoli. Some 60,000 British, Anzac and Indian troops, outnumbering the Turks by about two to one, were involved in the major action, which stretched from Anzac Cove to Suvla itself, some distance to the north. The idea, yet again, was to reach the high ground which ran like a spine down the middle of the peninsula and which had so far been defended repeatedly against successive Allied assaults at various places, from Achi Baba at the bottom to the ridges above Anzac further up. Only one group of Lancashire Fusiliers was put ashore at Suvla and this was the 9th Battalion, the first of Kitchener's New Army units to be formed by the regiment, raised at Bury almost twelve months earlier from completely raw miners and factory workers in the area, with a few Regulars to stiffen them with experience. It had seen no fighting yet, had not even been given any special training for the amphibious operation ahead until it reached the Aegean, a couple of weeks before landing on Gallipoli; and that proved inadequate when the troops were invited to disembark more than half a mile from where they were supposed to be, in an uncertain depth of water. This was tested by lowering the shortest officer available, an unhappy Lieutenant Davies, over the side on a rope. They then "splashed their way ashore with hoarse cries of 'Remember Minden'". Under the Turkish fire, one company lost all its officers in the landing and in the next few days the battalion as a whole suffered so heavily that it was temporarily withdrawn, until it was flung into the assault again on August 21. Ordered to take a hill with Turkish troops on top it did so, and hung on for nineteen hours, awaiting reinforcements from the Anzac sector which never came. Eventually the 9th was beaten back to its starting point, with fewer than 100 men left and not a single officer. The 1st Battalion, having been brought round to Suvla to give the failing assault fresh impetus, became involved in an action amidst fiercely burning scrub, set afire by falling shells in the tinder dry conditions of high summer; but they, too, were forced into retreat, having sustained another 234 casualties.

The four Territorial battalions, meanwhile, had been taking part in a great push down at Helles, whose logic was intended to divert the Turks from the major offensive further north, and to prevent them from sending reinforcements from the southern theatre of the war. Once again the British set their sights on Krithia and Achi Baba and, as before, they were flung back at dreadful human cost.

In what remained of the 1st/7th Battalion, out of 410 NCOs and men going into action on this occasion, only 139 came back in one piece. The 1st/5th, too, had by now been reduced to a token of its original strength. It had landed in May with thirty officers and 1,000 men. When George Horridge returned to it on August 15, he found to his horror that it had shrunk to six officers and 150 men. Quartermaster-Sergeant Yates was one who had disappeared during Horridge's absence in the Egyptian hospital. In Cairo, before they set sail for the peninsula, Yates had confided in the young Second Lieutenant his belief that he would die sometime during the months ahead. But he had come through the landing and Third Krithia without a scratch. The night before the Helles diversion he spent several hours quietly alone, at prayer. He went over the top next morning, carrying a walking stick, with a pistol in his other hand. He returned from that engagement, too, unharmed. During that night a shell landed in his trench, and that was the end of him.

Nothing was achieved at Suvla or in the diversions but more dead and more mutilated. And as it became clear that there was stalemate between the opposing armies, the Gallipoli campaign settled down into a less spectacular form of hostility, not much different from the trench warfare simultaneously taking place on a much larger scale across northern Europe. Snipers on both sides were permanently on the look-out for the incautious head raised above the parapet, and periscopes were widely used to reduce the hazard they presented. Shelling became a regular feature of everybody's life. Saps were dug and mines were laid by both Turkish and Allied forces, and from time to time there would be an abnormally heavy explosion, which would bury men alive when a trench caved in or was blown apart. The strain of being perpetually braced against sudden catastrophe, together with the exhaustion that had been mounting since they arrived on the peninsula, added to the debilitating effects of permanent diarrhoea and filth, were drastically reducing the men's effectiveness for any form of warfare. The commanding officer of the 1st/6th Battalion, Lieutenant-Colonel Lord Rochdale, noted at this time that courts martial were becoming a regular occurrence, almost always because a man had fallen asleep while on sentry duty. The kindlier officers would pretend not to notice a defaulter but would kick away his rifle as they walked past him, in order to wake him up. Some old sweats seemed impervious to any hardship. One such in the 1st/5th was Private Dawber,

whose military service in both the Regular and Territorial Fusiliers
dated back to Kitchener's campaign in the Sudan, for which he had
a medal. He knew all the tricks for survival, including the most
vital knack of never being in the wrong place at the wrong time.
But he irritated the younger, far less experienced men, when he
crooned – almost as though he were testing their already stretched
nerves, or even mocking them with his apparent invincibility – a
wry old Army song none of them had heard until now:

> Side by side like a crimson tide, in the days of long ago,
> In we dashed as our sabres flashed, and we conquered every foe;
> One by one till the day was done, I saw my comrades fall.
> Till I was the only one of them left to answer the last Roll Call.

The prevailing mood of most Fusiliers on Gallipoli was expressed
perfectly by Private John Taylor, who had been wounded in one of
the 1st/5th's early actions and was invalided out to Egypt. Just
before he was due to return to the fighting he wrote to his mother:
"I have been three weeks in hospital but I am going to the firing
line tomorrow. I suppose you will have got word by now about our
George and Jim dying out here. I saw our George get hit, but I had
no time to think; I had to do my duty . . . I think Bury should be
proud of her soldiers, for what they have done. They used to call
us 'Saturday night soldiers' but they have no need to now. We have
done as much as anyone in the Army, perhaps more than a lot. I
believe there are fellows on street corners yet. They ought to be
ashamed of themselves when lads of only fifteen or sixteen are
fighting for their country. I don't think the war will last long . . ."

It was an abrupt change in the weather that stopped the fighting
altogether. The blistering heat of summer gave way to the most
beautiful early autumn any of them had ever known, with clear
skies still, but with the heat cooled by breezes coming fresh from
the sea. Then, quite suddenly, the coming of October was accompanied by fierce storms which wrought havoc around the coastal
landing places. W Beach had long since been organised into a small
port, with jetties running out into the water and a breakwater of
sunken hulks just offshore. On the beach itself were field workshops, ammunition dumps, a stockade for the mules and horses
carrying supplies inland, a field hospital, a telegraph station: there
was even a small airfield on the cliff above. It was invariably a busy
place, with lighters moving from the beach to the convoys of large

vessels anchored just out to sea. Its activities were periodically interrupted by Turkish bombardments, but afterwards repairs were made, wreckage was cleared away, and the bustle went on as before. But the October gales ruined the piers and flung several barges on to the shore, doing as much damage as several bombardments at once.

And this wasn't the worst of the Gallipoli weather that back end. On November 27 a tremendous thunderstorm swept the peninsula, followed by violent hail, then torrential rain; and after that, two days of raging blizzard. The first storms created flash floods across the entire battleground, in which men and animals and debris were swept along gullies and trenches, and in which many soldiers drowned. Others, enemies who had been trying to kill each other relentlessly for six months, leapt on to the parapets of trenches only a hundred yards apart, intent on nothing now but getting out of the surging water below. The blizzard was even more devastating, especially to some of the Anzacs and Indians, who had never seen snow before. No one was adequately protected against the swift sub-zero cold and, as everyone was soaking wet before the temperature dropped as low as even the British had ever experienced, the result was chaos. The 1st Battalion of the Fusiliers, which had lost twenty men drowned in the flood, had another nineteen frozen to death, and 536 treated for frostbite. At Suvla alone there were over 12,000 cases of exposure bad enough for medical attention; and similar figures emerged in every sector of the peninsula. The one distinct consolation of the snowstorm was that it killed every corpse fly on Gallipoli.

The storms, coming on top of the stalemate and the hideous casualties, settled the outcome of the campaign. Sir Ian Hamilton had been relieved of his command in October and his successor, Sir Charles Monro, had been brought from France to advise Kitchener and the British War Cabinet what to *do* about Gallipoli. Shocked by the shambles he found there, and concluding that the Allies had reached an impasse that no realistic number of fresh reinforcements could resolve, he had advised withdrawal; and the November weather made him press London for evacuation as soon as possible, before winter began in earnest, with consequences too awful to contemplate. On December 8, nearly six weeks after Monro made his first recommendation, the politicians at last accepted the need to swallow their pride and cut their losses in the Dardanelles.

And it was a famous withdrawal, executed with a skill that had never been matched in any of the offensives. Suvla and Anzac were the first two areas to be abandoned and at first, in order to preserve secrecy, the men themselves were given to understand that the garrisons were merely being reduced until the better weather of the following spring. Various ruses were adopted to persuade the Turks that nothing unusual was afoot. The troops were pulled out only when it was dark. For several nights there would be no firing from the Allied lines, but when the Turks began to investigate they were at first immediately repulsed; so that, supposing a new tactic was being tried, they became less vigilant, undisturbed by the lengthening silences. Soon, only a few Allied soldiers were left on the west coast, and these had rigged various devices to make a rifle fire without anyone pulling the trigger, which also lulled the enemy into a belief that everything was as it should be. In a soft drizzle of rain that fell upon the early hours of December 20, the last Anzacs came down from Lone Pine, from Courtney's, from Johnston's Jolly, and from Walker's Ridge; and one Digger, passing a cemetery where he'd buried some of his mates months before, said "I hope *they* won't hear us going down to the beaches."

There was a pause in the evacuation, when bad weather again hit the peninsula and turned Helles into a bog. The Turks subsequently said that at this stage they weren't quite sure what the Allies were up to, even after discovering how they'd been deceived up the coast. Nevertheless, they began bombarding Helles more heavily than at any previous time in the campaign, and followed this with an attack on Gully Spur. The British responded with a tremendous artillery barrage of their own, together with ferocious machine-gun and small-arms fire, which beat the attackers off; and it became apparent that the Turkish troops had no wish to sacrifice themselves if their enemy was about to leave their land voluntarily. So the final withdrawal began, again using the deceptions of Suvla and Anzac, with the warships and transports slipping up to the Cape at night, leaving the sea empty before dawn. The plan was for everyone to be off the peninsula by the morning of January 9, and each night after Christmas saw a few thousand more men taken out; also, more than three thousand packhorses and mules, as well as guns, vehicles and general stores. But a great deal of material was left behind, not all of it blown up at the end. What upset the soldiers much more was the slaughter of five hundred animals, who couldn't be evacuated by the deadline because of insufficient space on the ships. The Army was strangely unwilling to leave them for the Turks, though it surrendered enough food to victual four divisions for several weeks.

By New Year's Day all the Territorial battalions of the Fusiliers were safely away – the 9th had already been taken to Alexandria from Suvla – and the 1st Battalion, which had been on the peninsula from the very beginning, was pulled out on January 2. In the pitch blackness of yet another stormy night, its soldiers filed down the mule tracks to the shore and made their way to the jetties of V Beach, where the empty shape of the *River Clyde* loomed above them as a reminder of a landing there even more terrible than their own. But no regiment in the British or any other army had spent more of itself on this campaign than the Lancashire Fusiliers. They left behind 1,816 dead men on Gallipoli.

# PART TWO

# 4

# Profit, Suicide, Jealousy

At home some people were not entirely dismayed by these events, which brought them substantial profits that would continue to the end of the war. The thrifty housewives of Bury who had started to queue outside the food shops at the rumour of impending hostilities knew what they were about, for the price of flour had suddenly trebled at the first sniff of an excuse. Before August 1914 was much older, many local businesses were using the war to advertise their wares and drum up customers, with blatant innuendo and artful display. A prominent grocer took out an advertisement which was headed AT THE FRONT, an ironmonger promised that "We are making a determined *attack* on prices", and a furniture store simply attached itself to "God Save the King. Motto for Patriotic Britons. Business as Usual." With a similarly sharp eye to the main chance, an international company with a factory in Manchester swiftly addressed itself to the people of south-east Lancashire in the following terms: "FORD – WAR! and the urgent need for efficient transport." It would be years before those with such primary instincts took the hint that most people were sick and tired of everything to do with the war. As late as 1917, even, Bury's most fashionable emporium for the sale of shirts and hats was shamelessly announcing itself with a long and unctuous advertisement culminating in "Lest We Forget – and that means all of us – that we are absolutely dependent on each other for the keeping down of prices. The greater the quantity of customers, the lower the prices will be."

It took some entrepreneurs little time to realise that the war presented opportunities, non-existent before, to manufacture things that people would eagerly buy at almost any price you cared to name within reason. By mid-September 1914, Bury's principal toy-shop was in a position to offer "Patriotic brooches, Buttons, Flags,

Post Cards, War Games, War Flags and War Maps." Typical of the postcards was one which pictured a mother vigorously paddling the backside of her small boy with a shoe, above the caption "What the Kaiser wants – and the Lancashire Fusiliers will see that he gets it!" Eighteen months later, the Fusiliers were scarcely evacuated from Gallipoli before relatives of the survivors were being invited to purchase the Dayfield Body-Shield, "an invaluable gift to send your soldier father, brother, husband, son or friend. The shield measures 17 inches by 12 inches, is covered with khaki drill and is worn under the tunic. It is light in weight (36 oz), comfortable to wear and does not impede action. Four toughened metal plates, strengthened at the joinings by steel strips, explain the Dayfield's resistive power." At about the same time the Soldier's Parcel ("Just What He Wants") was widely touted, containing a number of things to digest after being squeezed out of tubes or dissolved in water, together with a writing pad, a heating device, and a tin of trench powder to keep down lice. The hustlers responsible for putting this catchpenny mixture together may not have intended to be so eloquent about the realities of life at the front.

None of the sales talk would have made the slightest impression if there had not first been a softening up of the customers, chiefly by awakening their patriotism and stirring their most bellicose instincts. Within a few days of the war starting, a Bury newspaper printed a long ballad by some local versifier, which began:

> Come now, ye sons of Britain
> Your country calls again;
> Over the grave of peace is writ
> "Acquit yourselves like men" . . .

It continued in this vein for forty-eight lines, with occasional breaks for a chorus:

> When Britain has to fight her sons are always willing.
> The King, when wanting soldier boys, can get them for a shilling.
> There's Sandy, Pat and John, with Taffy standing by.
> And when they've got their warpaint on, the foeman has to fly.

Similar verses by different rhymsters were published at regular intervals for many months, and they were so popular that not many weeks after the first appeared, a lecture was given in a packed Co-operative Hall on "Patriotism in our Ballad Literature". There were other forms of incitement, most of it very deliberately aimed at recruitment, like the long article published "by an officer" about the traditions of Bury's local regiment, which began: "To some of our most eminent officers, the failure of our elementary and secondary schools to teach military history has been a matter of sincere regret – in the elementary classes by an absence of a general application to the history of our nation. A judicious mixture would make the subject a most attractive one for the youth of the nation. Properly applied, particularly in a country where the Army has always been maintained by voluntary recruitments, military history would instal the best of national virtues, obedience and self-sacrifice. In every nation these constitute the essential characteristics of the highest ideal of patriotism. Country before self!"

Many people in the town threw themselves into some form of war effort the moment hostilities began. Prominent among them was the formidable Jane Kitchener, a spinster cousin of the Field Marshal and War Minister. As soon as the war was over she would retire after thirty-six years in charge of the local girls' grammar school, by then easily the longest-serving headmistress in England. At the outset, after a full day's teaching, she generally spent her evenings urging men to join up at recruiting meetings, until she decided that there was other war work for which she was even better qualified. She placed her spare time thereafter at the disposal of the League of Honour, which liked to think that it cut across the class barriers of England, its object being "to work among women and girls and influence them in the direction of discreet behaviour, purity and total abstinence, and to induce them to take the prayer pledge on behalf of the country and our soldiers during the war." Miss Kitchener wasn't the only one who hoped that "the influence of older and more staid women will have a great influence among those of weaker will, and will help them to resist temptation."

After exhorting his fellow citizens from time to time about the many forms their bounden duty might take, the Mayor announced one day that he had decided to follow the example of his sovereign and drink no more intoxicating liquor until the end of the war; and added that he hoped all the aldermen and councillors would also abstain and thus give a lead to everyone in Bury. An even costlier renunciation was made by a Mr Porritt, who carefully let it be known that he was allowing his tenants, 120 people all told, to live rent-free during the hostilities. Quite a lot of practical help was offered, one way and another, in the first few weeks of the conflict. The Corporation which may or may not have put itself collectively on the wagon did at least vote, on the second day of the war, to assist all municipal employees who enlisted by making up the difference between their Army pay and what they normally earned. Similar concessions were not unknown among private employers, especially after a strong and early lead had come from the millowner John Horridge, whose two elder sons were already commissioned in the Territorials, with their younger brother destined to serve as an airman later in the war. Messrs Horridge & Cornall's wider contribution to the cause was to keep every enlisted employee on half pay, in addition to his Army money, and to guarantee him his old job when he was discharged. Thus encouraged, forty per cent of their workmen between the ages of nineteen and thirty-five promptly joined up.

The Lieutenant Stonestreet who had declined to go abroad with George Horridge and the rest of the 1st/5th Battalion, quickly achieved promotion and became Bury's chief recruiting officer. Captain Stonestreet now, his was the name appended to the recruiting posters that appeared on walls and billboards everywhere, urging the local men to "Think of Your Brothers now Fighting for Your Freedom". At regular intervals he marched at the head of troops on a recruiting parade through the town, sometimes accompanied by the local Ragged School Band, sometimes by military musicians. These marches generally stopped outside all the local picture halls, where the films would be interrupted at the arrival of the officer and his men. The Captain would then address his captive audience from the stage, and he was a persuasive advocate of going to war: it was common for dozens of young fellows to volunteer on the spot and to turn up in the morning, as they had promised to the night before, at the recruiting office. When he set about raising the 3rd/5th Battalion of Fusiliers, he got 138 men to sign on in the first four days. Sometimes the recruiting was done in big meetings at the Drill Hall, which could hold nine thousand people, with one of the local brass bands to entertain the crowds who came to be harangued by Members of Parliament as well as the recruiting officer. Patriotic smoking concerts were given in church halls and workingmen's clubs, and they did their bit for the war effort, too. It was after attending one of these that Harold Sale, a young millworker, joined the 1st/5th with his Uncle Albert in time for both of them to be at the Territorial landing on Cape Helles, which the older man survived but his eighteen-year-old nephew did not. That very week it was announced at home that Captain Stonestreet and his colleagues had already helped to send no fewer than 7,000 Bury men to war. One family alone had supplied three sons, two sons-in-law, five nephews and a grandson. Most of the recruits were destined for the local regiment, as the figures from one Bury parish testify. Just over two months after the outbreak of war it had seen seventy-four of its young men go off to fight. Two had joined the Navy, the rest were in the Army; and of these, sixty were Lancashire Fusiliers.

It was not long before the people at home understood that war was a more serious matter than the newsprint verses managed to suggest. Within a month of the outbreak, Bury's first two casualties were reported; a couple of lance-corporals of the 2nd Battalion, slightly wounded in France. Before the end of September, two men had been killed on the Western Front, both of them officers, and at the end of October wounded soldiers had started to arrive at the sick quarters of the Barracks, after initial treatment at military hospitals in the south of England. A hint that the conflict was turning very serious indeed came in a letter to the local press in November, from the officer commanding the 3rd/5th Battalion of the Fusiliers, which was still short of 500 men to complete its establishment. "Are we to do it all?" he wrote, "while you read the papers at home and go to picture palaces and football matches? Play the game and come and help us. The country is in a tight corner, but not so bad that if every able-bodied man will do his share we shall not come out on top." But the old year had ended and 1915 was well advanced before there was any sense of disaster in the air.

The first news of Gallipoli was deceptive. The landings of British troops on the peninsula were reported in the papers three days after they happened: "and despite the serious opposition of the enemy, who were strongly entrenched, proved completely successful. The War Office state that the landing of the Army and the advance continue . . ." The Lancashire Fusiliers were not mentioned. Three days later there were even better tidings: "The news from the Dardanelles is good. The British troops who landed on Sunday have made sure of their ground. They hold securely the sea end of the Gallipoli Peninsula, occupying some five square miles of ground, which will provide an excellent base for an advance upon the European shore of the straits . . . An unofficial report says that the Allies have taken some thousands of prisoners, including many German officers." There was still no reference to the local regiment. But on May 5, the first clue was dropped about the reality of Gallipoli, though it was coated with optimism: "three military forces are now fairly established in Turkish territory. They had to overcome desperate resistance but are now steadily advancing. The Australians and New Zealanders had the hottest fighting. The Allied fleet, having covered the landing operation, has now turned its attention to the forts. Our casualties are reported to be heavy. The King has congratulated all ranks on their splendid achievement."

On that day it was possible to deduce that the Fusiliers had been present during these events. At the very end of a long report about the war generally, it was mentioned that Captain Tallents of the 1st Battalion, in the Expeditionary Force, had been wounded in action. Nothing more. Not until May 15 did the propaganda machine reveal that the four Territorial battalions had also been in action and had suffered casualties. Days later, someone countermanded that release of information, having been apprised of the truth, perhaps, and having recoiled from it in alarm at the effect it might have on civilian morale. "Many baseless rumours have been circulated with respect to the Territorial forces in the Dardanelles, and as a result large numbers of families in this district have been put to needless anxiety . . . at the Drill Hall last night a notice was posted at the entrance door, 'No casualties have been reported yet'." But the truth would not be suppressed much longer; too many families were beginning to receive official news privately, all of it grim, and too much of it heartbreaking. Yet the authorities did their best to conceal the extent of the disaster in the Dardanelles. From the middle of May 1915 until after the withdrawal had been completed in January 1916, the Gallipoli campaign ceased to exist as far as Bury newspaper readers were concerned, for it was never once described in all that time. All the public had to go by were the mounting lists of casualties, which the papers faithfully recorded, often only because bereaved relatives kept them informed.

Neighbours were the first to know that someone had lost a man. They would see the telegraph boy cycling down the street, with the shiny black leather pouch slung over his back, and they would twitch their lace curtains aside and peer to see where he stopped, which unsuspecting door was opened to him. When they were good neighbours, close to the poor woman about to receive that ominous envelope, they would come running so as to arrive with the telegraph boy, to give the help that she would need straight away. The women next door were so swift that they almost caught Sarah Scowcroft when she fainted with the shock of reading that James had been killed in the Third Battle of Krithia; they helped to bring her round, stayed with her all day to comfort her, bathed young Alice and Joseph James and put them to bed that night. When Sergeant Harry Braund's wife received the news that he, too, was now dead, she became so violently ill that two doctors were summoned by the neighbours to attend to her. Then the curtains were drawn in every house along that part of the street, as a mark of respect and mourning for the dead. This was an old Lancashire custom, in peace as in war, and the habit was to open them again when the funeral was over. In 1915 there were few funerals but so many families mourning a lost soldier in turn, that parts of Bury seemed to have their curtains almost permanently closed.

After the telegram there invariably followed, sooner or later, a letter written by some superior of the dead man. Private James Hamer's company commander, a captain, sent a message which was the work of someone doing his duty and not enjoying it very much, largely because it had become repetitive: "I am writing you these lines to tell you that he died a soldier's death, doing some dangerous and heroic work on top of the parapet. The moon, which was behind the clouds, appeared suddenly and exposed him to view. His death was instantaneous – not a murmur and not a pain. He was one of my best men, always willing and cheery, and as brave as a lion. Men like him make our Army. I am sending with this letter Princess Mary's gift box, which was found on him."* Chaplains usually attempted a bit more warmth than that. When Private Joe Simpson died at sea somewhere between Gallipoli and Valletta, the Rev. H. P. Dawson wrote to his father: "I have the sad news to tell you that your son passed away on this ship about 10 o'clock this morning. He was severely wounded, poor fellow, in the back, and there was not much hope for him. I was glad to be with him until the end, to pray with him. Dear fellow, with almost his last words he repeated the Lord's Prayer with me. He has died for his

---

* Princess Mary's gift box was a royal version of the Soldier's Parcel, widely distributed to servicemen. An important difference was that it was free, and its contents were more cheerful, with cigarettes, biscuits, chocolate and the like, as well as useful things.

King and Country and I am sure this will be a help to you in your great sorrow. He will be buried at sea this afternoon as we are on our way to Malta. May God rest his soul!"

Occasionally a ranker would write to some dead friend's nearest and dearest, but it could be very clumsily done. When Fred Brockle-hurst was killed at Third Krithia, Private Ralph Horridge composed a long letter to the dead man's fiancée: "I am awfully sorry to write this letter of sorrow to you. I am writing to let you know how Fred got killed . . ." He then described in great detail the ins and outs of the action ("our nerves were strung up to the highest pitch, and the order was given to charge"), the night that followed and the next morning, before getting to his point, when he and Fred encountered each other in a trench. "Fred was sat down talking at the time and he told me to keep low, as there was a sniper about. When I got back, everyone seemed to be shouting 'Keep down, there's one man been shot.' Later on I discovered it was one of my pals who'd been killed – Fred. No one knows what I went through after discovering Fred had been killed. Afterwards I was told that he was sat down talking when a bullet hit a sandbag and then went straight through his head; he was instantly killed. He died for his country and had gallantly done his work. I must say we have had heavy losses, but I have been one of the lucky ones. All the pals send their sympathy, and I think I can include the officers."

Before May 1915 was out, the papers had started a new feature that would continue without interruption until the end of the war. In every edition it appeared under the same heading, "Local Heroes who have given their lives for their Country". At first, the matter underneath amounted to no more than half a column of type, but very soon this grew until it occupied full columns, eventually a whole page or two of the newspaper, with brief notes on each man, often accompanied by a photograph of his head and shoulders, usu-ally in uniform, sometimes with his khaki cap on; and then, more often than not, the badge of the Lancashire Fusiliers could plainly be made out above the peak – a smoking grenade engraved with the sphinx and the word Egypt, above a scroll with the regimental name. The first of the Local Heroes to be pictured were seven men who had either been killed outright at Gallipoli, or had died in Alexandria as a result of their wounds: Private Thomas Wall, who had been a nineteen-year-old apprentice draughtsman at a factory which made looms and spinning machines; Private Fred Collinson, an old soldier from the Boer War, who had been a half-back for Bury Football Club before becoming a gas meter inspector, and who left a widow and two children; Lance-Corporal Harold Partington, an eighteen-year-old who played cricket for his local team and worked in his parents' corner shop; Private James Turner, a pawnbroker's son; Private Wilfred Scotting, who lived with his parents; and two millworkers who also left wives and children behind, Corporal John Barton (thirty-four) and Private Harry O'Brien (thirty-one). Their faces had been dutifully expressionless as they posed for the garrison's tame photographer, so that the marks of their age and experience were almost the only things that distinguished them from one another. The older men wore moustaches; the younger ones looked achingly innocent and virginal.

Elsewhere in the paper, the obituary notices appeared with verses usually selected by the family from a book of samples that the local undertakers happily supplied. Occasionally these had clearly been composed with the losses of the Great War in mind, like the one lamenting the death of Private William Nabb, of the 1st/5th Fusiliers:

> Only a private soldier
> A true pal to the end,
> Buried in the field of battle
> We know his duty he has done.
> He has served his King and Country,
> God knows he has done his best
> And now he's asleep in Jesus
> A British Soldier laid to rest.

More often than not, however, the verses read as if they had come from some all-purpose catalogue; like the bleak little lines which were published to mark Sarah Scowcroft's grief at the death of James:

> We did not know his end was near
> We did not see him die
> We only knew he passed away
> And did not say goodbye.

The role of the undertakers was more limited than they might have wished it to be, because very few bodies ever came back to Bury, either from Gallipoli or from any other theatre of the war. It was possible for them to undertake other matters in the absence of burial, though, and offering samples of obituary verse was only one of these. More and more, as bereaved families became aware of the possibility, the funeral parlours of Bury instigated memorial services for dead servicemen and an early one was held for Lance-Corporal Richardson of the 1st/5th, whose corpse lay two thousand miles away at Cape Helles. A requiem was said for the repose of his soul at the Holy Trinity church, and that same evening vespers for the dead was sung. The organist had been recruited to play the Dead March and, significantly, "two buglers were in attendance, by permission of Captain Stonestreet, and sounded the Last Post."

There was a funeral for Stanley Sanders, who had worked in the mill and joined the Territorials as soon as he was old enough; and, at the age of nineteen, he had become a corporal with the 1st/5th at Gallipoli. Badly wounded and taken to Alexandria, he had subsequently been brought back to the military hospital at Netley, near Southampton. His parents were informed by telegram and rushed down to Hampshire, but he died before they got there and would have been buried in the vicinity had they not persuaded the Army to release his body. They brought him home to Bury and there he was given all the last rites of the Anglican Church, as well as full military honours. The clergy and the choir turned out, and the organist again played the Dead March. Hymns were sung – "For All the Saints", "On the Resurrection morning", "Jesus lives, no longer now". The coffin was covered with a Union Jack, a large oak cross and an arrangement of wild hyacinths, and it was carried by half a dozen Fusiliers. At the graveside, three volleys were loosed over the Corporal's remains by a firing party, Sergeant Holder and Private Whalley sounded the Last Post; and Captain Stonestreet, present on this occasion, saluted the young man who had gone to fight in the war that he himself had missed.

There were other casualties, not so glorious as those sustained on the battlefield, but laden with quite as much tragedy. Early in December 1914, the police were called to a billet in Southport, where the 3rd/5th Battalion of the Fusiliers were being prepared to go to France. They found in a room upstairs Private Bolton, who had tried to cut his throat with a razor but had made a hash of it. He was stitched up at the local infirmary and in due course he was sent to the Western Front; where, one day, a German howitzer performed for him the service he had been unable to manage himself. Private Ryan was more successful, only two months after joining the Army, slashing his neck in a public lavatory, where no one would be aware of him; until another soldier came in and saw blood running across the floor from under the locked door of the cubicle. Some men survived all the horrors of Gallipoli, eventually came home on leave, and there decided that they could face no more of this war. Corporal Billington, who had been an insurance agent before joining up, returned to Bury complaining of pains in the head and suffering the after-effects of acute bronchitis. His own doctor saw him and so did the MO from the Barracks. He stayed in bed one morning, after locking the door, and there gassed himself through a rubber tube connected to the lamp bracket on the wall. The coroner sympathised with his wife and said "it was one of those sad circumstances connected with this horrible state of affairs, but we must just put our teeth together and get on with it."

Private Elliott had almost finished his leave, having appeared quite normal, cheerful even, since the day he came home. His wife and three children had noticed nothing untoward and she had just come down after taking him breakfast in bed as a treat because that morning he was due to return to the war. She heard a loud bang and rushed back upstairs, where she screamed. A neighbour ran in and found Elliott on his hands and knees, with his rifle on the floor. The soldier tried to speak to the man but couldn't; his jaw was shattered and the bullet had gone through the back of his head. But, the neighbour told the inquest later, he still took five minutes to die. The coroner's verdict was suicide while insane. Private Schofield chose an end much less messy than that: having been a dentist before joining up he was more accustomed to neater ways and means. He had told a friend that he would rather sweep the streets than go back to the front, and that night he sent his wife to bed, while he stayed below and took a strong solution of cocaine, sitting in his fireside chair. Mrs Schofield told the inquest that her husband had been strange in manner for some time and had suffered from "ringing noises" in his head.

Some men, not quite so close to breaking point when they came home on leave, chose to prolong their absence, sometimes to desert.* Within a year of war beginning, most days of the week saw soldiers appearing in court at Bury charged with these offences.

---

* In the Great War 264 British soldiers were shot for desertion, eighteen for cowardice.

More often than not it was pleaded on their behalf that they had not intended to desert, but had overstayed their leave for a variety of reasons, which might include illness or other difficulties in the family. The police were always on the look-out for defaulters and they generally received a reward for catching them, which was invariably deducted from the pay of the wretched absentee. Eventually the authorities decided to make an example of someone, and she was Amelia Hallam, who was hauled before the Bury magistrates in the summer of 1917. Someone had informed on her, doubtless because she was married to a soldier who was in France, whom she hadn't seen for twelve months or more. The police knocked on her door just after midnight and asked if there was a soldier there, which she denied. "PC Hunt warned her to be very careful and went into the back kitchen and there saw a private of the Lancashire Fusiliers on the sofa without his jacket or his cap. He asked the man for his pass and he replied that he did not have one and did not need one." The soldier was arrested and before he was taken away Mrs Hallam gave him some cigarettes and some biscuits and a kiss. She said later that she'd known the Fusilier for eight months, but claimed not to know that he'd gone missing from his unit. She was charged with concealing an absentee. In court there was a great deal of discussion between the Bench and the police about the nature of the relationship, which one magistrate tried to end by declaring that "This is not a court of morals". But, in part at least, that's precisely what it was, as Superintendent Pickering admitted in a sidelong way. It was becoming quite common for women like Mrs Hallam "to detain men when on leave", while at the same time drawing a separation allowance because their husbands were away. "The women were drawing money from the Government, their husbands were allowing them something and it was very unfair to the men fighting at the front . . ." The magistrates wrung their hands with remorse, but said they had come to the conclusion that the defendant knew the Fusilier in her back kitchen was an absentee "and at the present time, when our existence was at stake, it was a serious offence." They sent Amelia Hallam to prison for a month, and she was taken down to the cells weeping bitterly.

There was quite a lot of spite beneath the patriotically united surface of the town, waiting to be vented on any men of military age who were not obviously bound for or back from the fighting. It sometimes took the form of a letter to a newspaper, whose author

94

never identified himself with more than initials and certainly never revealed his address. Thus it was coyly "N.D." who, during the weekend of the Gallipoli landings, wrote as follows: "Perhaps the query I am asking ought to be addressed to the gentleman who conducts the medical column in your paper; but can anyone else inform me of the reason for the increased bad eyesight which has suddenly affected a number of young men in Bury? Frankly, I have nothing but sympathy for those who are really so afflicted; but, conversely, nothing but contempt for those who resort to eyeglasses merely for effect or, worse still, as a means of evading the responsibility which faces the young men of today. Which reminds me: why is the Volunteer Defence Corps in Bury being used by a large number of young men, in every way fitted physically for the Regular Army, as a means of showing their patriotism?" The Volunteer Defence Corps was for purely local protection: its equivalent in the Second World War was first raised as the Local Defence Volunteers; better known, from July 1940, as the Home Guard.

The local poetasters, too, could sneer at the laggards with the same gusto they had shown for flag-waving at the outbreak of war. Here are the first and last verses of "The Shirker's Soliloquy", composed in the summer of 1915 by "E.W.":

> I'm a bachelor healthy and strong
> But my life's just a long misery.
> For everyone insists I ought to enlist
> But then, who knows better than me?
> What a rotten time they have drilling
> Digging trenches or marching all day
> Besides, I've a job where the money beats hollow
> The pittance they call Army pay . . .

> . . . So I don't care a toss for the gossip
> While I'm safely at home with Mamma.
> When I see the recruiting sergeant
> I bolt round the corner "Ta-ta!"
> Let all go and fight, then, who like it.
> The Germans will never come here.
> While England's the pride of the ocean
> And an Englishman never shows fear.

Young Territorials in uniform, lads who had volunteered for foreign service but whose battalions had still not moved off from the depot town, occasionally found themselves jeered at as "Mothers' Darlings" by young women lying in ambush along the main streets. It was as though the helpless in this war, the people who were disqualified from fighting because of their age, their infirmity or their sex, needed to lash out at someone, anyone, in order to confound their own impotence. When conscription was at last introduced at the beginning of 1916, it created the most obvious target of all for vilification in public and private. Life may have been difficult enough for those failing to volunteer in the first eighteen months of the war; but anyone who could conceivably be identified as a draft-dodger was now given a very rough time indeed, by the authorities and by his fellow citizens. The cruellest response was the result of collusion between these two, when the principal local paper began to publish the names and addresses of men who had failed to present themselves at Bury Barracks after being called up, right alongside the now regular list of Local Heroes who had given their lives. But ordinary working men could be vindictive, too. When a colliery engine winder of twenty-three was granted exemption from military service after some string-pulling by the mine's management, 200 men at a couple of local pits immediately went on strike. The police, naturally, became zealous in rounding up suspects. As a matter of routine they began to raid picture halls and other places of entertainment, and they would question any young man out of uniform and on the street, demanding to see his exemption card or be offered other valid explanations. One officer stopped 400 in one day. In a combined operation with the military police at Manchester's Victoria Station, the constabulary intercepted every male of age who arrived on trains from Bury during the rush hour one morning, and as a result five youths were taken into custody.

With the arrival of conscription came the tribunals set up to hear and adjudicate upon appeals made against the new obligation to do military service. In Bury, anything between a dozen and fifteen people sat on these bodies; a mixture of local councillors, other citizens from different parts of society, a doctor and, always, an Army officer. The reasons usually put forward by the applicants for exemption were various forms of hardship, some more obvious than others. Among the early cases was that of a printer, asking to be excused because he supported his eighty-one-year-old grandmother; but when the tribunal heard that the lady had an old-age pension and also received two shillings a week from her son and daughter, exemption was refused. Also turned down were the secretary of a local mill, who said that his chief clerk and two juniors had already gone to war, leaving only himself, a typist and a youth to do all the paperwork; and the manager of a firm of timber merchants, who claimed to be indispensable. But a man who supported a sick aunt was exempted, as was a thirty-eight-year-old weaver with a wife and seven children to keep. Men who had actually been in the Army appeared sometimes before the tribunal. One such was a nineteen-year-old jeweller's apprentice who had served four months before being discharged sick; he was exempted from further service for six weeks. A thirty-year-old tram driver who had been with the Fusiliers at Gallipoli, and was wounded there, was exempted on condition that he joined the Volunteer Defence Force. The most extensive interrogation of supplicants occurred when the man said that he had a conscientious objection to military service. In Bury, such people were virtually never excused, whether their objection was on religious or some other grounds. A typical example was that of a tackler – a power-loom overlooker, a skilled workman in a cotton mill – who had no connection with any church but declared himself to be a socialist, and claimed exemption because "I cannot accept the right of the state to dictate to me that I should take life or help in taking the life of any other man." The military representative on the tribunal immediately went on the offensive:

How long have you had this conscientious objection? Since the war commenced?

Conscientious Objector: I had these views before the war.

Military Representative: I suppose you are aware you are seeking the protection of the Fleet and it is a question of if we had not the Fleet, whether you would have work as a tackler, and yet you are not prepared to do anything yourself?

CO: As a citizen I am prepared to do all I can to help my fellow men, but I do not regard the question of the Fleet or armies as anything I am responsible for. I cannot do away with them.

MR: We have got our brothers fighting in the trenches. I suppose you'd be prepared to give non-combatant service making munitions?

CO: I don't think it right for me to object to killing and then to make munitions with the special object of enabling other men to kill.

MR: Do you object to non-combatant service at all?

CO: I cannot say I do, but I object to being placed under military rule.

MR: Are you one of those goody-goody men who, if assaulted, never retaliate?

CO: No.

MR: I suppose when struck on one side of the face you would turn the other?

CO: No, I should probably strike the individual back.

MR: You would act in self-defence, and we are asking you to do the same for your country.

CO: I regard war as being made not by the people of the country but by their governors, and someone distinct from the people of the country.

The Chairman of the tribunal, a local alderman, joined this dialogue:

You don't think this country could have prevented this war?

CO: I'm not blaming this country more than any other country involved.

Another Member: Do you propose taking any benefits of the war?

CO: I don't think there will be any benefits of the war.

AM: Do you believe in accepting the advantages of civilisation and a well-governed country, and are not prepared to make any sacrifice to defend the rights and privileges of that country?

CO: I regard the rights and privileges the people enjoy as having been won not by militarism but by constitutional methods, by the people organising and using their own constitutional methods.

AM: The same constitutional authority as is conducting this war?

CO: I grant that.

AM: And you don't agree with them?

CO: No.

His application was refused.

The animosities against people who were not strictly conforming to all the patriotic models of behaviour established by the authorities and public opinion, continued until the last days of the war. Some self-appointed vigilantes actually exceeded the standards expected of them by authority, and found themselves on the windy

The Six VCs Before Breakfast, who brought great glory to the Lancashire Fusiliers after the 1st Battalion of the regiment landed at Cape Helles, Gallipoli. At the time of the action, Willis was a Captain, Grimshaw was a Lance-Corporal and Keneally was a Private. The pictures are taken from a recruiting poster used by the regiment after 1918. It portrayed all the eighteen officers and men who won Victoria Crosses while serving with the Fusiliers in the Great War.

The "Lancashire Landing" at W Beach, Gallipoli, in the dawn of April 25, 1915. The drawing, by Samuel Begg, Special Artist of the *Illustrated London News*, appeared in the magazine on September 4, 1915. The officer waving a walking stick in the centre of the

picture is supposed to be Captain R. R. Willis VC, who supplied Begg with an account of
the landing which was the basis of the artist's work.

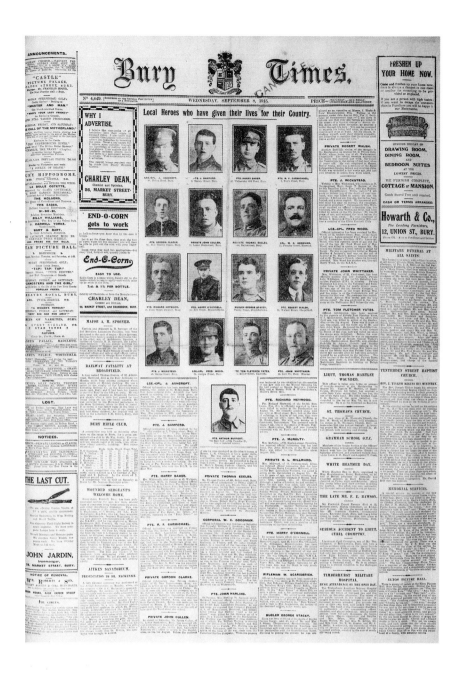

As the Gallipoli casualties were notified to next of kin, the *Bury Times* began to publish photographs and potted biographies of the local men who had been killed, with the connivance of their relatives. No such details were released officially in public until long after the disastrous campaign was over. The newspaper continued to feature its Local Heroes until the end of the war. Sometimes their photographs occupied two or three pages at a time.

side of the law. Only a few more months of the conflict were left when eighteen millgirls were taken to court for insulting behaviour liable to cause a breach of the peace. A young woman called Alice Prestwich had been abused by them outside the mill, and they had then chased her home, where they surrounded her house and continued to boo and shout epithets. This was because a Mrs Yates, who had worked at the mill for twenty-two years, had asked for ten days' leave of absence when her husband came home after being with the Fusiliers in France without a break for over a year. The manager had refused her more than two days off work; so she stayed home and got the sack. Miss Prestwich, who had a mother to support, was given her job. The magistrates dismissed the case against the millgirls after each had promised to behave properly in future.

The Lancashire cotton mills were operated almost wholly by women and old men by then, so great had been the drain on their normal male workforce. Similar gaps had appeared elsewhere on the home front, causing an appeal for half a million men to fill vacancies in agriculture, in shipyards, in general engineering and in the construction industry. It wasn't clear where this manpower was to come from, but Bury was only one of many towns whose citizens were informed that "men with a knowledge of carpentry or mechanics, men used to working in power houses and foundries, are urgently wanted. We can no longer leave the War to the Army and Navy while the rest of us go on doing our business as usual. Germany is wavering. Let the men of England move against the enemy *en masse.*" There were other shortages. In the spring of 1917 there was enough concern about the food supply for note to be taken in this corner of England of a suggestion from a retired Army officer in Aberdeen. He advised that young crows, abundant in his part of the world, made a tolerable substitute on the table for game birds, chicken or other fowl. Before the end of that year, it was announced that tea and margarine were to be rationed, and shortly afterwards meat was also put under government control. A Ministry of Food had been established and it described how to use potatoes in order to supplement available supplies of butter ("The potato butter may be improved with a few drops of butter colouring . . ."). In food, as in every other commodity, the profiteers were even more active towards the end of the war than they had been when they saw their chance at the beginning; "the general public are being fleeced – for such a word is not too strong to apply to the methods of some of those who are causing the price of articles used in the household to soar to heights which make it difficult indeed for people with slender financial resources to purchase them . . . It is high time strong action was taken by the powers that be . . ." That was an indignant Bury newspaper editor saying what all but a few of the townspeople thought.

They had, by then, given much to the war effort, especially in the amount of blood their men had shed. They had at last understood the heroic efforts made by their local regiment at Gallipoli, though it would be a long time before they discovered the awful truth about the catastrophe there, how it had come about, and its full disgrace. What they knew, from the stories the survivors told when at last they came home on leave, was that the Lancashire Fusiliers had been in the thick of the fighting and had acquitted themselves as honourably as anyone, at greater expense than most. They were also aware that the Victoria Cross – the highest award the sovereign could bestow for courage in war – together with other decorations, had been won by soldiers of the regiment for their bravery on the peninsula. The town had become extremely proud of its Gallipoli Fusiliers, even in its distress for those of them who would not be coming home.

An unfortunate consequence of this pride, and the concentration of the entire community's concern as the Gallipoli casualties mounted week after week, was that other units of the regiment serving elsewhere felt neglected and devalued. Shortly after the evacuation from the peninsula had been announced, and a sort of relief seized the town, a Sergeant Stanley Dixon, serving with the 2nd/5th Battalion, who were then up to their knees in the mud of the Somme – and were shortly to acquire a VC of their own – wrote the following letter to the same editor who was to castigate the profiteers: "Sir, It is with regret that I notice that the people of Bury and District do not realise that a local battalion have been fighting in the firing line for over six months . . . We have now been out here ten months, and when our lads go to England on seven days' leave the people still continue to ask 'Have you been in the trenches?' I put this down to ignorance on the part of the people at home, or they do not take an interest in what this battalion is doing. We deserve all the credit you can give us, and I feel confident in saying that if the people at home only knew what the lads out here had done . . . they would realise what kind of fighting we have had to do both in France and Flanders ... If ever a battalion was deserving of any credit at all it is the 2nd/5th Battalion Lancashire Fusiliers, and I hope that the people of Bury and District will see that we get it at home."

The Gallipoli survivors, too, were to know the score in France and Flanders before they were much older. As the first anniversary of their now famous landing on W Beach approached, the 1st Battalion were also on the Somme, entrenched at Beaumont Hamel. The 9th Battalion, which had participated in the failure at Suvla Bay, followed them to the Western Front within a couple of months. The 1st/5th and the three other Territorial battalions spent much longer in the Middle East after being withdrawn to Alexandria and Cairo. They took part in various operations along the Suez Canal, elsewhere in Egypt, and especially in the Sinai Desert; and although they were not once involved in a fight, there were several occasions when they and the Turks played catch-as-catch-can amid the sands. Towards the end of February 1917 they sailed from Alexandria for the last time; and two days later the ship carrying the 1st/5th and 1st/6th narrowly escaped being sunk, when a torpedo passed between the vessel and its log line, missing its target by only a few yards. Then the Terriers, too, spent the rest of the war in northern Europe, as did all the battalions of the Fusiliers except the 12th, which had nearly three years of campaigning in Macedonia. During the European war, there were Fusiliers at the Battle of the Somme, at Ypres, at Menin Road, at Polygon Wood, at Broodseinde, at Poelcappelle, at Cambrai, at Amiens. They won much honour, time and time again. But nothing ever quite matched their association with Gallipoli.

# 5

# Counting the Cost

It was unseasonably fine in Bury the day the war came to an end. There wasn't a touch of damp or fog, both normal in November, and the breeze which stirred the flags carried only a faint autumnal nip. When news of the Armistice broke on Monday the 11th, Union Jacks and banners bearing St George's cross were raised above buildings throughout the town. Street sellers emerged with trays full of little flags on sticks, promoted by people as eager for patriotic profit at the end of the bloodshed as they had been at the beginning. Otherwise, the town carried on as normal for a little while, before the schoolchildren were given a holiday and the mills, the workshops and the foundries also closed. Some of these had already been decorated in anticipation of the peace, and at one mill – owned by a Methodist family who liked to employ good chapelgoing folk as much as possible – they had stopped the looms on Friday afternoon; whereupon the operatives had started spontaneously singing "Praise God from Whom all blessings flow", and "O God our help in ages past". There were to be services of thanksgiving in many parts of Bury, including one in the Drill Hall, which two thousand attended; and at the County Court there was general applause when Judge Spencer Hogg interrupted proceedings to announce the news, at which a couple of litigious tradesmen decided to withdraw their case in deference to the occasion. At the Theatre Royal, the Monday evening performance of *Maid of the Mountains* went on as usual, but it was preceded by the orchestra playing "The Allies March" and the National Anthem to a standing ovation by the audience. The trams had stopped running at noon, and there was no afternoon postal delivery. By the middle of the day the main streets were full of people dressed in their best clothes. Wartime songs could be heard here and there, but most citizens were noticeably restrained in their celebration of peace. They roamed the streets with their little flags in a mood that was somewhere between elation and blankness, as though they were not quite sure what to feel. A handful of soldiers were among them, for the depot establishment at the Barracks had been stood down that morning for a couple of days. There was a glow in the sky all the way up Rossendale when darkness fell, as bonfires were lit on hillsides above each of the villages and small milltowns.

It would be months before there was a ceremonial return of the troops from war comparable to the exodus of the Fusiliers in 1914, when crowds had followed their progress from the heights of Turton to the railway station, at the start of their long journey to Gallipoli. The fourth anniversary of the landing had almost come round before the 1st/5th Battalion officially came home, and then it was only a token cadre of five officers and thirty-three men. Yet, in truth, out of the one thousand or so who had left the town at the beginning of the war, not many more than these members of the battalion were still on active service at the end: the rest were either dead or had been declared no longer fit to fight. And of those who landed at W Beach on April 25, 1915 in the 1st Battalion, only forty-three men were still fit for front-line service by Armistice Day. Crowds had seen the soldiers off anxiously four years earlier, but there was nothing but exuberance at the 1st/5th's return, with the streets around the station and the town centre solid with humanity. People knew when the train was approaching because it detonated a series of fog signals that the railwaymen had placed on the track, to warn the bandsmen on the platform to hoist their instruments. They were playing "Home Sweet Home" as the engine steamed up and, as the troops got out, the musicians switched to the regimental march, which could barely be heard in the hubbub of cheering voices all around.

The Mayor and Corporation were there to greet the men, together with other dignitaries; the Mayor in his official red robes and gold chain, and the Town Clerk in his dark robe and his bobtailed grey wig. Then the dignitaries, led by an attendant carrying the town's elaborate mace, went in procession directly to the Drill Hall; while the soldiers formed up behind the band and marched with rifles at the slope around the central streets, applauded every yard of the way by crowds standing five and six deep. The marching ended at the Drill Hall, too, where this remnant of the town's most cherished battalion was given a full-blown civic welcome at a homecoming banquet. This was a small token of relief and gratitude, after four and a half years of almost overwhelming pain. The Lancashire Fusiliers had lost 13,642 men in the Great War: and no one had managed to keep count of the merely wounded soldiers of the regiment.*

The most poignant losses were those which came right at the end, when men who had fought and managed to survive for four years had been killed only days, sometimes hours, before the Armistice. Private Oddy's wife had just finished reading a letter from him saying that he expected to be home soon, when there was a knock on the door and the telegraph boy brought the message that Oddy had died of wounds on October 31. Private Newton, a millworker before he joined the 1st/5th, and the father of three, was killed by machine-gun fire on November 8, in the battalion's last engagement of the war, in which he had fought since February 1915. The chaplain later wrote to his widow: "It does seem hard luck to be knocked out so near the end. This battalion had the honour of being one of the last to make an attack, and it was at a time when every man was asked to give of his very best. Victory was obviously within reach and it was just a question of striking such a blow as would make it certain. No man could have done better or given more than he did, nor yet have died more gloriously." Perhaps Mrs Newton did obtain some comfort from those impeccably constructed sentences; and from the various testimonies to her husband's manhood that in due course came to every widow.

First to arrive was usually a small illuminated scroll, lavish with draped flags, and with a steadfast Britannia counterbalanced by a sorrowing maiden. This was "a tribute from the Mayor, Aldermen and Burgesses of the County Borough of Bury to the Honoured Memory of_____who died for King and Country in the Great War. Greater Love Hath No Man Than This, That a Man Lay Down His Life For His Friends. *Pro Patria Mori.*" Subsequently, the Government sent a brass plaque which had the dead soldier's name

* Of the Fusiliers who went to Gallipoli, the 1st Battalion had lost 1,300 men in the war as a whole, the 1st/5th 539, the 1st/6th 480, the 1st/7th 543, the 1st/8th 549, the 9th 559. The 2nd Battalion, which was the first to see active service, lost 1,510 men. Of the other two Bury Territorial battalions, the 2nd/5th lost 838 and the 3rd/5th 179.

engraved between Britannia's raised arm and an adjacent lion, above the legend "He Died For Freedom And Honour". Finally, as the ultimate acknowledgement of widowhood, there came an unilluminated scroll bearing the royal arms above the following sentiment: "He whom this scroll commemorates was numbered among those who, at the call of King and Country, left all that was dear to them, endured hardness, faced danger, and finally passed out of the sight of men by the path of duty and self-sacrifice, giving up their own lives that others might live in freedom. Let those who come after see to it that his name is not forgotten." Rolled inside the scroll was a slip of paper, headed Buckingham Palace, and beneath, a reproduction of George V's signature.

The pain was almost as bad, and sometimes it was worse, for the families of men whose deaths had not been verified after they fought an action, but who had simply been posted missing. It was nearly three years after Harry Bullough's last battle in November 1916 before his sister received a message that "he is now officially regarded as having died on that date or since . . . A letter from an officer of his company shortly after he was reported missing states that he was with a bombing party which met with a warm reception, and that many did not return. Many were, however, thought to have been captured when held up in the enemy's wire." No such luck for Private Bullough; and not much more for Private Heyes, who had been at Gallipoli with the 1st/5th and was eventually taken prisoner in Belgium early in 1918. The Germans released him after the Armistice, but left him to make his own way to the Allied lines on foot. A couple of days later he was found wandering aimlessly, too exhausted to speak, and was taken to a civilian hospital, where he shortly afterwards died, though his wife and five children didn't hear about it for another seven months. Newspapers in Lancashire regularly carried pathetic messages from women whose men appeared to have vanished into thin air – as they literally had sometimes, if they had been hit by an artillery shell – without their comrades knowing how they'd died. Thus, in March 1919, "Mrs Harrison, of Rochdale Road, Bury, would be grateful if any returned soldier could give information regarding her son Private Herbert Harrison, 2nd/5th Lancashire Fusiliers, who was reported missing France, November 20, 1917." Another mother was anxiously enquiring for news of the 9th Battalion's Private Airton, whose wife had died about the time he went missing two years earlier, leaving four children in their grandparents' care. Most people eventually received some official communication which presumed the soldier's death, as in Private Bullough's case, but some had to wait a long time. It was the end of 1921 before the Ashworth family heard that the remains of young Tattersall Ashworth, who joined the Fusiliers in 1915 and was posted missing the following year, had been placed in Delville Wood Cemetery on the Somme.

Some Fusiliers reached the sanctuary of home before fate struck at them maliciously. Nothing in the war itself was crueller than the end awaiting John Holliday, who had been in the thick of things at the front for four years before being demobilised in 1919. He was a miner and he went back to his old job at Outwood Colliery, on the outskirts of Bury, one Monday morning. On the Wednesday there was a roof fall at the coal face, which crushed and killed him instantly. George Allen had been in the war even longer, having joined the 1st/5th during those heady days of recruitment in early August 1914. Three weeks after demobilisation, he started work he'd never done before, as an oiler and greaser in a Bury dyeworks. Twelve days later his jacket snagged on a moving pulley, he was dragged into the machinery and he, too, was crushed to death. Fred Butterworth's death could only be surmised after the gruesome discovery of his remains. He'd been discharged from the Fusiliers in the last summer of the war and hadn't been able to settle down to anything, had made no attempt to return to his job as a coal heaver. At one of the farms on the outskirts of Bury the winter threshing had begun, when bits and pieces of a body began to come out of the threshing machine. The appalled farmworkers stopped it and saw what was left of a man underneath. So much had been eaten by rodents before the machinery started up that a doctor found it impossible to determine how Butterworth had died; but he thought it likely that the ex-Fusilier had taken shelter in a thunderstorm several weeks earlier and there suffered a fatal heart attack.

Some men died because the war caught up with them after they had tasted, for a little while at least, the relief of getting home alive. Ernest Fletcher had been so badly wounded with the 1st/5th at Gallipoli that he was discharged from the Army at once and spent the rest of the war in Bury, where he died the night before the Armistice was declared. Bill Newsham lost a finger and a toe at Gallipoli but he had soldiered on for the rest of the war after a period in hospital, and it was "malaria and other ailments" which did for him in the end, after his demobilisation. Fred Lomax had come through Gallipoli intact, but he had been discharged shortly before the end of the war, suffering from shell shock after too many artillery barrages in France. Two years later, at the age of twenty-four, he died of bronchitis and pneumonia, related to the epileptic fits he'd suffered ever since the shelling; so the Fusiliers buried him with full military honours provided by coffin bearers, the Union Jack, a firing party and a bugler.

A number of men took quite a long time to die from the effects of the war. It was 1932 and Charles Cadden was in middle age before Gallipoli at last brought about his end. He had been a healthy man, a bricklayer's labourer, when he joined the 1st/5th, but in the Dardanelles he was wounded in the spine, the left shoulder and the ribs. He had spent the next six years in various hospitals before being discharged in 1921, with his right leg so paralysed that he dragged it when walking. He got a labouring job again, but after a few months had to give it up. He then obtained employment as a canteen assistant in a Bury cotton mill, but in 1929 he collapsed there one day and was sent to the hospital attached to the Jericho Institution on the outskirts of the town, the workhouse where local indigents were, after a fashion, provided for. He was discharged from this hospital, too, in time, and returned to life on a disability pension of twelve shillings a week with his wife Susannah and two unmarried children. One day in 1932, Charles collapsed in the street and never again left his bed. Two months later he went blind. For a month he took no nourishment except a little brandy. One morning he became semi-conscious and died in the evening of the same day. The doctor who conducted the post-mortem examination said there was scarcely any superficial fat on the body. He gave the cause of death as heart failure, anaemia, cancer of the stomach and fibrosis of the lungs, the last being attributed to the previous existence of a septic wound in the left side. He also mentioned his discovery of a piece of lead near the kidneys, about half an inch in diameter. It looked like a bullet, though it appeared to have caused nothing more than slight irritation. Nevertheless, the doctor concluded – and the coroner accepted his advice – that Mr Cadden's death "was directly due to wounds received in action in May 1915, in the Dardanelles and Gallipoli." The regiment gave him a military funeral, too.

As in the early days of the war, some men were spiritually

crushed by their experiences and one day put an end to themselves, long after the hostilities had ceased and there was no danger of their having to face machine-guns, snipers, mines or shellfire again. The only detectable pattern common to them all was that they had returned from war depressed, and nothing ever lifted them from the slough of despond. John Galloway had been wounded at Gallipoli, and in Europe he had been taken prisoner. Years after he returned to Bury he went into hospital for a minor operation, which was completely successful. A few days later he suddenly got out of his bed, went to the lavatory at the end of the ward, and there took a header through the window, thirty feet above the ground. Bert Peachey came home from France shell-shocked, spent time in the local Prestwich Asylum, returned home, and some months later hanged himself in the cellar: the coroner "thought it possible it was caused by his service in the Army". James Scott had been with the 12th Battalion of the Fusiliers, which spent so much of its time in Macedonia, and there he contracted dysentery, malaria and insomnia. He also complained of head pains and alternated between extreme restlessness and periods of abnormal lassitude, which alarmed his mother and his brother – also a returned Fusilier – so much that they took it in turns to keep an eye on him. But in the middle of the night he got up and, before his mother could intercept him, he went to the bathroom and cut his throat.

Those who committed suicide often went to extraordinary lengths to end their lives. Jonathan Corlett, who became a gas meter inspector after his Territorial service, waited till his wife went out one afternoon before fetching the zinc bathtub into the kitchen and filling it by hand with a basin, from the tap above the sink. When there was 4½ inches of water in the tub he got into it fully dressed and face down, and in the somewhat greater depth caused by his displacement he just about managed to drown. Even more bizarre was the death of Harry Howarth, a baker who had gone to war in 1914 and returned from it to the Armistice. He had been twice wounded and was buried once in a shell hole, where he had almost suffocated. He had been discharged as neurasthenic and in this still shell-shocked condition he had lived with his brother and sister for seventeen years after being demobilised; until one day he went down to the cellar and there improvised a bed beside the gas bracket. He went back upstairs and carefully bathed and shaved himself. He put on a white shroud and white socks, to save the undertaker the trouble of doing so. Then he returned to the cellar, lay down on the makeshift bed, and turned on the gas.

Some had returned from the war so utterly disturbed in mind and spirit that they had no sense at all of their own identity. At the end of 1919, the parents of Private Herbert Worrall, a Fusilier who had been missing for years, heard from another Bury family that at the military hospital in Warrington, about thirty miles away, there were three soldiers the authorities had not been able to identify. Outwardly unmarked, they were living there in a kind of daze, an emptiness which no treatment had yet managed to reach. There were, at about this time, over 6,000 such ex-servicemen lodged in British lunatic asylums. Mr and Mrs Worrall set off without delay, hopes raised, but perhaps not too high; mercifully, for none of the three was their son. One of them insisted that his name was Albert Wilson, that he had worked at the Peel Mill in Bury before the war, had lodged in Nelson Street; that he had a brother named Frank, who worked at the Bridge Hall Mill . . . When the Worralls went home they reported this to the local newspaper, which prominently ran the story in the hope that Wilson's relatives might respond. A number of people visited the hospital and saw the man, but no one ever recognised him. Nor did anyone ever find out who he really was.

Bury's leading citizen voiced his concern for many who survived the war. Sir James Hacking was a self-made man who had started life as a half-timer in the textile industry (a child whose life was divided between rudimentary education and menial work for a pittance in the mill) and had risen to become a millowner himself. He had lately been knighted for his civic leadership, which had been extended annually ever since his first term of office at the start of the war. On Armistice Day he let it be known that he hoped the terms of the peace settlement with Germany would be as severe as could honourably be imposed. More attractively, he turned his thoughts to those who would be coming back from the war with wounds that would prevent them from living normal working lives again, and to those whose breadwinners would not return. There must, he said, be training of some sort for both; and in this he was merely echoing what the local branch leaders of the Discharged Soldiers and Sailors Association had been saying for a year or two. They recalled the Boer War, when hundreds of men had returned to Bury and district to nothing better than begging and selling bootlaces on the street, some of them destined to spend the rest of their lives in the workhouse at Jericho. That was one of the reasons why the Lancashire Fusiliers had opened a Compassionate Fund in 1902, the first regiment to do such a thing, copied by many others afterwards.

The officials of the DSSA were quite clear about the requirements of 1918, starting with an adequate pension for those who had been "maimed, disabled or broken in health by the war". Moreover, "the widows and children of the private soldiers are as much entitled as the widows and children of the Generals to be maintained in the same manner as before the war." They also wanted artificial limbs supplied free of charge to the men who had been damaged for their King and Country, instead of at the current cost of £25 for each appliance. They were not impressed by a recent debate on the pensions issue in the House of Commons, when only forty-seven MPs had bothered to turn up. Six months after the war ended they would be given even more grounds for pessimism, at the opening of a hostel for limbless ex-servicemen in London. A Lieutenant-Colonel T. H. Openshaw was on that occasion to say, quite seriously, that a man who had lost one leg was likely to live longer than if he had not, that a man who had lost two legs would probably live longer still. "The heart has to carry the blood to the extremities and, other things being equal, will continue to work longer if the legs are taken away. A man who has lost both his legs can be a better swimmer than before his loss."

Nearly a year after the war, 1,266 men were registered as officially disabled in Bury, suffering from tuberculosis, heart trouble and neurasthenia, as well as limblessness. Courses for such ex-servicemen had started at the local technical school; in book-keeping, practical mathematics and English (which included commercial correspondence and office routine). The cotton industry had agreed to accept up to two per cent of its male work force from the disabled, though the Government had asked for this to be five per cent; but the millowners had argued that, as there were many more women than men working in the mills, two per cent in their industry was the equivalent of five per cent in any other. Other employers were even less sympathetic to recruiting such ex-servicemen, and so were a number of trade unions. At a meeting of the local War Pensions Committee in September 1919, the representative of the National Union of Clerks complained that his occupation had become a dumping ground for the disabled. Someone else said that the training schemes so far adopted had not been very successful, partly through a shortage of tutors in technical schools and other institutions, partly because there was a notable reluctance to help in practical training on the floor of the factory or workshop by the employers and the existing work force. Nor did the disabled ever receive quite as much assistance as they thought they deserved. At regular intervals some failure in the system would be publicised by one or other of the groups lobbying on their behalf, or an individual would make an indictment of his own. Someone signing himself A Crippled Ex-Serviceman wrote a letter to the press in 1931 about the treatment offered by the Bury Employment Exchange. According to him, six temporary clerks required by a local charity were recruited through the exchange. "Not one was taken from the disabled men's section, yet there are men signing on who have held very good positions in life before being crippled. I know one who held the position of managing director . . . yet he is told he is not capable of being a clerk by the manager of the exchange. What have cripples to do? Sign on for ever?" A couple of decades later, there was still bitterness in the disabled ranks. The Second World War had been over for eight years when the Bury branch of the British Limbless Ex-Servicemen's Association lobbied for special allowances on behalf of those damaged in 1914–18, "to compensate them for their increasing disability arising from the effects of their amputations, their age and the strain of wearing artificial limbs for more than thirty years." It was said that, of the 45,000 British ex-servicemen who had lost limbs in the First World War, only 23,000 were still alive. So much for Colonel Openshaw's prognosis.

No similar pressure group ever challenged the nation on behalf of the war widows with anything like the same vigour, as Sarah Scowcroft and others like her gradually discovered. Such help as they received came, in the main, from their neighbours; but their survival most of all depended on their own strength of character, their energy, and their luck in obtaining a part-time job which gave them a little money and the time to look after the children until they were old enough to take some care of themselves. Shortly after the news of James's death at Gallipoli, Sarah's war pension came through; sixteen shillings a week for her, six shillings for Joseph James and four shillings for Alice. That wasn't nearly enough to live on as respectably as the Scowcrofts had always prided themselves on doing, and Sarah supplemented it in various ways. She continued as caretaker at the local Methodist chapel, the work that she and James had shared before the war. She took in washing, and she did cleaning for two different families of millowners who had large houses on the same side of Bury as the Scowcrofts' terrace home. There was another advantage in this arrangement, because one of the families had a boy and a girl just a little older than Sarah's children, who consequently received many cast-off clothes and toys. Other garments came from the jumble sales at the Sunday school where Sarah, being caretaker, was invariably allowed first pick. There was just one more source of income while the children were of school age. Sarah occasionally took in lodgers, men from out of town who worked on contracts in Bury from Monday to Friday before going home to their families for the weekend. When Joseph James became an apprentice at the age of thirteen, his six shillings a week from the Government stopped; as did Alice's four shillings when she began to work in a toffee factory. She had been bright enough at the elementary school to be offered a place at the Bury High School. But you needed a special uniform for that, gym slips and other things, which Mrs Scowcroft could ill afford, so the opportunity was missed.

They were always conscious of just making ends meet; as at breakfast time, when there was usually a boiled egg apiece for the children, their mother's share being the top, broken off each. Yet there were organised pleasures in the midst of all this dogged and frugal respectability. Once a week the Methodists gave a Happy Home concert, with sing-songs and recitations. Once a year, the Lancashire Fusiliers gave a party in the Drill Hall for all the widows and orphans of the regiment who lived locally, which meant games and a meal and a present, usually a packet of sweets. Somehow or other, every summer Sarah Scowcroft managed to take her children to Fleetwood, less expensive than the more popular Blackpool, for a short holiday. And in this manner she made the best of her widowhood and tried to compensate for the absence of James.

She would probably have said that there were women much worse off than herself; and by this she would have meant those who had got themselves into trouble while their men were away at the front, and paid for it when the soldiers came home. The ugliest domestic aspect of the war, from its outset, had been the letters sent to serving men about the goings on in their enforced absence; often written anonymously, but sometimes composed by a sanctimonious friend happy to reveal his or her identity. In many cases the stories were fabricated slanders; in others there was at least something of the truth. In Ada Lord's case, the informant was her mother-in-law, who decided to dispense justice herself while her wronged son was in France, setting about Ada so fiercely – and being counter-attacked vigorously in turn – that the police were forced to haul them apart, swearing furiously, at ten o' clock one night. But the infidelities did not often contain elements of farce. Rachel Hayes had married her husband in 1916, just before he went to France, and in the spring of 1918 she had somebody else's child. She wrote to her husband "Now, Will, I have had a dreadful fall. Do for God's sake forgive me." But he was not in a forgiving mood when he came home, and divorced her at the first opportunity in June 1919. Isabella Hardman was in the workhouse during her husband's time away in the Fusiliers, together with half a dozen children that were theirs, and another she'd conceived after he went abroad. One day she absconded from the workhouse, leaving the illegitimate infant behind. She was put on trial for that and for walking off in clothes belonging to the Bury Guardians, who ran the place. For these two offences she was given a month's hard labour in prison. Some women were unfaithful to no one, yet contrived to make a tragedy of their lives. One such was Bertha Collier, an unmarried munitions worker to whom romance with a soldier on leave came at the age of thirty-six and resulted in pregnancy. She aborted herself with a mixture of pennyroyal and sweet nitre, and shortly afterwards died in Bury Infirmary from septic peritonitis.

Mary Jane Boardman personified the full wretchedness of women whose lives became complicated by a wartime relationship out of wedlock. Her husband had been a miner at the same pit that killed the demobilised John Holliday, but David Boardman went missing at Gallipoli shortly after the 1st/5th went ashore, and it was a year or more before he was officially listed among the dead. By then Mary Jane was pregnant by Jack Turner, a lodger with her parents. The child was born in the summer of 1916 and within a few hours its body was found in the sluice of a local bleachworks. Mary Jane was eventually charged with its murder at Manchester Assizes, where a jury heard her sad story of misery and loneliness; and also of betrayal. She had told Turner she did not want to disgrace her parents and would go away. He said he would go with her and find work to support the three of them. But instead he enlisted and went off to the Army without another word to her. He appeared in court in uniform, denied that he was the father, declared that he had nothing at all to say. Mary Jane Boardman broke down at that point, shouting that he was telling lies. Her counsel pointed out that she had given birth without anyone's assistance and had nearly died as a result. A police inspector said she was a steady hard-working young woman, with nothing against her before. The prosecution accepted her plea of not guilty to the murder charge and she was sentenced only for concealing the birth. The Judge said; "You were a married woman and at the time when your husband was abroad and at the time when he was reported to be missing and when you ought to have been hoping he might yet be found alive and return to you, you were unfaithful to him . . ." He sent her to prison for six months.

Hopes that ex-servicemen would fare better after the Great War than their predecessors had done in 1902, were quickly dashed. Within five months of the Armistice, the number of unemployed in Lancashire and Cheshire was rising by 10,000 every week and in Bury there were by then 6,229 people out of work. This was remarkable, when the cotton industry was enjoying a boom that attracted a great deal of speculation from London investors, who were persuaded that high profits would follow in Lancashire for five full post-war years. The average dividend paid by 150 Lancashire spinning companies was 16.25% in 1918, 21.25% in 1919 and 40.21% in 1920; normal returns were between 5% and 7%. The boom collapsed in 1921 and, from then on, the unemployment figures rose steeply until they reached a peak in Bury of almost thirty-one per cent in 1932: a bit further up Rossendale, in the smaller milltown of Rawtenstall, forty-eight per cent were out of work by then. Even before the cotton slump began, men back from the war were finding it difficult to obtain jobs; and, as in the case of the disabled, trade unions as well as employers often stood in their way. Recently demobilised men who tried their luck at local collieries found themselves turned away because the Lancashire and Cheshire Miners Federation threatened to bring the pits to a standstill if anyone was employed who hadn't been a skilled miner before the war. It mattered not that some of the soldiers had worked in the industry as unskilled youths, before going off to the Dardanelles and the Somme: the union's position was that "no man shall be employed in mining unless he has been brought up in the trade."

The desperation of many ex-servicemen was reflected in statements made at this time by various officials who were trying hard to find them work. In June 1921, the Director of the Ministry of Labour Appointments Department for the North-west was appealing to anyone who could offer work "not necessarily on his own staff, but within the circle of his acquaintances. Will any reader who is willing thus to act as 'godfather' to one or more ex-servicemen let me know when he thinks he can help? He may be so situated that he can best assist a clerk; he may be in contact with firms who engage salesmen or travellers; or he may know an architect who is looking for an assistant ... I believe that if the commercial community will give this assistance, 'adopting' individuals as English towns have 'adopted' French towns, a large percentage of these men will speedily be found work when trade begins to improve; and I believe, too, that everyone who succeeds in placing an ex-serviceman in a situation will feel that he has done something towards paying off a national debt."

As the third anniversary of the Armistice approached, another officer in the department wrote as follows: "On Friday, November 11, the nation will join in remembering those who laid down their lives in the war. May I ask your readers to give, also, upon that day, a moment's thought to those who survived and are now without work? The department with which I am associated is charged with the resettlement of ex-servicemen of superior qualification and education, of whom thousands are unemployed, and my first concern is of course for them, but the concern of the nation should extend to all who returned from the fighting forces, and in their ranks the unemployed are counted by hundreds of thousands. Will every employer who reads this letter consider for a few minutes the possibility of finding or creating, a post for an ex-serviceman? A special effort on Armistice Day, for the sake of the living, will be a recognition of our obligation to the dead." By "ex-servicemen of superior qualification and education", the man from the Ministry meant, of course, officers and senior NCOs. In this one region alone, more than 2,000 of these were on his books by then. Some had been there for three years and "the number is growing steadily".

At the other end of the line, soldiers who had less glittering recommendations were among the hundreds who demonstrated on

PART TWO

Bury Fairground repeatedly in these years. After one mass meeting they sent a deputation – including Joseph Nuttall and William Leach, both labourers who had served with the Fusiliers – to see the Mayor and to ask for assistance from the Corporation. They made it plain to His Worship that they weren't asking for charity and they didn't want to make trouble. Charity, however, is what many of them had to accept, and the Fusiliers' Compassionate Fund did what it could to help. In 1914 it was disbursing £360 a year to survivors of the Boer War and stricken dependents of Fusiliers killed in South Africa. By early 1922 the figure had risen to £5,000 and the fund was so nearly empty that a public appeal was launched to replenish it. Nuttall said he had been to his old employer "times without number" but hadn't been able to get a job. If only he could obtain three days' work a week it would be better than nothing. Then the deputation rejoined the men who had been at the demonstration, and everyone marched in an orderly fashion, four abreast and with Police-Sergeant Hill leading the way, to the rooms of the local Labour Party, which 370 men immediately joined. Of that number, 218 were returned soldiers, fifty of them receiving Army pensions of some sort, most of which amounted to less than ten shillings a week. On that occasion, the Mayor remarked that he had seen reports of damage done by rioting unemployed men in other towns: he thought that in Bury the men had more sense and "appealed to them to carry on in the future as they had in the present". And they did. There was another Fairground meeting a few days later, after which hundreds again marched through the town, this time to the Council offices, where they lined up to impress the elected worthies who were arriving for a meeting inside. The tactic paid off to some extent. The Corporation later announced that it was offering a total of 300 new jobs; a couple of men with the Fire Brigade, six labourers at the gas department, thirty for street-cleaning, a dozen to wash the filter beds at the Sewage Works ... It would probably mean that almost all would work no more than alternate weeks; but, as Joseph Nuttall had said, that was better than no work at all. Six months later the council announced plans for a new road to be built between Bury and the adjacent town of Radcliffe, specifically to help the unemployed a bit more.

Some became so discouraged by the reality of coming home from the war that, after enduring it for a year or two, they decided to try their luck elsewhere. The Ministry of Labour found an increasing number of servicemen in the area signifying their willingness to emigrate to Australia, New Zealand, Canada and South Africa or other commandingly white parts of the British Empire. There were 200 such men on the local office's books in the summer of 1920, and many of these were officers, too: like Captain G. H. Yapp, who had survived France with the 2nd/5th Battalion of the Fusiliers, was fortunate enough to obtain employment as executive officer at the nearby Territorial firing range, but who announced one day that he was off to Alberta, to try his hand at farming instead. And then there was Captain Robert Hall, who had been at Gallipoli with the 1st/5th and in 1921 declared himself "fed up with Blighty". To rid himself of this melancholy he embarked on what was described as a voyage of discovery up the Amazon with two other ex-officers who also found the peace less invigorating than the war. Periodically thereafter, Bury was treated to reports of their adventures, which included firing Verey lights to scare off Indians, and almost drowning when their canoe capsized and lost them, among other things, 2,000 rounds of ammunition for their Winchester rifles. Just over a year later, and a little sorry for themselves, because they were covered in insect bites and not very clean by then, they were on their way back to Bury with talk of perhaps returning to Brazil one day to look for gold.

Meanwhile the slump dragged on in Lancashire. When a great march of the unemployed from Glasgow to Westminster came through Bury on its way south, a score of local men joined it and took part in the angry demonstration outside Parliament at journey's end. That was in 1922, and there was a lot more poverty, hopelessness, disappointment, bitterness still to come. There were soup kitchens in Bury every Tuesday and Thursday night in the winter of 1934, with volunteers dishing out fifty gallons to the needy each time. The same winter also saw a paving stone hurled through the window of a herbalist's shop on Union Square in the early hours of one morning. The shop was owned by the Mayor for that year, Alderman Thomas Evans, brother of the corporal who had caught smallpox in Egypt and rejoined the 1st/5th Battalion at Gallipoli just in time to be killed the next day. Like the men who returned from the war in South Africa, ex-servicemen had been begging on the streets of the town for some time by then. Three who were drunk when they started soliciting, and turned nasty when anyone refused to give them something, were given three months in prison in 1922. They were not the only old soldiers who got into trouble after trying to remedy their situation illegally. William Townsend, a Fusilier since the outbreak of war and a railway porter after demobilisation, stole five pairs of ladies socks, worth 1s 3d, from a case at Knowsley Street Station, from which the local Territorials had left Bury in 1914. He was married with four children, his wife was ill, and he himself was suffering from consumption. Six months earlier he had been up before the magistrates for stealing empty bottles from the station, in spite of which the railway company had not sacked him. For his second theft, the magistrates sent him to prison for three months, but stipulated that the sentence was to be served without hard labour; not because he was less than fully fit, but so that he would continue to receive his Army pension of thirteen shillings a week when he came outside again. It would have been terminated with the stiffer penalty.

Magistrates quite often made allowances for men who had come back from the war, especially if they had been to Gallipoli. Stephen Johnson had served with the 1st/5th in the Dardanelles, where he had been the battalion's barber, but could only get a labouring job after the war. He and his wife were tenants of a Bury paper mill and in 1919 they received notice to quit. Mrs Johnson approached the mill manager in the street, asking him to have the eviction stopped, but the manager said he couldn't and wouldn't even if he had been able to. Johnson then appeared and the manager was beaten up. Assaults of that order almost always meant imprisonment, but the Bench merely bound Johnson over to keep the peace for six months. Albert Hoyle, another survivor of Cape Helles and a tram conductor since the war, was accused of an indecent offence against a fourteen-year-old girl. He was given the benefit of the doubt and the case was dismissed. James Wrigley, a miner who had won the Distinguished Conduct Medal, was arraigned for assaulting his wife and persistent cruelty, which caused the Magistrates Clerk, a former officer in the Fusiliers, to say "With the distinction you have won you should be heartily ashamed of yourself . . . Good God, man, your pals would have struck you if they had seen you." Or perhaps not: for it was subsequently revealed that Mrs Wrigley had given her husband venereal disease on his return from the war, and the magistrates did nothing but make a separation order against him.

Juries, too, could be lenient to old Fusiliers, as Norman Howarth discovered to his benefit. Although he had never received a medal for it, he had performed heroically at Gallipoli and was lucky to be alive. Everyone in his platoon apart from himself and two others had been killed in a charge on the Turkish trenches, and when he reached the second line of the enemy defence he was three times hit by explosive bullets, and bayoneted while lying on the ground. Eventually rescued, he was in an outpost receiving first aid when it was blown up by a shell burst, but he survived that, too, though in no condition ever to fight again. Discharged from the Army before the end of 1916, he returned to Lancashire but was unable to resume his trade as an engraver. He lived on a pension of twenty-five shillings a week. Among other disabilities, he had virtually lost the power of speech: when he appeared at Manchester Assizes, his replies to questioning had to be written down. He was charged with attempting to procure a sixteen-year-old girl, whom he had met casually on the train between Bury and Radcliffe, and subsequently invited to join him and a party of people in Brighton. A policeman said in court that until this, Howarth had led a most respectable life and had an excellent character. His Army discharge papers carried a recommendation from his commanding officer, who wrote that Howarth had had a good influence on the other men. A doctor told the Judge that Howarth's shell shock, from which he still suffered, would to some extent take away his sense of responsibility. The fact that the case had been sent by the Bury magistrates to the superior assize court indicated the gravity of the charge; and Howarth never denied that he had written incriminating letters to the girl. The Judge went out of his way to say that there was not a blemish on her character, nor had she enticed the accused in any way. The jury, nevertheless, found Howarth not guilty and he was discharged.

The community had other ways of acknowledging its indebtedness to Fusiliers who had survived Gallipoli. Bob Spencer eventually came home as a man who had been wounded on the peninsula and had returned to do battle again. Nothing in his life afterwards would ever compare to those four years of fighting, principally for his own survival; for they achieved an intensity that his civilian existence would never remotely match. He would never marry, would live quietly for many years with his brother, who had been a sailor in the war, would take a succession of jobs, which included making bread for his two sisters in the bakery they ran, and lived above, in one of Bury's dependent villages. His greatest excitement after 1918 would be to have one of his loaves displayed at a London exhibition. He never knew the miseries of unemployment that so many suffered after the war. The worst thing about his homecoming was being asked, so many times that he lost count, by Mrs Schofield to tell her everything he could remember about her Billy's last hours, last few days. But he remembered nothing about the attack on Krithia that took Billy's life. There was too much confusion, too much noise, too much gut-rotting funk about his own predicament. Billy was there before they charged; he had gone when the battalion was pulled out. So Bob Spencer came home without his mate: to be pushed to the head of queues as long as he still wore his uniform, to be bought a drink as long as everyone remembered who he was and where he'd been, to be told he was good old Bob. He enjoyed that warmth. He was glad, now that it was over, he had been to Gallipoli.

So was Will Hoyle, who had a weakness for responding to the bugle when King and Country called. He had volunteered for South Africa, where he had earned campaign medals for fighting in the Transvaal, in the Orange Free State, in the Cape Colony. When he returned home he got a job on the railways, greasing the engine wheels and the piston rods, but retained his Army connection through the Terriers and was one of the first to report to the Drill Hall when the 1st/5th Battalion was mobilised. He came through Gallipoli and the rest of the hostilities with nothing worse than dysentery and trench foot; and he picked up some more campaign medals as well as a lance-corporal's stripe. He was one of those who, seeing the state of things in Lancashire after the war, decided to emigrate with his wife and daughter for a better life. He went ahead to Canada, to find a job and a home, before sending for Annie and the little girl. But his wife suddenly went blind, and disabled migrants were not wanted in the white Empire. So Will Hoyle came back. When the honorary chaplain to the 1st/5th Battalion heard what had happened, he did something to help. He was the Rector of Bury and the Hoyles were among his parishioners. He made Will his gardener and handyman; which was a small social advance on being a railway cleaner, and offered greater security. Quite a lot of Fusiliers were given a leg-up like that.

But no one profited from the Gallipoli connection as much as

Charles Ainsworth. He belonged to a millowning family at Holcombe, where the Pennines came nearest to Bury and a hilltop
tower commemorating Sir Robert Peel was a notable landmark. He
was, in fact, chairman and managing director of the local bleachworks when he joined the 1st/5th Battalion at the outbreak of war.
If Lieutenant Stonestreet had not ducked foreign service, then Ainsworth would probably have gone to France with the 2nd/5th
instead, but it was he who took Stonestreet's place in the Dardanelles. He was wounded at the Third Battle of Krithia, declared unfit
for further foreign service, and spent the rest of the war training
recruits at home. When a general election was called almost as soon
as the Armistice was declared, Ainsworth was nominated to stand
for the Bury constituency on behalf of the Conservative and Unionist parties to oppose the sitting MP, Sir George Toulmin, who had
represented the Liberals in Parliament since 1902. The challenger
was Captain Ainsworth by then and he played his military record
for all he was worth in the campaign. At every election meeting he
was introduced as the man who had been wounded at Gallipoli,
while his political opponent had been voting for the interests of
the conscientious objectors at home. Ainsworth himself did not
hesitate to say that Sir George had "jeopardised our chances of
winning the war" by voting against conscription. The returned hero
was in favour of Germany paying the entire cost of the conflict and
said he "would brand the conscientious objector the coward he is
all the days of his life and would not let him have the ordinary
rights of citizenship or the franchise." He was very good at handling
potentially tricky questions from his audiences. Asked whether he
was in favour of officers and other ranks receiving the same pensions, he coolly replied that "he had often been told he was entitled
to a pension but he had never asked for one." Toulmin never stood
a chance of retaining his seat, which Ainsworth won quite comfort-
ably with forty-six per cent of the vote against the Liberal's thirty-
one per cent, Labour trailing behind with twenty-three per cent.
On the night of his victory, the chairman of the local Tories said
that the Captain "had had the sympathies of the ladies, inasmuch
as he had come forward so gallantly – although over military age
at the time – not as a pressed man, but as a volunteer to fight for
his country." Not many women had the vote in 1918, but the
sentiment doubtless reflected the truth.

Almost the first thing Charles Ainsworth did after his election was to re-emphasise his connection with the Lancashire Fusiliers. On New Year's Day 1919, he made a point of entertaining to tea at the Shoulder of Mutton Inn, bandsmen who had served with the 1st/5th and 2nd/5th during the war, after they had played selections of music on the lawn of Higher House, Holcombe, where Ainsworth lived. The bandsmen had by then been discharged from the Army but had kept in practice to await the official homecomings of their battalions later on. Bury's new MP was one of the dignitaries who was standing on the station platform with the Mayor and Corporation, when the 1st/5th came steaming back amid detonating fog signals in the spring of the year. He was always to keep his Territorial credentials in good repair, periodically taking promotion as it fell due until, in 1928, he was Lieutenant-Colonel Ainsworth and in command of the 5th Battalion, with two sons and a nephew serving under him. He was also, by then, Master of the Holcombe Hunt, for his war wounds had never been so serious that they stopped him from riding to hounds. He was much less vigorous in Parliament, where his most notable act was to move the second reading of a bill which would have made it more difficult for trade unions to levy a contribution from their members for the benefit of Labour Party funds. His amendment was defeated, as Ainsworth himself never was at the polls. He won six elections, one after the other, in Bury, whose voters did not see another MP until 1935, when Charles Ainsworth had retired. This was a remarkable achievement in an increasingly depressed town in the Lancashire industrial belt. He even won in 1929, when Labour swept the country and formed a government for the first time, under Ramsay MacDonald.

The depression was weighing heavily when Edward, Prince of Wales, visited Bury in 1921. On the morning of the visit, an editorial in the local paper regretted the fact that the heir to the throne was not arriving "in happier public circumstances". It then made the point that although "the loyalty of this large-hearted manufacturing population is unimpaired ... the strenuousness and prosperity of the people are very much impaired by many months of trade depression and trade dispute ... the manifestations of joy due to the Prince's coming that will be observed along the line of the route, absolutely honest and loyal though it will be, will reflect the real life of the people less than will the queues of workless men and women who throng almost daily the steps of the Textile Hall or the Temperance Hall ..."

Half an hour late in arriving, the car carrying the Prince swept into the Market Place with church bells ringing, troops presenting arms in a royal salute as the National Anthem was played, and thousands cheering everywhere in the centre of the town. Two hundred ex-servicemen, some of them disabled, survivors of Gallipoli among them, had been mustered in front of a platform on which stood the Mayor, the Member of Parliament and other welcoming personages. When the Prince's car came into sight, these stepped down to greet him, and he was then conducted along the line of veterans, standing in their Sunday best suits, with billycocks, trilbies, caps and even a straw boater on their several heads. The paper was to make much of the Prince's time with these men, the firmness of his grip when he shook their hands, his grin "when some remark showed the lighter side of a soldier's life", the way he seemed to lose his shyness "and to be actuated by a feeling of comradeship." Then he was off to a civic luncheon, and by mid-afternoon he had left Bury to lick its various wounds again. Some citizens were comforted in the knowledge that their sacrifices had not been overlooked by the royalty on whose behalf they had lately been drummed up to go to war.

# 6

# Six VCs Before Breakfast

There were many disinterested testimonies to the bravery and other fighting qualities of the Lancashire Fusiliers at Gallipoli. Mostly they praised the 1st Battalion's landing on W Beach in that first dawn of the campaign. The warmest and most unaffected tribute was contained in a signal made shortly after the event by HMS *Euryalus*, which had taken the soldiers on the last stage of their voyage from Egypt to the peninsula. "We are as proud as can be to have had the honour to carry your splendid regiment. We feel for you in all your great losses as if it were our own ship's company, but know the magnificent gallantry of your regiment has made the name more famous than ever." Vice-Admiral de Robeck, the commander of all naval operations, endorsed this in an official despatch which said: "It is impossible to exalt too highly the service rendered by the 1st Battalion Lancashire Fusiliers in the storming of the beach; the dash and gallantry displayed was superb." The Allied Commander-in-Chief, Sir Ian Hamilton, recorded his own view in a despatch which included the following observation: "So strong, in fact, were the defences of W Beach that the Turks may well have considered them impregnable, and it is my firm conviction that no finer feat of arms has ever been achieved by the British soldier – or any other soldier – than the storming of those trenches from open boats . . . and it was to the complete lack of the senses of danger or of fear of this daring battalion that we owed our astonishing success . . ."

Before 1915 was over, it had become apparent to the people of south-east Lancashire that their soldiers had not only suffered heavily in the Dardanelles, but had covered themselves with glory there. The local troops were also to be much decorated in acknowledgement of their performances. In the thirty-seven weeks of the campaign, the six battalions of Lancashire Fusiliers which were involved in it won no fewer than six Victoria Crosses, four Distinguished Service Orders, five Military Crosses, two Companion Orders of the Bath, thirteen Distinguished Conduct Medals, and forty-three Mentions in Despatches. This was an impressive haul by any standard. Of these awards, all the VCs, one DSO, two MCs and four Mentions went to officers and men of the 1st Battalion for what happened on April 25. What captured the imagination most of all, of course, was the award of those half a dozen Victoria Crosses. They became famous far beyond the regiment itself as the "Six VCs Before Breakfast", a ringing phrase that has been current for well over half a century, though no one knows who originated it. They contributed more than any other single thing to the enduring myth of Gallipoli in Bury and the other traditional recruiting grounds of the Fusiliers; who were, in fact, to win more VCs in the Great War than any other regiment.* But the total never counted for quite as much as the Gallipoli Six.

The highest award for gallantry that the British and their imperial helpmates would ever know was not only instituted in the reign of the Queen whose name it bears. Victoria took a great interest in its design and vetoed the original inscription "For the Brave" on the grounds that this would seem implicitly to exclude bravery in those who had not won the award. So the Maltese cross (technically a cross *patté*) simply bore the words "For Valour" instead. Every one was to be cast in bronze from the metal of a Russian field gun captured at Sevastopol in the Crimean War and, originally, the ribbon to which it was attached was red for the Army and blue for the Navy; but from 1920 this was changed to a uniform red for all services. The VC was instituted in 1856 but the first awards were made retrospective by two years in order to cover the war in the Crimea. The Queen's intention was that the new decoration "should be highly prized and eagerly sought after" and that neither rank, nor long service nor any other consideration should be

---

* The regimental count is eighteen VCs; but the War Office always maintained that the VC won by Lieut. Col. J. N. Marshall, while commanding the 16th Battalion, Lancashire Fusiliers, in France just before the end of hostilities, must be credited to the Irish Guards, to which he normally belonged. Even seventeen VCs, however, was many more than the number awarded to anyone else. The Rifle Brigade, the Royal Fusiliers and the Yorkshire Regiment came next with ten apiece.

adduced in determining an award; only that the recipient should have performed some feat of outstanding gallantry in the presence of the enemy. She herself made the first investiture on June 26, 1857, at a ceremony which was held on a perfect summer morning in Hyde Park. A very large parade of troops had been drawn up there to await the arrival of the Queen, and the sixty-two men to be honoured that day stood beside a table on which the crosses lay. Victoria came to this occasion on a horse, from which she never dismounted. As each winner of the decoration was announced and stepped forward, the Secretary of State for War picked up the cross and handed it to the Queen, who then leant down from her charger to pin it to the breast of the recipient. The intention was that the Victoria Cross would always be received from the monarch's own hand, either by the winner in person or, if awarded posthumously, by his closest relative. It became customary, however, in due course, for the monarch's personal representatives – that is, a Viceroy or a Governor-General – to make the award when the recipient lived far from the British Isles; eg in India, Australia or New Zealand. Gallipoli was to result in thirty-five such decorations by George V, and although the half-dozen awarded to the Lancashire Fusiliers became the most frequently invoked by posterity they were not, in fact, unparalleled: they were not even unequalled on the peninsula. The Royal Navy also won six VCs in one day at Gallipoli, awarded to a commander, a sub-lieutenant, two midshipmen and two seamen for their bravery at V Beach on the morning of April 25, during the disaster of trying to land troops from the *River Clyde*. The record haul of Victoria Crosses by one unit in the same action – a record which still stands today – had already been established by a lieutenant, a corporal and five privates belonging to the 2nd Battalion of the 24th Regiment (better known later as the South Wales Borderers) at the defence of Rorke's Drift in the Zulu War in January 1879. Four other VCs were won at the same time by men not of that regiment. Of the Gallipoli VCs, nine went to Australians, one to a New Zealander, the rest to various British units, including Navy and Marines.

The first the people at home in Bury knew about their regiment's VCs came almost exactly four months after the landing at Gallipoli, in August 1915, when it was announced that three Fusiliers had won the highest decoration of all. The announcement said that the winners were Captain Richard Raymond Willis, Sergeant Alfred

Joseph Richards and Private William Keneally, but it didn't reveal that Keneally's award had been made posthumously. There is some small confusion about the date of Keneally's death, even in the relevant file at the Imperial War Museum. One source gives the date as June 29, 1915, another has him dying of wounds in Malta in September. His headstone in the Lancashire Landing Cemetery at Cape Helles offers the date in June. By then he had been made Lance-Corporal. The newspaper article breaking the news was quite brief in its reference to the NCO and the ranker, but spread itself fulsomely on the officer. "Captain Willis, who belongs to Totnes, has been associated with the Lancashire Fusiliers for about twenty years. He is the band president and is known as a capable musician. About twelve years ago he was stationed at Bury Barracks. While home on furlough about a week ago he visited the Barracks and met some of the men recovering from wounds . . . Captain Willis is a typical British officer of the best type – quiet, handsome, obviously capable . . . He is excessively modest, and to the interviewer who tried hard to get his personal adventures out of him he said, always with a smile, 'Please, please, keep me out of it.' . . . Captain Willis was wounded beneath the heart in an attack made upon a Turkish position on June 4 . . . When Captain Willis came, a convalescent, to Bury Barracks, where the writer met him, he had to hold a sort of levee, for he has so many friends who were glad to see him again . . . Captain Willis has made a good recovery from his wound and was expecting to return to the Dardanelles. 'Tell me,' said the writer, 'what are the sensations of a soldier on returning, after being wounded, to the firing line?' 'Well,' said the Captain, 'it's rather like walking a long way to see your dentist for the third time after he has given you a bad tying up twice before. It's not pleasant. But by far the worst of it in my case is that all my brother officers and most of my men are gone.'"

Willis was, above all his fellow VCs, always the one picked out for particular attention. The most celebrated pictorial represen-tation of the Lancashire Landing on W Beach, shows an officer urging his men on through the surf and the barbed wire at the water's edge, waving nothing more dangerous than a walking stick in the air. The figure is supposed to be that of Willis. Many years later, when only a handful of Gallipoli survivors were still alive in old age, the last remaining member of C Company recalled approaching the beach in the next cutter to Captain Willis. "I saw him stand up and everyone in the boats heard him, above the noise of the bullets and the guns, shout 'Come on, C Company! Remember Minden!' That was it. Whenever we were in trouble, whenever we looked like going under, the cry 'Remember Minden!' brought us back to our senses. Captain Willis could not have timed it better."

For all the excessive modesty attributed to him by the reporter, Willis appears to have been assiduous in promoting the legend of his personal heroism at the beachhead. Apart from talking to journalists when he was back in England that August, he also managed to secure for himself the central role in the famous picture of the Lancashire Landing. This, "Drawn by S. Begg from Material Supplied by One Who Took Part in the Action", appeared in the *Illustrated London News* in September and, as Willis was presented with the original after it had been published, there can be no question that it was he who told the artist how things had been on April 25. The caption beneath the illustration was lengthy and informative about the award of three VCs, but Willis was the only soldier named in a description of what was supposed to have happened as the Fusiliers attacked. "The men sprang overboard and, up to the armpits, waded ashore, where a long stretch of barbed wire faced them. Captain Willis and a number of men with him daringly got through the obstruction, and the survivors sheltered behind a mound, whence they returned the Turkish fire. They had first to clean their rifles with pull-throughs and even with toothbrushes, to get the sand out of the barrels. Meanwhile, others of the regiment lay down close to the barbed wire to fire – only to be suddenly decimated by more hidden Turkish machine-guns posted to flank the beach. With fresh men, they eventually made their way round the ends of the entanglement, and joined Captain Willis. All thereupon charged the Turkish trenches . . ."

This account by the caption writer doesn't quite tally with the impression formed by the artist after he, too, had listened to the Captain's summary. The barbed wire entanglement provides a classic artistic diagonal across the composition, with sand cliffs looming in the background and surf frothing to the fore, on the viewer's side of the wire. In the water are men at the moment of being shot, some already lying dead, others stumbling towards the beach, with their rifles held high to avoid getting them wet. In the middle of these figures, at the emotional and compositional heart of the picture, is an officer who is half turned towards the viewer, cap tilted jauntily to expose the whole of his face and his brow. His right hand is cupped by his mouth: he is shouting encouragement to his troops. His left hand is waving the walking stick: another stirring gesture by a superbly nonchalant man. Whenever we look at Begg's picture of the Lancashire Landing, our eyes settle on this officer. We do not need the regimental historian's assurance that he is Captain Raymond Willis, performing the deed that won his Victoria Cross. Everything about the picture tells us that this is so.

But hold on a minute . . . Although the caption strongly suggests that Willis and his company were the very first Fusiliers to breach the defences and to shelter behind a mound of sand until reinforcements could join them, the drawing makes it equally plain that no such thing has occurred. Apart from Willis and his troops, who are actually in the water, in this version of events there are others who are struggling with the wire ahead of them, and even more who have got through the entanglement and are trying desperately to get to some refuge from the Turkish fire. It is possible, in fact, to make out a faint line of figures who are already crouched in the lee of rising ground below the sand cliffs. Moreover, Willis appears to have been beaten to it by another officer brandishing a walking stick, who has broken through the wire before him and is urging his own men to follow him. The gallant Captain was not, of course, responsible for the pictorial and written versions of his story contradicting each other. He had merely so fired both the artist and the caption writer with his testimony that each, in his own way, was moved to make Willis the most prominent character in the awful drama of W Beach. They had no other eyewitness they might have turned to, either for inspiration or for corroboration of what they had been told.

The Lancashire Fusiliers had not only taken a mauling by the time Willis was interviewed in August 1915; they were also a very disappointed regiment at that stage. For shortly after the landing on April 25, the commanding officer of the 29th Division, Major-General A. Hunter-Weston, directed that the 1st Battalion should submit six names for the VC. He was doubtless taking advice from his General Staff Officer, Colonel O. C. Wolley-Dod, who happened to be a Lancashire Fusilier himself, and who was on W Beach in person from two o'clock in the afternoon, in overall charge of operations there; whereas the divisional commander was never closer than his grandstand seat in *Euryalus*, some distance offshore. The names were given to Wolley-Dod by the commanding officer of the 1st Battalion, Major H. O. Bishop, and in addition to those of Willis, Richards and Keneally, they included Captain Cuthbert Bromley, Sergeant Frank Stubbs and Lance-Corporal John Grimshaw. Major Bishop nominated the six after consulting "the officers who happened to be with him at the time and who did not include either of the officers awarded the Cross." According to a Lieutenant Nightingale, of the Royal Munster Fusiliers, the rumour going round Cape Helles at the time was that "they all drew lots among the officers as to who was to get it, and a fellow called Willis got it." Wolley-Dod passed all the names to his divisional commander and Hunter-Weston in turn submitted them to his Commander-in-Chief, Sir Ian Hamilton, with the following endorsements: that the landing by the 1st Battalion "is a deed of heroism that has seldom been equalled" and "Their deed of heroism took place under my own eyes." This was true, though Hunter-Weston was watching at greater range than perhaps Queen Victoria and her military advisers had in mind when they drew up the Warrant for the Victoria Cross. Nevertheless, Hamilton had no hesitation in accepting the recommendation and in transmitting it to London with his own weight behind it. His covering memorandum, however, had a slightly defensive note, as if he was expecting trouble from the military bureaucracy at home. "Recommended. These six Decorations for one battalion may seem excessive. But only one other VC recommendation has been made for all the Southern landings."* Hamilton knew his War Office well enough: its hierarchs were very quickly scribbling memos to each other, clearly bent on preventing the award of six VCs.

On June 11, Major-General F. S. Robb wrote to Hamilton from Whitehall that "I am directed to return the enclosed recommendations for the award of the Victoria Cross with a request that you will be good enough to state whether the selection of these individuals was made as directed by the 13th paragraph of the Statute governing the grant of the VC. In the event of the pro-

---

* He was, obviously, discounting the six naval VCs, whose bravery was being evaluated by the Admiralty, not the War Office. The only other soldier referred to was Corporal William Cosgrove, of the Royal Munster Fusiliers, who earned his VC at V Beach.

cedures not having been followed I am to request that it may now be resorted to, unless such specific acts of bravery can be recorded against each of those recommended, that each can be considered on its merits." The 13th clause referred to had not been invoked since the Boer War, and it had been applied on only one occasion since the Indian Mutiny. It allowed a body of troops (or a ship's company) to elect people to the VC, so long as the commanding officer took the view that everyone under his command had been equally brave and that no one had been outstandingly more gallant than his comrades: VCs thus awarded, therefore, signified a collective as well as an individual valour. The clause further stipulated that one officer should be elected by his fellow officers, one NCO by the other NCOs and two private soldiers by all the privates. In short, it wasn't possible for a unit to be given more than four VCs under the elective principle. The clause ended with the injunction that "the names of those selected shall be transmitted ... to the general officer commanding, who shall in due manner confer the decoration *as if the acts were done under his own eyes*" [author's italics]. It was, perhaps, in anticipation of a quibble that Hunter-Weston had vouched for the heroism of the six Lancashire Fusiliers having taken place "under my own eyes".

There were, in fact, two quibbles raised by the War Office in this matter. Having told the regiment that it must supply distinctively separate citations for each of the six or accept the fact that there could not be more than four awards, the bureaucrats then informed the Fusiliers that they could not include Grimshaw in addition to Willis, Richards and Keneally if they went for an elected four, as the rule about one NCO and two privates in such a quartet must be strictly observed. Again the signals shuttled back and forth between Whitehall and Gallipoli. On July 14, Hunter-Weston was writing testily that "I am aware the Warrant lays down that only one NCO can get it, but in view of the fact that only one private's name instead of two is being sent forward and that it is the wish of the privates themselves that Corporal Grimshaw should take the place of the second private, I hope the men's request may be acceded to." Before the month was out, Wolley-Dod was making another cogent point: "I have consulted with the officer commanding the 1st Lancashire Fusiliers and he informs me that it is not possible for the few surviving privates, now with the battalion, to select another name. They naturally have a very hazy notion of what actually occurred, and during the fight parties of the battalion were widely separated . . ." He appealed for each of the six recommendations to be considered separately. But the War Office would have none of it. On August 24, 1915, the *London Gazette* announced the award of the Victoria Cross to just three Lancashire Fusiliers.

Over a year later, with the campaign in the Dardanelles no more than a bitter memory, the climate in Whitehall had altered to some extent, largely because of changes in personnel at the War Office. Wolley-Dod had not only picked up one of the CBs awarded to members of the Lancashire Fusiliers at Gallipoli, but he had been promoted to Brigadier and had become Inspector of Infantry in England. More importantly, the peremptory Major-General Robb was no longer Military Secretary to the Secretary of State for War. At that focal point in the bureaucracy now stood Lieutenant-General Sir F. J. Davies, another old Gallipoli hand, who had succeeded Hunter-Weston when the latter collapsed from exhaustion and sunstroke at the end of July, and was invalided off the peninsula. Towards the end of 1916, Wolley-Dod, sensing that he might now be addressing a more sympathetic ear, brought up the case of the unacknowledged three yet again on behalf of his old regiment. Davies at once promised to do what he could to have the matter reviewed; and in due course informed Wolley-Dod that he had brought to light "a case of gross injustice". On March 15, 1917, the names of Bromley, Stubbs and Grimshaw were added to those of Willis, Richards and Keneally under the same citation. The Lancashire Fusiliers at last had their "Six VCs Before Breakfast". This was the only example of a collective award being made in the Great War. It is the only occasion in the entire history of the Victoria Cross when the strict terms of paragraph 13 were waived to allow so many men to be decorated.*

One other quibble even Davies was unable to resolve. In his despatch of May 20, 1915, Sir Ian Hamilton added a rider to his applause of the 1st Battalion for their action on April 25. He ordered

---

* Grimshaw had been awarded the DCM, after the War Office vetoed his VC, in November 1915; and the medal was withdrawn when his VC was subsequently granted. It is an indication of how sensitively this matter of the Six VCs was regarded in the War Office that the normal thirty-year rule for the release of state papers into the public domain was suspended here. The papers did not become available to the Public Record Office until 1968.

W Beach to be renamed Lancashire Landing, just as Z Beach on the west coast of the peninsula had been officially redesignated Anzac to honour the Australians and New Zealanders who landed there. Probably for very good political reasons, and doubtless fearing Antipodean wrath if they blocked this suggestion, the bureaucrats in Whitehall chose not to stand in the way of the Anzac appellation. But they forbade the implementation of Hamilton's other proposal. Nor would the Fusiliers be permitted to use Lancashire Landing as an official battle honour in their regimental history and heraldry. They would have to be content with "Landing at Helles" instead.

The Six VCs were to be the most potent expression of regimental pride from the day they were fully and officially acknowledged; and nowhere would that pride be flaunted more vigorously than in the regimental depot town. As long as the war continued, there were limits to the amount of rejoicing that was thought appropriate, and military bounce was in any case repeatedly subdued by setbacks like Gallipoli and the First Day of the Somme. But once peace arrived, the Six VCs were invested with an aura that the citizens of Bury in particular were never in future allowed to ignore for long. They became the topic of sermons in churches throughout the town. Grammar School boys in the OTC were implicitly – sometimes explicitly – encouraged to dwell on their symbolic heroism. Whenever anything to do with the Victoria Cross anywhere in Great Britain attracted the attention of a journalist, however provincial, sooner or later the item would appear in Bury's local press, however irrelevant it might be to life in Lancashire. National events were followed in full detail. In 1929, the British Legion gave a dinner in London to 321 holders of the VC, and the guest of honour was the Prince of Wales, whose speech was reported verbatim in Bury. It began: "I feel probably as uncomfortable as you do, because it is not our national habit to invite men to dinner in order to tell them how brave they are . . ." The national habit, in fact, was to pretend diffidence while advertising the bravery or other virtue most assiduously in a minor key, which Americans were apt to regard as the charming British art of understatement. The Prince's speech, and the reporting of the speech in Bury, were both fine examples of the affectation. The report in the Bury papers served to remind the readers of "their" Six VCs. But they were not, strictly speaking, theirs at all. Not one of the six belonged to Bury and surrounding district. Only one could be described as a Lancastrian.

He was John Grimshaw, who had been born at Abram, near Wigan, and had worked at the pithead of a local colliery until he joined the Fusiliers in time to serve with the 1st Battalion in India for two years before the war. William Keneally also had a connection with Wigan, for his family had moved there from Wexford when he was a child. His father had been a Colour-Sergeant with the Royal Irish Regiment before migrating to England, where he became a weighman at a Wigan colliery. Keneally followed him to work down the pit before enlisting in the Lancashire Fusiliers in 1909. He was one of six fundamentally Irish brothers who fought for King and Country in the Great War, and one other besides himself did not return to the peace.

Of the other four VCs, Alfred Richards had a stronger regimental connection than anyone, his father having been a Colour-Sergeant in the 2nd Battalion of the Fusiliers. Like all Army families, this one had moved around a good deal, which meant that Richards was born in Plymouth and received most of his education in Newcastle-upon-Tyne before joining the 1st Battalion as a bandboy in 1895, just after his sixteenth birthday. Frank Stubbs was another old sweat by the time the Great War began, born not far from the Oval cricket ground in London and, like Richards, into the Lancashire Fusiliers as a boy. He had never married, and it was his mother who received his VC from the King in May 1917. Cuthbert Bromley came from Sussex, was the second son of Sir John Bromley, and had been educated at St Paul's before joining the Fusiliers in 1898, when he was twenty. When the 1st Battalion was in India he was largely responsible for its exceptional record in boxing tournaments, as well as in football and cross-country running; and he went to Gallipoli as Major Bishop's Adjutant. Raymond Willis was another southern Englishman and the only VC who was married when the regiment went to Gallipoli. He was also another public schoolboy, from a military family (all four of his great-grandfathers had been generals), educated at Harrow before Sandhurst, joining the Fusiliers in time to serve in the Nile Expedition in 1898 and to take part in the Battle of Omdurman.

Only three of these men survived the Great War. Stubbs was the first to die, on the day of the landing itself. He was a member of Willis's C Company whose objective, once they had got ashore and through the wire, was Hill 114 above the beach. (The numbers given the various hills at Gallipoli denoted their height in feet.) It was topped by a solitary tree and Stubbs had managed to lead the remains of his section up to it before he was hit. Keneally almost certainly died of wounds at Gully Ravine on June 29, though there is no regimental record of the circumstances: the confusion at the Dardanelles was so great that such details became lost or were destroyed – and only about one fifth of all the imperial dead have known graves there. Bromley was slightly wounded in the leg on April 28, in the first attack on Krithia, but stayed on the peninsula and was fit enough to lead what was left of the 1st Battalion in the disastrous assault up Gully Ravine. Major Bromley by then, he gave his troops "a stirring address which was warmly applauded", before they set off up the narrow and steep defile. He was wounded in the foot shortly after the attack began, seriously enough this time to be taken off Gallipoli next day and sent to Egypt for treatment. A few weeks later, though expected to convalesce further, he persuaded the doctors to let him return to Gallipoli and he sailed aboard the transport *Royal Edward* from Alexandria. On August 13 she was torpedoed and Bromley – normally a strong swimmer who had once made the crossing from Malta to Gozo – was drowned.

Richards should have died on Gallipoli, along with Stubbs and Keneally. He, too, was in Willis's company and on charging ashore from the cutters was hit so badly by machine-gun fire that his right leg was almost torn off. Somehow he managed to get through the wire and find shelter until first-aid could be brought to him; but that was the end of his Great War. The leg was amputated; and this mutilation brought him sustenance as well as pain during the rest of what turned out to be a fairly long life. He married the girl who nursed him in a Surrey hospital where he was recovering from his wound, and at their wedding other wounded soldiers formed their guard of honour. He spent the rest of his active life working for the employment of disabled soldiers, in a scheme sponsored by another holder of the VC, Lord Roberts. He lived until several years after the Second World War came to an end, by which time he was well into his seventies. But he rarely came to the North of England after his Army time, and he was buried in Putney Vale cemetery, London.

Grimshaw always kept in touch with his native county, though he only once lived there again after the war. On the day of the Lancashire Landing he was a signaller whose job, once the cliff above W Beach had been reached, was to send messages by semaphore to the divisional command aboard *Euryalus*; and in doing so "he distinguished himself by his coolness and gaiety". He came through April 25 unharmed but was one of the Fusiliers badly frostbitten during the November blizzard, and he was evacuated from the peninsula then. After doing time as a sergeant musketry instructor in England he rejoined the Fusiliers and spent the rest of the war in France, where he received a commission. After the Armistice he went to India, on attachment to the Indian Army, returned to the Fusiliers in 1921, but twelve months later ended his active association with the regiment for good. Until he retired in 1953 he worked as an Army Recruiting Officer in Cardiff and elsewhere in Britain, and eventually became Lieutenant-Colonel Grimshaw. Even when he and his wife had settled into retirement in Twickenham, he would regularly return to Bury for the annual commemoration of Gallipoli; and when he died in 1980, his widow asked that there should be no flowers at the funeral, but that donations should be made instead to the Fusiliers' Compassionate Fund. Grimshaw was the last survivor of the Six VCs.

Willis had died fourteen years earlier, in a Cheltenham nursing home. After his hero's welcome in Bury, he had not returned to Gallipoli, but had been drafted into the 2nd Battalion of the Fusiliers and with them saw service in France. He was Major Willis when the Armistice came, but he had been a temporary Lieutenant-Colonel commanding, in turn, the 1st Royal Inniskilling Fusiliers, 8th West Riding Regiment, and 6th York and Lancaster Regiment at various times before the peace. His movements after he left the Lancashire Fusiliers in 1920 were also erratic, his earlier home in Devon being succeeded by addresses in Buckinghamshire, Berkshire, Norfolk, Worcestershire before ever he reached Gloucestershire. He became a teacher in private schools, sometimes tutor to private pupils, except between 1923 and 1929, when he was an education officer in the Royal Air Force. He became a Fellow of the Royal Geographical Society in this period and he belonged to the Junior Naval and Military Club in London. He and his wife had two sons and a daughter and the boys, coincidentally, each became Major Willis, too. Both eventually emigrated; one to South Africa, the other to Southern Rhodesia.

The last twenty years of Willis's life were depressing, partly because he became extremely hard up. Between 1947 and 1959 he applied for and received a succession of grants from both the Fusiliers' Compassionate Fund and the Officers' Association, which totalled £427. In 1957, he placed an advertisement in the *Daily Telegraph*, appealing for the loan of £100, indicating that he was "in desperate need" of the money; and the sum came to him from the sister of a dead VC who wished to remain anonymous, together with other monies from various well-wishers. This exposure of a hero's penury led to a Question in the House of Commons by an MP who had been at Gallipoli with the Worcestershire Regiment, which had followed the Lancashire Fusiliers ashore on April 25, 1915; and, by chance, Willis was living in Worcestershire in 1957. Mr Simmons asked the Prime Minister, Harold Macmillan – himself a Great War veteran, well known for his public agonising over the human cost of that conflict – whether he did not think it disgraceful that a VC "who held commissioned rank in the British Army" should have been reduced to beggary. The Prime Minister's reply was a perfect example of political evasion: "I am sure that the case is one which would be equally deserving of attention whether he was the holder of the VC or not. There are all sorts of ways in which help is made available to officers. As for the point of the Question, there is no distinction, because officers are eligible for their reward if they are in need. That is the rule. I should like to point out that the provision of the old normal annuity of £10 (for winners of the VC) can now be increased to £75."

Willis was then eighty-one years old, his wife seventy-seven. By 1962 she had died and Willis was accompanied by his married daughter when he went forth to a garden party given by the Queen at Buckingham Palace that summer, for people who had won the VC or the George Cross. Three months later, writing from Faithful House, the Cheltenham nursing home, he told an old acquaintance "I am so nearly blind now that I can hardly read at all . . . When I think of the demand, cheerfully paid by the youth of England during three centuries for no reward and little recognition, I am furious with the people who run down 'teenagers', hateful word, but who would cheerfully sacrifice them once more, if there were still an Empire . . . My brother is still alive and more active than me. I did thirty-seven years teaching, from royalty to ploughboys, till my sight failed, and I enjoyed it even though the pay was a third of today's. AND I had four languages . . ." Four years later he was gone. The Lancashire Fusiliers sent a Brigadier and a Major down to the funeral in Gloucestershire; and Lance-Corporal Carroll, who sounded the Last Post and Reveille beside the old hero's grave.

The regimental depot town did, in fact, give one of its native sons to the Great War in exchange for a Victoria Cross. Private George Peachment was an eighteen-year-old apprentice fitter in Bury when war came and he enlisted, not in the Fusiliers but in the King's Royal Rifle Corps; doubtless because his brother was a Regular soldier in that regiment, a quartermaster-sergeant by 1914. In September 1915 the younger Peachment was killed when he went over the top in France to rescue a wounded officer lying in no man's land. The town's acknowledgement of his gallantry was slight; nothing more than a mention of the posthumous VC in the paper, together with the text of a very thoughtful letter to Peachment's mother from Sir George Toulmin MP. After that he was virtually ignored for more than forty years until Mrs Peachment, who was then eighty-six, went to a memorial service at her local church.

There was a stir when James Hutchinson won the VC, though, not entirely accounted for by the fact that he came back to tell the tale. He wasn't a Bury man – he came from Radcliffe, a few miles away – but he was a Lancashire Fusilier. He was a piecer in a local mill when war came and he joined the 2nd/5th Territorial Battalion with his older brother, who was married and who only enlisted to keep an eye on Jimmy. During an attack on enemy trenches near Ficheux in 1916, Frank was killed and, judging by the citation and an eyewitness report, Jimmy appears then to have gone off his head; clearing out a trench single-handed, covering the withdrawal of the Fusiliers alone, bayoneting and shooting one man after another, seemingly unaware that he had been wounded in the face. He wasn't quite twenty-one years old when this happened. When he came home, Radcliffe turned out *en masse* to fête him, with a civic welcome, a procession through town behind the local band, the presentation of a gold watch and chain from the community, a suitcase from his old school, £50 worth of Savings Certificates from his bosses at the mill. There was also, inevitably, a celebration of his gallantry in awful verse, which began:

> Proud Hero! Bury welcomes thee
> Back from the trench, bravest VC.
> Your courage, Jim, hath turned this lay
> To swell this great auspicious day . . .

The Mayor of Bury had been invited to attend the homecoming celebrations, but had pleaded other commitments. Hutchinson wasn't quite Bury's man, after all, in spite of the poetaster's efforts to claim him for the regimental town. He was close enough to being a native son, to be sure, which was why his occasional public appearances were dutifully logged in the local press; a garden party for VCs here, a London dinner for war heroes there; even though by 1929 James Hutchinson had moved away from Lancashire and was living beside the sea in Devon, where he died in 1972, at the age of seventy-six. Bury was hungry for a living hero of its own, whom it could adore unsparingly. It was being carefully drilled in the art of hero worship by the traditions of the Lancashire Fusiliers, by those awful weekly columns listing the latest Local Heroes who had given their lives, by the tremendous new example of the Six VCs. It wanted such a winner who was blood of its blood, and whose blood was yet unshed. George Peachment might have done, in spite of the fact that he was a Rifleman and not a Fusilier; but he was just another dead hero and Bury had plenty of those. So it made what it could of Jimmy Hutchinson; even more of the Six VCs, because they were the greatest source of regimental pride, which the town was being painfully taught to share and to glorify, far above any sense its people might have had of their own civic worth.

James Hutchinson, five foot four inches in his socks and a cocky twenty-one-year-old, left us with one of the very few descriptions of what it was actually like to receive the Victoria Cross from your sovereign; having none of the inhibitions that officers and gentlemen shared about the propriety of revealing what went on in the sovereign's house. It was like this, he said: "There were only two VCs, and while we were talking together an officer came and attached a small pin to our tunics, just over the breast pocket. A few minutes later my name was called and I was shown in to the King. He looked in the best of health and wore khaki uniform. I advanced two paces and bowed to the King, and the officer commenced to read out the details of the little affair that gained the cross for me. 'A very fine piece of work,' the King commented, when the officer had finished reading. His Majesty then asked me how my right eye was progressing and I told him that the doctors did not give me any hope of getting my sight back. He expressed regret and said he was sorry that it would not be possible for me to rejoin my battalion. Meanwhile, the officer had placed the VC on a cushion near the King, who then pinned it on my breast. He then shook my hand and congratulated me on gaining the honour."

There never was much warmth in George V, which has often been given as a reason why his son Edward went rather seriously off the rails, and why the much more likeable Bertie had such a pronounced stammer when he succeeded his abdicated brother and became George VI. When the Great War was over, plans were afoot to issue a campaign medal to every man who had fought in the Dardanelles: the plans got as far as the production of a ribbon, which combined dark blue for the Navy, red for the Army, yellow for the Australians (the colour of their wattle) and grey-green to symbolise the fernleaf of the New Zealanders. But neither the Gallipoli medal nor the ribbon was ever issued, because George V forbade them. "We do not," he is supposed to have said, "issue medals for retreats."

Victoria would have done much better than that.

# 7

# Church Militant

The regiment always enjoyed the blessing of the Church in its depot town, where the two had grown exceedingly close by the time war was declared. This was only to be expected, when the Army's sworn allegiance to King and Country involved it by extension in alliance with the established Church of England. Lancashire, in fact, had been a notoriously irreligious area in the mid-nineteenth century compared with other English counties, though its Roman Catholic population was one of the strongest in the land, having kept the faith assiduously during the worst of the penal times. At the 1851 census, only five English counties had lower levels of church and chapelgoing and only four returned more depressing figures from the Church of England's point of view. More than half the regular worshippers in Bury were Nonconformists at that time. But the adoption of Bury by the Lancashire Fusiliers, as the last quarter of the century began, had coincided with a degree of resurgence among the Anglicans.

The Parish Church of St Mary the Virgin not only stood in the centre of the business area, with the main roads out of town all radiating from the Market Place in front of the church steps, but was at the heart of much in the life of the community, especially at the major religious festivals. These the populace celebrated with some gusto, even when they marked a melancholy rather than a joyous event in the Christian calendar. On Good Friday morning there would be an appropriately mournful liturgy in the Parish Church, but immediately it was over most of the congregation would take themselves off to Holcombe Hill, where thousands would be gathered by mid-afternoon, to walk across the summit and ascend the memorial to Sir Robert Peel, to listen to bands play, to gossip with acquaintances, to flirt, to play games which included the local tradition of pace-egging with real but artificially coloured and hard-boiled eggs.* There were always queues to climb Holcombe Tower, because at Easter the mill chimneys were inactive and visibility improved so much that on a fine Good Friday it was sometimes possible to see the Irish Sea, more than thirty miles to the west.

But not even Easter compared with Whitsun for spectacle swirling round the Parish Church. A quarter of a mile away stood the open expanse of Union Square, whose four sides consisted of old terrace cottages for the most part, generally dwellings, but with a few converted into shops. Among these was Tommy Evans's herbal emporium, with its gigantic coloured flasks in the window, and its chests of small drawers inside, containing sticks of root liquorice, dried camomile flowers, knobs of ginger, sprigs of feverfew, and all the other remedies Culpeper catalogued. A few doors along was a front room window with a tilted white marble slab on which the Casewell family displayed the original version of Bury black puddings; and a little bell clanged behind the door when customers went in and out of what would normally have been the Casewell parlour, but had been fitted with a small counter and shelves at the back. For most of the year, Union Square was a fairly quiet enclave just aside from the bustle of Bury's main streets. But at Whit weekend it was transformed. That Friday, all the Anglican and Nonconformist churches held an open-air service there, with hymn-singing accompanied by the massed brass bands of the town, and prayers conducted from a special platform in the middle by the Rector of Bury and Free Church ministers in turn. When the service was over, the various congregations walked out of the square one after another in a long and vivid procession which moved past the Parish Church for a start and then round all the main thoroughfares. Each congregation was led by a band, booked months beforehand; and behind this came its choir and then its banners – Sunday School, Mothers' Union, Bible Fellowship and others – with long coloured ropes and ribbons attached, so that people could hold on to them and stop the wind billowing the huge embroidered pictures away. The yard of the Parish Church was raised high above street level

---

* "Pace" was a corruption of Paschal. Children would roll their eggs downhill in competition, with prizes for the winner. "Pace-egging" in the vernacular of Lancashire came to mean, by extension, playing about instead of attending to serious matters.

and many people lined its railings for a better view; and so as to be well placed for the customary throwing of small coins to the children in the parade. The Parish Church choirboys were especially well equipped to catch these, for they alone were not only tricked out in cassocks and surplices, but with academic mortar boards as well; and with these they fielded the pennies and threepenny bits that came their way through the air. It normally took the Whit Friday procession the best part of two hours to pass from Union Square, down the side of the church, and out of the Market Place. And then, on the Sunday, the same thing happened all over again, when the Roman Catholics of Bury held their own Whit Walks.

The churchyard was also the perfect grandstand whenever there was a military parade through the town, which became a regular feature of Bury life after the regiment made its home there in 1873. There was a statue of Sir Robert Peel in the middle of the Market Place and the plinth on which this stood made a perfect foundation for a saluting base, where a military commander or some civilian luminary would acknowledge a march-past of troops on their way to or from a war, or merely making a public display of their discipline, their gorgeous full-dress uniforms, and their musical instruments. In 1905, Peel's statue was counter-balanced, on the other side of the tramlines which bisected the Market Place, by a monument which had been commissioned to celebrate the part the Lancashire Fusiliers had played in the recent South African War. This new figure in bronze was not bowed with grief for the men who had been lost in the calamity on Spion Kop: he was a Fusilier standing upright with pride, one hand firmly on his rifle, the other brandishing his head-dress at arm's length in the air; he seemed to be urging his comrades on, or perhaps calling for general applause. Hundreds turned out to watch this memorial being unveiled, and to see the soldiers in their red tunics, their blue trousers and their bearskin busbies, their white belts and rifle slings, standing stiffly at the Present all round the Market Place, in rank after rank. The crowds were so great that not only was the churchyard full, as well as the streets, but some were perched on its walls and even on a parapet over the great south porch.

All the proportions of this Victorian Gothic building were large, except for the spire, which had survived from an earlier church, but looked rather as if it had been added when money lavished on nave and chancel had almost run out. Inside, the overwhelming impression was one of great height and length, and dim light filtering through the yellows, blues and reds of the stained glass. Walls which on the outside were of stone that was gradually blackening in the dirty industrial air, were on the inside faced with a brick that produced a glowing warmth. But the interior also had stone pillars and tracery, and galleries which rose high above the patterned tiling of the floor. There was an intricate screen of wrought iron separating the congregation from the choir, and another marking the entrance to the Lady Chapel behind the decani choir stalls on the southern side. Bury Parish Church was really rather grand for a town of 50,000, most of whom did not in any case subscribe to the lenitive doctrines of the Anglicans. Its Rector usually had one and sometimes two curates to assist him. Its musical tradition was one of the finest in the land outside the great cathedrals. It had the scale, and some of the characteristics that distinguish cathedrals built a little later in Sydney, in Christchurch and in other cities of the Antipodes. And, well before the Great War, the military had made their mark in it. One of the first things to catch the eye, once it had adjusted to the subdued light on entering the church, were the flags hanging from the clerestory just under the steeply pitched roof of the nave. They jutted out on poles over the congregation. These were the most precious heirlooms of the Lancashire Fusiliers, for some of them had been woven early in the history of the XXth Foot. One or two were so ancient that not only had the colour been leeched out of them, but the fabric itself had been decayed by wind and smoke on many a battlefield, by rain and by sun on parade grounds in remote parts of the world. These hung transparent as cobwebs, frail talismans of a warrior past. As battalions of the Fusiliers were raised and then disbanded after they had served their purposes in war, their colours were brought to the Parish Church to be laid up in the custody of its priests. The time would come, after the Great War, when the regimental banners were ranked closely one after the other from the chancel arch, on both sides of the nave, all the way to the main west door. Even the most casual worshippers could never be unaware of this heraldry's significance.

The Rector of Bury when the Great War began was John Charles Hill, who had been appointed in 1909 when he was in his late forties. He was a southerner who had gone to Harrow and Trinity College, Cambridge, an education not at all unusual for someone occupying such a post: but it was exceptional that Hill had spent time working in a bank before deciding to become a priest. He had held curacies in London and in Yorkshire before becoming incumbent of a parish at Halesowen in the Midlands, which immediately preceded his appointment to Bury. This was yet another step up the ladder of preferment. It was customary for Rectors of Bury to be marked out for higher things and Hill was to become suffragan Bishop of Hulme in 1923; as was his successor, more than twenty years after him. Hill was regarded as a moderate churchman in the doctrinal traditions of the living, which meant that incense might be used in the Parish Church on high feast days like Easter and Christmas, but rarely otherwise. It meant that vestments tended – until episcopal rank was reached – to be no more decorative than a coloured academic hood hanging behind the surplice, and that the tendentious skullcap and cape worn in the street by the most enthusiastically Anglo-Catholic priests were eschewed. It meant choral performances of Orlando Gibbons, Stanford in C and other classical settings of the communion service, which began and finished in the distinct assumption that the congregation must be seen and not heard: this hoi polloi was barely tolerated in the splendidly pointed versions of the Canticles and Psalms, and it was encouraged to open its lungs only in the less subtle music that accompanied the hymns. In such an atmosphere of genteel and aesthetically satisfying piety, Rectors of Bury were expected to make spiritual and other pronouncements from time to time that would strike some chord in all sections of the wider community and deeply offend none. They were also saddled with a number of temporal appointments that went with the job. Charles Hill was chairman of the Infirmary Board, chairman of the Governors of Bury Grammar School and – perhaps because of his very first expertise – on the Board of the local Savings Bank.

On the first Sunday of the war, Hill climbed into his pulpit and took as his text a line from the forty-sixth Psalm: "God is our hope and strength; a very present help in trouble." He then preached a sermon that was as full of unabashed patriotism and bellicose intent as any of the verses that were beginning to find their way into the public prints. Its core was a passage which began: "There is no need to protest our love of peace, peace which means so much to our hearths and homes, to our happiness and well-being; peace which is Christ's own gift. But there is a peace which is 'devil-borne', a peace gained at the price of truckling and treachery and dishonour.

And there is a war which Christ allows; nay, which we believe He approves, a war of honour, of duty and of right. We would not, we could not, consent to a shameful and a treacherous peace; and so we have been plunged into war – a war of duty and honour, a war for freedom and right, and only God knows what and when the end shall be." From there it was but a short step to a cruder form of jingoism. As the congregation filed out of the Parish Church that day they remembered, as much as anything, their Rector invoking the spirit which flung back the Spanish Armada at sea and which "broke the insolent aggression of Napoleon" on land.

A little later that month, the 5th Battalion of the Fusiliers attended church parade in St Mary the Virgin, just before setting out for the Turton camp. Hill was their honorary chaplain and on this occasion he quoted Sir Galahad: "My strength is as the strength of ten. Because my heart is pure." He was fond of attributing to Lancashire Tommies the merits he perceived in Arthurian and other quintessentially English folk heroes. The day on which the 1st Battalion were landing on W Beach at Gallipoli was just another wartime Sunday to the Rector of Bury at home in Lancashire, but he dwelt extensively on St George, whose feast day had been celebrated two days earlier. George, he told his congregation that terrible April 25, was "the personification of chivalry. He stood for us as the splendid example of courage in the face of danger that might lead even to the loss of life itself . . . We men of England must be proud indeed of St George, our patron saint, the chivalrous champion of the weak against the strong, the one who asserted right against might."

The Rector threw himself into the recruiting campaign from the very beginning of the war. In November 1914 he was writing in the parish magazine: "The war has been going on for three months; and I do not think it is any exaggeration to say that the end seems further on now than it did three months ago. Then, a good many people spoke confidently about peace being well in sight by Christmas. Now we sadly wonder if we shall be able to speak of peace being made when next year's Christmas comes. The plain fact is that the Germans have proved to be more powerful than anyone anticipated. What can we do to hasten the downfall of Germany's ill-used might? First and foremost, we can and must provide the War Secretary with MORE MEN. Recruiting is not as brisk as it ought to be." A couple of weeks later he was on the platform at a great

Gallipoli Sunday 1923, with the Fusiliers marching past the saluting base beside the statue of Sir Robert Peel, Bury's most famous son. The troops had just attended a service of commemoration in the Parish Church, which has been held annually ever since 1916, together with the military parade.

In 1921 the Prince of Wales – subsequently and briefly King Edward VIII – visited Bury, where he shook hands with a number of Gallipoli veterans. Also in the picture are (stroking his chin) Charles Ainsworth, the local MP who had been elected largely on an inflated reputation for heroics at Gallipoli; Bury's Mayor (in gold chain) and Town Clerk (in wig); and, on the right, the 17th Earl of Derby, who at the time owned almost all the town.

The memorial to Lancashire Fusiliers who fell in the Great War, outside the Wellington Barracks, the regimental headquarters. The memorial was the work of Sir Edwin Lutyens, who was busy designing New Delhi at the same time. He gave his services free because his father and other members of his family had served in the XXth Foot, as the regiment had formerly been known.

Two aerial views of central Bury, taken between the world wars. Top is the Market Place, with the Parish Church and the bulk of the Drill Hall nearby. Bottom is Union Square, where the annual Whit Walks traditionally began, surrounded by the terrace housing, the cotton mills and other factories then typical of the town.

Two Rectors of Bury who became closely identified with Gallipoli Sunday and the Lancashire Fusiliers. LEFT is Hugh Leycester Hornby, who won a Military Cross while serving as a chaplain in France. RIGHT is John Charles Hill, whose only son was reported missing on the first anniversary of the Lancashire Landing. The two men were in Bury, one after the other, from 1909 to 1953; and each, in his latter years as Rector, was simultaneously suffragan Bishop of Hulme.

BELOW In 1938, Bury's great patron, Lord Derby, laid the foundation stone of the new Town Hall. Here, afterwards, he reviews Territorial troops of the local 5th Battalion of the Fusiliers. These were almost always paraded on notable civic occasions, as well as military ones.

recruiting meeting in the Drill Hall, which had seating for 4,000 and standing room for 5,000 more, and which was packed with citizens who were entertained by a band between the speeches made by Army officers and a brace of visiting politicians. One of these, Admiral Lord Charles Beresford MP, brought the house down when he informed his audience that "I know the Lancashire Fusiliers. When their ammunition is expended they will use their bayonets, and when their bayonets are broken they will use their fists."

And yet the Rector of Bury was to know as piercingly as any man what the Great War really amounted to, and what was its terrible cost. He had an only son, also named Charles, who had been educated at Harrow like his father and had left Cambridge after his first year at Trinity in order to enlist in the Highland Light Infantry. He was only twenty-one when, towards the end of April 1916, his parents received the telegram that told them he was missing after some action on the Tigris Line in Mesopotamia. A few days later, there was a big service in Bury Parish Church to commemorate those who had fallen at the Lancashire Landing at Gallipoli twelve months earlier. Unable to face the ordeal of a public appearance, Mrs Hill locked herself in her room so that the Rectory servants could not see her, and did her grieving in solitude. The Rector simply carried on with the planned ritual in a church that was overflowing before the service even began. The Mayor and Corporation were there, and so was a contingent of survivors from Gallipoli, men from the 1st/5th Battalion who would later go to France. And although many in the congregation were in tears, knowing the blow that had befallen their priest, which added to the wider lamentation of that day, the Rector himself maintained his composure throughout, a slight, white-haired figure whose voice never quavered, never gave the slightest hint of personal tragedy.

He began his sermon by reminding people that the King had just attended a service in Westminster Abbey, and that three thousand Anzacs had paraded through the streets of London in order to commemorate the Australians and New Zealanders who had fought and died in the Dardanelles. "But, men of Lancashire, while we pay the honour due to those gallant men who came from the dominions beyond the seas to fight and fall on our behalf, we don't and dare not forget the part played on the same day and on that same shore by the sons of England, Scotland, Wales and Ireland and, as in duty bound, we especially commemorate the immortal heroism shown by the officers and men of the 1st Battalion, Lancashire Fusiliers, our own regiment, whose home is here in Bury, whose colours hang proudly in this fair church, whose memorials speak to us from these walls. If they did not find mention in the Abbey, at least they shall find it here, for they are ours, our brothers and our flesh, and the record of their deathless deeds is the heritage of our country and of our town for all time." He then embarked on a detailed recapitulation of the action on W Beach and the following hours, full of phrases that would not have disgraced the war correspondents of the day ("Under a hail of fire from hidden guns they landed from their open boats and by their dauntless courage fought their way on . . ."). He quoted Admiral de Robeck's paean to the Fusiliers and savoured the award of the three VCs – all that had been conferred when the Rector spoke – and the manner in which the valorous trio had been chosen by their comrades in the regiment. At length he came to a resounding conclusion which was also, given Charles Hill's own personal agony at that moment, an heroic one. "Their deeds will be remembered ever more, their memorial is inscribed in our hearts: in future ages some of our country will seek to follow their example of daring and courage. We are resolved that by God's gracious favour, these our brothers shall not have laid down their lives in vain. 'Greater love hath no man than this, that a man lay down his life for his friends.' Leaving us an example. O God, to us may grace be given to follow in their train."

Thus was born Gallipoli Sunday, which was to become a central point in the calendar of the entire community, irrespective of individual religious affiliations: a mixture of glorification and lament that would afterwards be observed without fail each year by the people of this ordinary milltown in the lee of the Pennine hills. This initiative was followed almost a month later, and on a Monday, in Manchester. There, a parade was first held in the pleasure gardens at Belle Vue, followed by a march past the Town Hall through Albert Square and a service in the cathedral. Two thousand people attended this, including 100 Territorials who had been in the Dardanelles. These soldiers were guests of honour at a civic luncheon given by the Lord Mayor and Corporation. On the tenth anniversary of the Lancashire Landing, Charles Hill made it plainer still that it had been conceived in a sense of injustice which he, a Hertfordshire man, felt as keenly as any Lancastrian. He mentioned again the honouring of the Anzacs by the King in London, though he did not note the fact that this had been a political sop by the Motherland to His Majesty's increasingly disillusioned subjects in the southern hemisphere. "It was right and fitting that their gallant deeds should be celebrated by a service of memorial in Westminster Abbey, and we grudged nothing of that; no, nor did we grudge the fact that the 25th of April was called after them Anzac Day. It was right that what they had done should be kept in mind, telling to all generations that the ties of Empire when this greatest war of all time was being waged meant much indeed, and produced something else in our hearts. Anzac Day for the Empire was Lancashire Fusiliers Day for us: our men no less than those from the southern lands achieved the impossible, and Lancashire Landing stood as their memorial to all time . . ."

The death of young Mr Charles – as the Rector's son was known to the congregation of Bury Parish Church – was saluted in full some time after the first Gallipoli Sunday. When his birthday came round in July a commemorative communion service was held, at which the choir sang Woodward in E Flat and Walter Williams, the autocratic genius who presided over the church's music-making, played the Good Friday music from *Parsifal* on the organ. Later still, the Rector and his wife donated a reredos for the high altar as a memorial to their son, a strikingly golden triptych, full of descending angels and their beating wings; and in each panel the emblem, in turn, of Harrow School, Trinity College, Cambridge, and the Highland Light Infantry. The Hills had one other child, their daughter Katharine, and almost predictably she was to marry a young lieutenant of the Lancashire Fusiliers. The wedding took place in 1924, in the anniversary week of the Gallipoli landing.

Charles Hill's patriotism never faltered in the years after the Great War, even though he had been hurt as much as anyone who had not been to that war: "The scars that it has made will be on our hearts all our life long," he said, when preaching at a service hurriedly arranged the day the Armistice was announced. At a more lavish thanksgiving later in that first month of the peace, personal grief was again subordinated to an exultation of nationality, to the ideal of Britishness. "And what of our own dear land? Isn't she a nobler land than the land we loved four years ago but which, by all that her sons and daughters have done, we must love much more now? Because in truth they have made her great, those who have fought and died for her, gladly giving themselves for their country and their country's cause. They tell us on our Sunday of thanks-giving that we must not be unworthy of them, that Britain has been saved that she may be fairer, sweeter, purer, more chaste, more free, happier, in the right sense of the word merrier, than she has ever been before. All have joined in the fight for her, or have given their sons to fight and die for her, and all must join with such powers as God has given us so that the land for which so much has been sacrificed may be – dare we say; yes we dare, without boasting, but with humble thankfulness – the joy of the whole earth." When, on the first anniversary of the Armistice in 1919, the town came to a mute standstill for two minutes on the stroke of eleven o' clock in the morning, as did communities all over the land, the loyal Rector of Bury referred to this gesture of recollection as the King's Silence. That very week saw the Dardanelles Commission publish its final and damning report of all that had happened in the planning and execution of the Gallipoli campaign, most especially "a breakdown of the War Office system". This item of news was buried in three short paragraphs at the foot of a page in the *Bury Times*, which made no editorial comment either then or in subsequent issues.

Yet for all his sentimental and wholly uncritical attachment to King and Country, the Rector of Bury did not fail to remind his parishioners – and, by extension, because of his position as the town's chief Anglican priest, the whole community – of the raw deal many ex-servicemen were getting as the great post-war slump began. On Gallipoli Sunday 1920, he told a story from the pulpit about an encounter he'd had on the train coming back from London, with a local man who had been blinded at Suvla Bay. He had been a cotton spinner before the war but, that now being impossible because of his lost sight, he had been trained at St Dunstan's to repair clogs instead. The Rector had asked him how he was getting on and the man said he'd done very well at first, less so now, because his pension had been reduced on his learning a trade and not many people brought their clogs to him because the big differ-ence between his work and that of a sighted clogger was that his took four or five times longer to do. Also, the man said, the war was over now and people had forgotten. "As I heard him say that," the Rector told his congregation, "not bitterly, but sadly, I felt something of pain and shame, because there was a man who a short time ago all England was acclaiming as a hero, and was saying that nothing was too good for him and others like him, that we shall never forget them, and that not one of them shall suffer, because of what they have gone through and lost for our sakes." He put the matter no more bluntly than that: his commission, after all, was never to cause grave offence.

Hill's successor, in 1930, brought even more impressive credentials to the post. Hugh Leycester Hornby was not only a Lancastrian by birth, whose family had lived in the county for three hundred years, but two of his kinsmen had been Rectors of Bury before him, in the nineteenth century. He himself came to the town from the village of St Michael's, in rich farming country near the coast, where a Hornby had been parish priest without interruption since 1789. The family progression of clerics therefore, for the third time, took a Hornby from the village in the Fylde to the milltown at the bottom of Rossendale, and this was not only a hierarchical advancement but a stipendiary one, too. Hugh Hornby was exchanging a living worth £563 per annum for one that would bring him £2,000 as well as the large Georgian Rectory standing in its own grounds behind a high brick wall. Not many Anglican priests below the level of archbishop were more amply provided for in 1930. He was a very tall man with a scholarly air of authority, who carried himself like a bishop long before he became one. He was a patrician both by ancestry and training. His grandfather had perished on Sir John Franklin's expedition to the Arctic, and another relative had been the dashing A. N. Hornby, of Lancashire and England, the first man ever to captain his country at both cricket and Rugby. Hugh Hornby had been educated at Rugby School and Balliol College, Oxford; and he had one other irresistible commendation. He had been through the Great War as a chaplain, from start to finish, first with the King's Liverpool Regiment, later with the 6th Brigade of the 2nd Division in France. He had been in the fighting many times, and from Vimy Ridge he had come home with the Military Cross, for tending the wounded under heavy fire.

Perhaps it was because he knew what it was like in the trenches, out of his own experience and not from hearsay, that almost from the start he struck a notably less aggressive note than Charles Hill's utterances in praise of British soldiery. On his first Gallipoli Sunday he told his people that "No one, unless he is a fool or a knave, wants to glorify war, or look for war, or perpetuate national hatred; but it is an act of at least equal folly and knavery to wax eloquent in the cause of peace and at the same time ignore the loyalty and devotion shown in war and transfer the hatred and suspicion, which caused war, into the sphere of politics or industry. The true way is to keep alive, by every means we have, the memory of the mutual trust and self-sacrificing devotion which carried us through the war, and to foster that spirit in facing the problems of peace." Twelve months later he took the proposition a stage further, by trying to explain what the Lancashire commemoration stood for philosophically. "There are some who, mistakenly I think, but quite sincerely, rather deprecate this kind of commemoration on the grounds that it tends to glorify or idealise war; and certainly, if it were true that anything at these services were calculated to make men desire war, then we ought not to hold them. But that is not true. What we commemorate and idealise today is not war – far from it – but the unequalled self-sacrifice and devotion that were shown in the war; and we dwell on the memory with the hope and prayer that such sacrifices may never be called for in war again, and with the resolve that, God helping us, we will harness that same spirit of self-sacrifice and devotion to the tasks and the deeds of peace. It is not a glorifying of war any more than the keeping of Good Friday is a glorifying of crucifixion."

Hornby's sermons were more cerebral than Hill's had been and he was less wary of using theology to illuminate the contemporary for fear of preaching over the heads of his congregation. He made Gallipoli Sunday in 1935 the occasion for pointing out – in the year of Zinoviev's first trial, and a month after Germany repudiated the disarmament clauses in the Treaty of Versailles – that evil was abroad in the world again; but he did not do this by appealing to emotion as his predecessor would have done. "We cannot separate the thought of the past from the thought of the present; and, if we could, it would to my mind be very undesirable that we should. For the value of memories of the past consists in the spirit that they can generate for facing the calls of the present: but unless we do so use them – if we indulge the memories without harnessing them to anything – then the indulgence becomes weakly sentimental; for the truest definition of sentimentality is emotion divorced from action." Where stood the commemoration of the Lancashire Fusiliers in all this? "They felt, we all felt in those years, that we were fighting to crush an evil spirit that was threatening the world, and so to make the world a securer, happier, better and more peaceful place for ourselves and for those who should come after us. And yet there is this chaotic turbulent world of 1935. It reminds one of that very grim and very suggestive parable which Our Lord once told, about an evil spirit going out, a house being left empty, and the evil spirit coming back with others. Something very like that has happened. Through the gallantry of those whom we commemorate today, and thousands more like them, the evil thing was checked; its wings were clipped. And yet something very like a reinforced edition of it is abroad in Europe now; and that is the challenge which the world of 1935 offers to our commemorations."

The day was to come when this Rector of Bury stood in his pulpit and, pointing to the military banners hanging from the galleries of his church, invited his parishioners and many pews full of young Lancashire Fusiliers to consider the proper significance of such heraldry. "All these emblems and memorials speak of the loyalty and gallantry of generation after generation of men in this regiment, and the presence of these things in this church speaks of the loyalty and the gallantry and the faith for which the Church stands. If there were no such connection, the presence of these emblems and memorials here would be a hollow sham, as would the holding of a service like this. For a Christian church is not a national Valhalla; it stands for a cause much wider and deeper and more far-reaching than national power and prosperity . . ." At a drumhead service for the Grammar School's OTC, he was to warn the adolescents who were potential officers against "unsanctified patriotism". As the Second World War approached, this Rector of Bury arranged a meeting at the local Athenaeum, whose purpose was to suggest that if Church leaders of every denomination throughout Europe could be persuaded to act in concert, then the impending war ought to be impossible. "Is it really worth while," he asked, "spending all our time, thoughts, and energies preparing to give a good account of ourselves in the next war?" The war was but four months away when he shared a platform in the Textile Hall with a medley of people representing various pressure groups including the Communist Party, to repudiate a Government plan to introduce conscription – which, said Hugh Hornby, "actually brings nearer the very danger which conscription is meant to avoid." He wasn't the only Englishman to hope until the very last minute that war against Hitler might be averted.

And for all that his stance was close to that of an unqualified pacifist in 1938 and 1939, a difference was that this Rector of Bury embraced the traditions of the regiment whose spirit was regularly exalted in his church, but tried to give the community, including the soldiers themselves, a vision of the future notably different from that of the past. He accepted the notion of the just war, as a pacifist could not; but he tried to define more clearly than before what, in fact, was just. He also attempted to make people rethink their patriotism. "This service is founded on memory and memories are subtle things," was how he began his sermon for Gallipoli Sunday in 1938. "You cannot live, no one can live, healthily on memories of the past. If we try to do so, the result will be that we become weakly sentimental or conceited by compliment, and neither of these states of mind is a healthy one . . . But the memories of yesterday can be a great help in the task of today if we dig the right kind of things in the right kind of way out of them. What, then, are the right kind of things to dig from the memory of the Gallipoli landing? Few of us, I hope, would wish to remember any part of it for its own sake or for the sake of stirring up a desire to repeat it. There is as much room in the commemoration for shame that men should have been asked to do these things as for admiration of the way they did it . . . The thing it is worth digging up and clinging to from these memories is the fact that, first, the task to which those men set their hands is still an unfinished task. Secondly, that its completion will call for the same qualities of self-sacrifice, loyalty and comradeship that they showed . . . And what, then, of the future? Of all the dangers and difficulties which surround us at present, the greatest is that we may do what a Latin poet once explained by the line which meant 'preserve your existence at the cost of everything that makes it worth preserving'. That is our risk. We inevitably think and hear and read a great deal about rearmament and ARP and the like.* There is a real danger that we may forget there is something else that matters far more than these things. That 'something else' is the soul of England rather than her body. More important even than her safety is her standing, and continuing to stand, for the true values in life."

The two great anniversaries bequeathed by the Great War

---

* Air Raid Precautions was a civilian auxiliary service in the Second World War. Its wardens were charged with ensuring that buildings and streets were without lights that might assist enemy aircraft, with supervising air-raid shelters, and with helping to rescue people from bombed buildings.

developed patterns that endured for later generations. That first Armistice Day in 1919 was announced by the blaring of factory hooters all over the town, which marked the imminence of 11 a.m. On the stroke of the hour, when there were hundreds of people in the Market Place, men removed their hats and everyone stood in silence. Some soldiers were there and they remained at attention for the two minutes suggested by George V. At the Barracks, the Guard turned out and the Last Post was sounded by a bugler. In the schools of Bury, the children were assembled and, before the silence, heard a letter from the King which was addressed to "all my people". A year later, the Mayor arrived in the Market Place before 11 a.m. and a number of people entered the Parish Church to spend the two minutes in prayer. By 1925, the local Provision Dealers Association had come to the conclusion that it would be seemly if all shops in the borough closed their doors and refrained from business between 10.45 a.m. and 11.15 on Armistice Day. At the same time, some citizens were wondering whether it might be permissible to temper the sobriety of the morning with some later jollification such as an Armistice Ball; which caused the combined churches of the town to urge on the populace "an atmosphere in which men will hate to be at variance and will long to understand." Armistice Day had become known alternatively as Poppy Day by then, and to be seen without a synthetic scarlet bloom produced by disabled ex-servicemen, was to be counted insensitive to the significance of the hour. At the war memorial which had lately been completed outside the church, wreathes of poppies were laid, as well as small wooden crosses with a poppy pinned to each intersection. Before the silence began, individuals – almost always women dressed in black – crossed the cobblestones to lay another cross or a swathe of flowers there. When the noise of the mill sirens stopped, so had all the traffic anywhere near the centre of the town; and for two minutes there was a silence such as no other day in the year produced.

Gallipoli Sunday became an altogether lustier event. It began soon after breakfast on the nearest Sabbath to April 25, when the stamping of Territorial boots in the Drill Hall could be heard, in response to sharp words of command. This was only a couple of hundred yards from the Parish Church, and not long afterwards the crowds would begin to gather in the Market Place and adjacent streets to watch what would become a full two-hour display.

Presently the sound of military music drifted faintly up Bolton Street, which meant that other troops were marching towards the town centre from the Barracks. They would be brought to a halt in front of the Drill Hall, for an ostentatious series of movements designed to impress spectators with the crispness of their parade-ground drill. Officers would move along the ranks, muttering to this man here, glaring at that unfastened button there, nodding briskly to the NCO in charge of each polished and gleaming file of soldiery. Officers' wives, most of whom were as thin as flagpoles and dressed in all the finery of spring that a commissioned salary and possibly a private income could buy, would line the pavement in front of the Drill Hall, where the public were not allowed, and gaze adoringly as their husbands encouraged, mildly chastised, and endlessly manipulated this phalanx of virile youth and durable old sweats. When the carefully calculated amount of time had been spent in these preliminaries, the troops would be marched into their garrison church, where civilian members of the congregation awaited them, as did also the regimental band, drawn up at the foot of the chancel steps to augment the organ and the singing of the choir. And in specially reserved pews were the men everyone had come to honour on Gallipoli Sunday; the survivors of the 1st Battalion, who had brought such fame to the Lancashire Fusiliers, although of the three surviving Gallipoli VCs, John Grimshaw was the only one who appeared with any frequency among his old comrades on this day. Last of all to enter the church came the dignitaries of the day; the Mayor and Corporation, the commanding officer of the regiment, the Member of Parliament, maybe a visiting general or other luminary from afar.

The pattern of the service varied little over the years between the wars. It started with a colour party marching from the west door of the church to the chancel steps, where the Rector and his curates accepted the banner and laid it on the high altar for the duration of the service. Then the liturgy devised for this day alone began to unfold. There were hymns that were sung more powerfully, perhaps, than on any other Sunday in the year. One at least, accompanying the offertory, was anguished:

> O Valiant Hearts, who to your glory came
> Through dust of conflict and through battle flame;
> Tranquil you lie, your knightly virtue proved.
> Your memory hallowed in the land you loved.

There were others whose words and melodies were less likely to catch the singer by the throat: "Onward, Christian Soldiers" for one, to the triumphant tune composed by Sir Arthur Sullivan. There were silences in which prayers and other phrases were dropped so disturbingly that those who knew what was coming braced themselves.

> They shall not grow old as we that are left grow old:
> Age shall not weary them, nor the years condemn.
> At the going down of the sun and in the morning
> We will remember them. *

There were lessons; from Corinthians, from Ephesians, from the Book of Wisdom, from Ecclesiasticus, from some other portion of the Bible that was thought appropriate. There was the sermon, which was almost always preached by the Rector, though one year saw a General offering a soldier's assessment of the Fusiliers instead, and another had the Chaplain-General mouthing platitudes of the most mawkish jingoism ever heard in Bury Parish Church. After the sermon came the offertory, from which the Fusiliers' Compassionate Fund did rather well: one choirboy with a large brass plate was normally quite enough to convey the offerings from the sidesmen to the altar, but on this day of the year, with the building packed as on no other, three of the choristers, heavily laden, were only just sufficient to take all the money up. Then the colour party marched forward to retrieve the regimental banner. Silence as they came to a double-stamping halt again by the west door. Broken, after a moment's stillness, by the sound of a bugle in the clerestory high above the body of the church; which rang and rang and rang again as the brazen notes of the Last Post and Reveille volleyed and ricocheted off the walls and the roof, and cleft the air around the motionless figures below, standing obediently with their memories.

There was a very rigid order of precedence in the next stage of Gallipoli Sunday. By the time the service was over and the congregation surged into the churchyard, the town centre was a mass of people, effectively with room for no more. The ones who had patiently waited the longest were those who had secured the best places to watch the parade that followed; opposite, or immediately beside, the saluting platform which had been brought from the Drill

* *For the Fallen (September 1914)* by Laurence Binyon (1869–1943).

Hall and set up in front of Peel's statue. The regimental band was drawn up near the statue, too, as the dignitaries arranged themselves around the platform, on which stood the Mayor and whoever was going to take the salute. Retired Fusilier officers were among this élite of spectators, distinctive still in a kind of civilian uniform: dark suit, black bowler hat, and regimental tie of primrose and rose stripes. Meanwhile, in The Rock, the street that ran along the length of the church, there was a great deal of shuffling and dressing of ranks, and men with loud voices shouting periodically. The bandmaster raised his baton, one last command echoed from The Rock, the bass drum boomed three times, and the parade stepped off as the musicians broke into "The British Grenadiers".

First came the men who were the excuse for this intricate display and for the religious observances that had preceded it; the ones who had landed on W Beach in the dawn of April 25, 1915. Their numbers dwindled annually and their marching became less military, more the proud carriage of those whose bodies no longer quite respond to every demand. As they drew level with the platform they snapped their Eyes Right, in a reflex drilled into them long before, towards the figure who was saluting them; and, as one, removed their hats and held these over their hearts, in acknowledgement of his courtesy. Behind them came another rank of ex-servicemen who had also been at Gallipoli, though not in the 1st Battalion; and as they strode and limped towards the saluting base, campaign medals glittering on every chest, they heard the music change above the cheering and the clapping of the crowds, to the trippling cadences of the "Minden March" which was, much more than the "Grenadiers", the Lancashire Fusiliers' very own tune. More men in civilian clothes marched up, whose bravery and endurance had been tested on the Somme, at Ypres and at the crossing of the Seclin Canal. There were even men who had come through the war against the Boers. And there were, finally, line after line of men in khaki, the serving Lancashire Fusiliers of the day, who might spend the rest of their lives in peace, or be obliterated in another world war, or merely be damaged by a vengeful bullet fired by some tribesman on the North-west Frontier. As they left the saluting base behind and turned out of the Market Place, their arms were still coming up to shoulder level with the precise regularity of metronomes, their legs swinging easily in ripples along each company. They were bound for the Barracks, on the outskirts of town; the bemedalled heroes of Gallipoli and Passchendaele and Spion Kop heading instead for their annual reunion meal, where long tables awaited them in the cavernous space of the Drill Hall.

As the bandsmen fell into step behind the troops, and the martial music began to fade away down Bolton Street, the crowds at last loosened themselves from the congestion of the pavements, to stream across the roads, to greet each other, to agree that it had been a good commemoration again. It had invariably been very much more than that, especially the part celebrated in the Parish Church. The annual service was at the very heart of local feeling for and pride in the Lancashire Fusiliers, the Church's rituals and its authority conferring a form of sanctity on "our regiment".

Of the two major anniversaries from the Great War, it was Armistice Day that was virtually forgotten first.

# 8

# King of Lancashire

The most powerful figure in the mythology linking Bury and its regiment with Gallipoli was Edward George Villiers Stanley, the 17th Earl of Derby. He was one of the King's greatest cronies, close enough to the throne to be able to criticise George V to his face for bullying his sons, and to get away with it. Derby did this one day when the King was staying with him at his home in Lancashire. The King was silent for several minutes before he replied; "My father was frightened of his mother; I was frightened of my father, and I am damned well going to see that my children are frightened of me." Derby was many other things as well as a devoted royalist, including one of the country's most active politicians. But he was, above all, a benevolently feudal figure who at one time owned most of Bury and its surrounding district. He was its hereditary lord of the manor, though his home was much closer to Liverpool. He looked as powerful as, in truth, he was. He was a big man with a thick neck who, in his prime, closely resembled a bull sealion which had acquired a walrus moustache.

The Stanleys originated on the borders of Cheshire and Staffordshire and they had added estates in Lancashire to their already ample holdings, as a result of a judicious marriage, long before their greatest stroke of good fortune in the Wars of the Roses. Thomas, the second Lord Stanley, brought 4,000 troops to Leicestershire from the North in 1485 to fight in what turned out to be the conclusive engagement of the Wars at Bosworth Field. He had answered the summons of King Richard III but, on arriving at the battlefield, he cunningly positioned his men at some distance from both the contending armies, until it became apparent that Henry Tudor was gaining the upper hand. When Stanley then threw his soldiers into action against the King's men, the battle was quickly over, Richard was dead and Henry VII was proclaimed. Stanley's reward for this assistance was to be raised to the earldom of Derby by the new sovereign and to be given yet more northern lands, including the area round Bury, which were forfeited by faithful supporters of Richard III. The title had nothing to do with the county of Derbyshire. It was associated with the hundred of West Derby, not far from what was then the minor harbour of Liverpool. From that moment, the Derby family was always to be in favour at court, numbered among the chosen few who had the monarch's ear and who could be counted on to give him or her unswerving allegiance, though not always advantageously: James, the seventh Earl, was beheaded in Bolton for his loyalty to Charles I in the Civil War. In less disjointed times for Englishmen the Derbys prospered mightily, both in substance and in influence. At Knowsley, the ancestral home the Stanleys had acquired through that crucial fourteenth-century marriage to the Lathoms, they were renowned for their lavish entertainment of royalty and nobility from many lands besides their own. They were more often than not involved when affairs of state were being settled, their authority reaching a peak when the 14th Lord Derby was three times Prime Minister in the nineteenth century. With their immense wealth they became generous patrons in many spheres, though conspicuously never in any of the arts: the turf was much more to the taste of successive generations and it was the 12th Earl who established one of the world's greatest horse races, the Epsom Derby, in 1780. Their patronage in the north-west of England was endlessly sought by all manner of communities and causes, and it was very rarely refused. They left their mark on Lancashire in many very obvious ways, and in some cases where the connection was only apparent to familiars: the Derby emblem of the Eagle and Child was responsible for the large number of public houses across the county which traded under that name. The 17th Lord Derby became so much identified with local as well as national interests that eventually he was known as the Uncrowned King of Lancashire.

As a young man he had gone to Wellington College before completing his education at Sandhurst, after which he was commissioned in the Grenadier Guards. Except in time of war this regiment never left London, where its officers fulfilled a largely decorative role; but Edward Stanley enlarged on this requirement by getting himself sent to Canada as aide-de-camp to the Governor-

General, who happened to be his father. On his return to England he began to nurse the Lancashire coalfield constituency of West-houghton and in 1886 – still a Guards officer – entered Parliament for the Tories, and did not abandon his commission until he had been in the Commons seven years and a Government Whip for four. When the Boer War started, he resigned from Lord Salisbury's administration and went to Cape Town as an honorary colonel and Chief Press Censor, but returned in 1900 at Salisbury's request and for political promotion as Financial Secretary to the War Office. He was briefly Postmaster-General after that until, in the 1906 general election, he lost his Parliamentary seat to Westhoughton's Labour Party candidate, a local carpenter. This was a severe blow to Stanley's pride, almost on his own doorstep, where his family was not accustomed to public rebukes from the working class. But a couple of years later he was back in Parliament without the assistance of the ballot box. His father had died and he was the new Lord Derby at the age of forty-three.

He instantly became one of the wealthiest men in the kingdom, partly because the 16th Earl left £2.75 million to his heir. Even more welcome were the properties Derby inherited, and especially the regular income they brought in. He was not by any means the landowner with the largest acreage in Great Britain: the biggest men in that sense were Scottish lairds and their English equivalents, who possessed vast tracts of the Highlands and Isles. The Duke of Sutherland could lay claim to more than a million and a quarter acres up there, the Duke of Buccleuch to half a million or so, and there were several more not far short of that figure, whereas Lord Derby's inheritance was just under  0,000 acres. But the lairds and the southrons owned land that was at best good for farming and often fit for nothing but cover for game birds and browsing for deer. Derby's estates were almost all much more productive than that as a result of the Industrial Revolution, with rent-paying tenants thickly populating them, and large numbers of factories that also yielded a return. It has been reckoned that the gross rent roll of the Derby estates in 1908, when Edward Stanley inherited them, was close to £300,000 a year, that he received from his landed properties alone a net income of £100,000 annually; and this, as his biographer pointed out, was at a time when the standard rate of income tax was but one shilling in the pound. There were probably seven noblemen in the realm with a somewhat bigger income than his, but there wouldn't have been more than that.

There were some smallholdings in the South of England, but most of the Derby wealth was accumulated in the North. Apart from a slice of rural Cheshire and a small piece of Westmorland, the estates extended throughout the length and breadth of Lancashire, and these included land and tenancies at Knowsley, as well as its great house. There was also much property in Liverpool, whose Lord Mayor its owner would be for a time. And there were the holdings in East Lancashire, 11,477 acres of farmland, and large urban properties, much of which had been seized from the Pilkington family after the Battle of Bosworth by Henry VII and handed to the man who backed the winner that day. In Bury, Lord Derby owned everything except for a tiny piece of Church glebe near the Rectory and a few acres elsewhere in the borough which belonged to the local Walker family. He was the landlord of some sixty farms on the outskirts of town; of five hundred houses, two thousand mills, shops and other commercial premises; and he had mining rents from the two Bury collieries at Outwood and Ladyshore. Lord Derby's predecessors had built Bury's Town Hall, its police headquarters and its court houses. When, in 1925, he stunned the town by announcing that he intended to sell his estates there, he also let it be known, in a typical Derby gesture, that he would donate the freehold of the Town Hall to the Corporation.

He was disposing of many properties at this time in order to reduce his taxes. The local sale was made to a firm of timber merchants fifty miles away, outside the county in Chesterfield, who were generally held to have paid £1 million for Bury, though Lord Derby always declined to reveal the amount. The purchasers acquired the land and properties purely as a speculation, the principal of the firm declaring that everything would be resold in small lots to the existing tenants or anyone else who cared to buy. Certainly they could never have hoped to replace the 17th Earl as an exemplary landlord, whose withdrawal from this relationship was widely regretted in the town, not least by its small farmers, who had often had their arrears of rent written off when times were bad. Even a local paper which prided itself on its forward-looking policy, generally hostile to the Tory interest, remarked that "To the people of Bury and surrounding district the Stanleys have long been popular representatives of an unpopular order, the just protagonists of an unjust landed system . . .''

Otherwise, the relationship continued unchanged, for it had always been based on something more than, as well as, the patronage of the landlord towards his tenant. Essentially it dated back to times when a powerful man offered his protection to the lowly against those who would pillage them, in exchange for their obedience in any cause he cared to nominate. Lord Derby had been bred in this tradition with regard to Bury, among other places, long before he succeeded to the title in 1908. His first public duty in the town had been performed when he was in his twenties and laid the foundation stone of its Technical School. A few years later he did the same thing at the new site of the Grammar School, which had previously been situated behind the Parish Church since 1625 (apart from the fact that it had no boarders, it was organised in the manner of the big public schools, and one of its pupil subdivisions was Derby House). There were few aspects of life in Bury untouched by the Derby influence, even when the 17th Earl did not appear at an event in person. He was not only lord of the manor here but he was also patron of the town's most important ecclesiastical living, which meant that it was he who appointed each Rector of Bury. He was the conduit for any dealings the town might hope to have with royalty, so that the first intimation the Mayor and Corporation had that the Prince of Wales would be heading their way in 1921 was when a message arrived some months beforehand, not from His Royal Highness's address in London, but from His Lordship's home at Knowsley; and throughout that breathless summer's day, the solid figure of the Earl was never more than a few feet away from the debonair young Prince. Derby's political preferences played a powerful part in shaping Bury's improbable allegiance to the Conservative Party, which continued for another thirty years without a break after the local Gallipoli hero, Charles Ainsworth, retired from Parliament: Edward Stanley had learnt a great deal about the art of patronising Lancashire working people more agreeably after his setback at the Westhoughton poll in 1906. The brass bandsmen who trailed across the county to entertain Derby's house guests at Knowsley one weekend in 1924, would have been much less biddable eighteen years earlier. The feelings the town entertained for him, its reluctance to see the back of him, were represented by the unanimous decision of the town council to make him a Freeman of the borough a few months after he had dropped the bombshell that he was selling up. His own feelings in return were gracefully expressed in the Town Hall some years later, when he referred to his connection with Bury in terms of "privilege" and "honour"; though, characteristically, he spent much more time speaking his mind about Mr Gandhi's call for a boycott of British goods in India, especially of textiles made in Lancashire. No one was more ardent in advocating all forms of imperial preference.

When August 1914 came, Derby threw himself wholeheartedly into recruiting Lancashire's young manhood for the war. All his public energies since entering the House of Lords had been spent in politicking within the Conservative and Unionist parties, which had not held office since the election that had cost him his seat as a Commoner. He was a frustrated giant in those circles and the war might almost have been the crusade he had been waiting to spend himself on. In its first five months, he raised five new battalions of the King's Regiment in Liverpool, just as Colonel Sir Robert Peyton had once raised the XXth Regiment of Foot in Exeter; a difference being that the 17th Earl of Derby quartered his men under canvas on his private estate at Knowsley, and presented each one with a regimental badge made of solid silver. In the same period he began to stride back and forth across the county, making speeches in which he used every form of pressure to bring in the volunteers: "I have only two sons. One is at the front. He has been home for a few days leave and went back to the front again on Thursday. My other boy is in the artillery, and when properly trained will go to the front. If I had twenty sons I should be ashamed if every one of them did not go to the front when his turn came . . . When the war is over I intend, as far as I possibly can, to employ nobody except men who have taken their duty at the front. I go further than that and say that, all things being equal, if two men come to me for a farm and one has been at the front, there is no doubt which is going to get the farm." The implicit threat was an especially calculated one when Derby was notoriously a large employer in his various enterprises: attached to Knowsley Hall alone was a domestic staff of thirty-eight and an additional thirty-nine gardeners. But this master knew well how to use the carrot as well as the stick. Employees of his who enlisted were told that they would have their Army pay made up to their normal wage while they were away, and that their jobs would be awaiting them when they came home.

He was perfectly willing to use his well-placed contacts for the advancement of almost anyone who was prepared to go to war; the network system on which the English gentry had always thrived. In an open letter published throughout Lancashire he noted that "I receive applications from men anxious to take commissions in His Majesty's Services but whose names I am unable to put forward as they have no military experience. I have now come to an arrangement with Colonel Errington, commanding the Inns of Court, an OTC duly authorised by the War Office, to take Lancashire men and train them for commissioning. The conditions are as follows – Men must be under thirty-five and must have been at a public or other well-known school. They must be approved of by Colonel Errington and after approval undergo a three-month course. They must undertake to give the first offer of their services when their military education is completed to Lancashire regiments . . . Although I am unable to promise that at the end of their course they will be given commissions, I personally undertake, to the best of my ability, to secure for them commissions either in Lancashire regiments or, if they are full, in regiments elsewhere . . ." This old boys' network, like every other one before and since, did not always feel constrained to abide by its own rules, and not everyone who made use of its services had attended "a public or other well-known school." One of the men to take advantage of Lord Derby's assistance was Joe Tinker, a leading member of the miners' union on the Lancashire coalfield, who had been loud in his condemnation of militarism before the war, but quickly seized the opportunity presented at the Inns of Court to improve his position in life.

The recruiting, which had exceeded everyone's highest expectations early in the war, dried up in the middle of 1915 for a number of reasons, including the discouraging news coming from both Gallipoli and the Western Front. There was also in Lancashire the effect of an order, lately issued by the War Office, which stipulated that a new recruit must be willing to serve with any regiment, and not only the one for which he had specifically volunteered. This was a blow at the very heart of the Territorial philosophy, with its emphasis on local allegiance to local regiments. Derby exploded when the order was promulgated, for he was totally committed to the Territorial ideal. Indeed he had been a member of the 1906 committee which proposed the Territorial arrangement incorporated in Haldane's reforms. He was the Chairman of the West Lancashire Territorial Association and Honorary Colonel of several Territorial forces throughout the country, including the 5th Battalion of the Lancashire Fusiliers. On hearing of the new policy he at once telegraphed his friend Lord Kitchener, the Secretary of State for War, and pointed out that it "has simply murdered recruiting in this district. We cannot get a man. It really is heartbreaking to find that some damned fool should send out this order without consulting anybody connected with the Territorial Forces ... recruiting is in a very parlous state even in Lancashire at this moment." The fertility of the county as a recruiting ground, normally much higher than the national average, was probably due at least as much to Lord Derby's local stature and authority as it was to innate Lancashire patriotism and belligerence.

He redoubled his efforts in the face of this setback. At the beginning of October, he went to Bury for a big recruiting demonstration, similar to others held elsewhere in an effort to revive the flagging enlistments. This one was something between an Army parade and the annual Whit Walks, an afternoon procession which started from the Drill Hall and made its way round the town before finishing up where it began. There were a couple of military bands supplied by the Fusiliers, together with soldiers marching with rifles at the slope, a number of National Reservists, and a group of Territorials from the 1st/5th Battalion who were recovering from wounds they had received in the Dardanelles. The full contingent of the OTC from the Grammar School had been mustered, as well as 200 Boy Scouts, the Church Lads' Brigade, and an array of hospital nurses, who worked the crowds along the route with collecting boxes, for this was a Red Cross flag day as well as a recruiting drive. The Rector of Bury was in attendance to give the occasion his blessing, and there was a massed choir which was conducted by the Parish Church's Dr Williams through two verses of "Rule Britannia" when the procession returned to its starting point outside the Drill Hall, where Lord Derby inspected a guard of honour. The choir then sang "Land of Hope and Glory" while the 17th Earl went up to the balcony of the building, to address the crowd that had gathered beneath. This is how his speech was reported later in the local press: "You have your 1st/5th Battalion at the Dardanelles, part of that very great Lancashire division for which no praise can be too high. The man who is commanding it, Sir Ian Hamilton, is a personal friend of mine, and I have had many letters from him. There is never one in which he does not speak in the highest praise of the East Lancashire Division [Applause]. He has, however, a complaint – and a very serious complaint; and it is that he has not got enough of them. It is up to you to see that that complaint no longer holds good. You have sent your kith and kin out there to fight for you and your homes, and it will indeed be a disgrace to you if you don't keep their ranks full to the fullest extent ... With regard to your Regular Battalions, gallant representatives of a gallant regiment with many gallant deeds on its colours, you have provided, since mobilisation, in this area nearly 10,000 men. It does not say, nor could it say in this return, how many of those came from Bury itself, but I venture to hope and believe from what I know of Bury, that the proportion that came from this town is as good as or better than that which came from anywhere else [hear, hear] ...

"It is at present a voluntary call. It is up to you to say whether the voluntary call is to continue or the reverse. It is up to all of you if you want to see conscription in the future a dream, to find the men now by voluntary means, because rest assured of this; that if there is an inconclusive peace at the end of this war, it will mean a certain war again in the immediate future, and it will mean by the very fact of its being an inconclusive peace that it will impose conscription on this country, not for you, not for the men who have gone to the front, but for your children and your children's children after you ... The women can help, too, in a way that perhaps they don't realise. It is a woman who can often keep a man back. She keeps him back – a mother keeps her son because of her affection for him and of fear that harm may come to him – but remember this, and I say it to every woman in this place: the men who are going to the front, the men who have gone to the front, have gone to defend you and your honour and your safety [Applause]. They have gone to prevent that happening to you that has happened to the women and girls and children of Belgium. They have gone to defend you and your honour: it is up to you to make your men go, your sons go to defend, to help to defend, the honour of the womenkind of this kingdom [Applause].

"Therefore they can help by letting their feelings of grief at the departure of their son be hidden, and only show to him the satisfaction they feel that their son is doing his duty. Please God that son will come back, but if he does not there will remain at all events with you the feeling that he went to do something to help you. He will have gone because honour called him, he will have laid down his life for that honour, he will keep his self-respect, which no young man will have unless he takes his position in the fighting line of His Majesty's forces [Applause].

"I feel that words of mine cannot really make an appeal to those who have not yet gone, but I would venture to ask them to see from whence the appeal is really coming. It is coming from the women of this country, to save them; it is coming from the men who are fighting in France, who say 'Come and assist us'; and it is coming, as a voice from the dead, from those who have laid down their lives for their country, which says 'Come and avenge us, come and be men, men of England.' That is the call that is coming to every young man: and I hope and believe that this town of Bury, with which my family has been so intimately connected, will be one of those towns which will not turn a deaf ear, but will say, one and all, 'We hear the call, we hear the call of England, and willingly we come to defend the honour of our country'" [Applause].

This was a perfect example of Derby's response when he had his back to the wall, in its mixture of every rhetorical trick used without scruple for anything but achieving the objective he had set himself: the name-dropping to impress the humbler folk, the threats of conscription and a second war, the stock flatteries and the easy familiarity, the call to honour and the harping on female vulnerability, the outright emotional blackmail of those who had not yet signed up. When he had finished the crowd gave him three cheers and, after thanking them, he astutely called for three cheers more – for the Lancashire Fusiliers ("The cheers were given with great heartiness"). After that, everyone sang "O God, our help in ages past", followed by the National Anthem.

Three days later, the Liberal Prime Minister Mr Asquith announced that the Tory Lord Derby was to be national Director-General of Recruiting. The decision, in fact, was Kitchener's; and he had discussed the appointment with Derby during one of the latter's frequent visits to London, some time before he returned north for the meeting in Bury. Derby had proved himself to be, in Lloyd George's phrase, "the most efficient recruiting sergeant in England" and was the obvious man to direct a new overall strategy at this crucial stage of the war. But he had not been entirely candid with the people of Bury at the demonstration of October 2, when he implied that it still lay within their powers to prevent the introduction of conscription. It did not, and he knew it did not, for both he and Kitchener had already agreed that compulsory military service must shortly be introduced. Derby later noted in his diary that Kitchener had said it would be his duty as Director-General "to prove to Labour that we had come to an end" of voluntary enlistment. The Labour Party inherently opposed the idea of conscription and so did many Liberals; so, too, for most of his life did Lord Kitchener, though on the grounds of fighting efficiency rather than moral principle. The supporters of conscription, however, had been numerous ever since the Boer War, in whose aftermath a National Service League had been founded, of which the popular Lord Roberts VC later became president. By 1911 it claimed to have more than 91,000 members, including grandees like Lords Curzon and Milner, more than a hundred Members of Parliament, and the nation's most eloquent patriot, Mr Rudyard Kipling. The league's objective was the peacetime compulsory service of every fit white man in the British Empire, for home defence against the threat of foreign invasion; and, for all that he spent so much of himself in raising volunteers, the 17th Earl of Derby believed in the league's ideals. Kitchener only accepted the basic premise when the flow of voluntary manpower began to dry up, while the front-line casualties continued to mount with every passing week.

In July 1915 a National Registration Act had been passed, which required every male between the ages of eighteen and forty-five to enter his name on something comparable to the electoral roll, so that the authorities would know precisely who was available to the recruiting officers if the need arose. Under the Derby Scheme which the new Director-General launched that autumn, a compromise was attempted between voluntary service and conscription; at heart, a last gesture to the former and a way of demonstrating to its supporters that the time had come for compulsion. All the men on the national register were invited to signify their willingness to enlist, and Herbert Asquith pledged that married men would not be called up until the unmarried had been recruited first. The Scheme foundered because the unmarried declined to offer themselves in sufficient numbers, and married men who had attested their willingness to serve on the assumption that this would only be required of them after the bachelors had done their bit, were formed into a pressure group to see that the Prime Minister's pledge was carried out. Grievance reached the point where the Attested Married Men's

Union held a meeting in the Manchester Free Trade Hall, where 3,000 men, claiming to speak for half a million more, demanded conscription and Lord Derby's resignation, coupled with an invitation to His Lordship to become their president. In May 1916, conscription was voted in by Parliament and the principle the British had held tenaciously through centuries of warfare was abandoned at last. The act had just been passed when a German mine took HMS *Hampshire* and Lord Kitchener to the bottom of the Atlantic, nor'west of Scapa Flow. Only days after this catastrophe, Derby was confiding to Lord Charles Montague that the War Office was the only job he had ever really wanted and that "I would do anything to have it now . . ." In fact, he had to wait his turn for six months. Lloyd George got the nod from Asquith to succeed Kitchener, and Derby was appointed his Under-Secretary. But in December 1916, Lloyd George was himself forming a Government, and Derby at last became Secretary of State for War. This turned out to be a less than happy appointment. Almost at once there was a furore over the Cabinet's decision to place the British Army in France under the French high command and Derby, who had been left strangely ignorant of the Cabinet's conclusion, sided with the British generals who resented it. Thereafter, Derby's relationship with Lloyd George was uneasy, and in April 1918 he was made British Ambassador in Paris, where he remained for the next two years. By 1924, he was finished with national politics and resumed the role for which his breeding and character fitted him best; northern potentate with an entrée at court, intermediary supreme between his native county and the capital.

He was such a man for pulling strings all his life that it would be surprising if Lord Derby had played no part in the War Office's reconsideration of its ruling on the award of Victoria Crosses to the six Lancashire Fusiliers after Gallipoli. When the original memoranda were flying back and forth between the Dardanelles and Whitehall in the summer of 1915, Derby was still playing the recruiting sergeant in the North. But he could scarcely have been unaware of the difficulty the regiment was having with the military bureaucrats: he was, after all, not only lord of the manor in the regimental depot town, but Honorary Colonel of its Territorial force. He was certainly in touch with the man who was doing his best to block the full six VCs recommended by Hunter-Weston and Ian Hamilton; the Military Secretary to the War Minister, Major-

General Sir Frederick Robb. Derby and Robb were in communication that summer about the granting of commissions to people who were not born and bred officer material. "I quite agree with you," Derby wrote to Robb one day in September 1915, "that it is iniquitous the way people put forward men for Commissions, but the case you mention fairly staggers me. To think that an officer of the Grenadier Guards should do such a thing as to recommend a Golf caddie for a Commission horrifies me and I am very anxious to know who it is."

When, in the latter half of 1916, the matter of Victoria Crosses for Bromley, Stubbs and Grimshaw was raised again by Wolley-Dod with the man who by then had succeeded Robb, Lieutenant-General Davies, Lord Derby was the Under-Secretary of State for War: it is inconceivable that he was not privy to the negotiations then going on between his immediate military subordinate in the War Office and the regiment with which he himself was so closely associated at home in Lancashire. The three additional VCs were gazetted in March 1917, several weeks after Derby had been promoted to War Minister, in whose gift the award penultimately lay on the advice of serving officers. There is, in fact, no available documentary evidence that he had anything to do with the award of the Six VCs Before Breakfast: not in the War Office files for those years which have been declassified, not in Lord Derby's own papers. But people of influence sometimes very carefully do not commit themselves to delicate matters in writing, as Derby himself once acknowledged in a message to his friend George V. He had just been made Under-Secretary and the King had sent his congratulations. In thanking him, Derby wrote: "With Your Majesty's permission I shall from time to time write to Your Majesty and also, if I may, ask for an audience. There are so many matters one can tell but cannot write!"

Although Derby saw little of Lancashire from the moment he became Director-General of Recruiting in the autumn of 1915, his patronage there continued throughout the war. He had 100 acres of the Knowsley grounds put to the plough to help the local food supply, and gave £200 towards the travelling expenses of wives and mothers of Lancashire Fusiliers who were prisoners of war in Switzerland. After going home to the county in 1920, and especially after he withdrew from all his national roles, his activities in Lancashire returned to the level the people there had always expected of him. He was in great demand for the unveiling of war memorials in the area, and performed this function in Bury more than once. He made other visits at regular intervals, when he was asked to lay yet more foundation stones, when he escorted the Prince of Wales in 1921, and when he was made a Freeman of the borough. Eventually, in spite of the fact that Lord Derby had sold off his Bury estate, he returned to the town at least twice every year; once for Gallipoli Sunday and once in his capacity as Lancashire's Lord Lieutenant, making an official call on the Mayor. He never forgot the smaller gestures of patronage. Just before Christmas he invariably sent a large box of cigarettes to the secretary of the 5th Battalion's Old Comrades Association, for distribution at the annual general meeting in the Drill Hall.

Curiously, he had ignored Gallipoli Sunday in the time of Charles Hill. But in appointing Hugh Hornby to succeed Hill as Rector of Bury, Derby was not only acting as patron of the living: he was also making a relative the incumbent. He and Hornby were distant cousins through marriage. The new Rector invited his patron to the Gallipoli service in April 1932, in order to unveil a tablet commemorating the part the 1st/5th Battalion had played in the Dardanelles and in the rest of the war. Thereafter, Derby scarcely missed an anniversary, in peace and war, until the day he died. Very often he read the lesson, frequently he took the salute at the march-past after the service in the Parish Church. One year he presented long-service medals to two veterans of the Terriers and addressed the current Battalion from the Drill Hall balcony where, years earlier, he had exhorted the young men of the town to be brave, to defend their womenfolk, not to disgrace their families. "You are all members of a great regiment," he told their successors in 1938, "and each of you bears a great responsibility, of keeping the good name of the regiment. The love for the regiment increases rather than decreases as the years go on. For myself, I love my regiment; I don't know whether more so now than fifty-five years ago, when I joined. You will feel like I feel, that the Regimental March brings back to you the memory of many friendships that you will keep all through your life. One of the greatest assets you can have is a love of your regiment. Keep and preserve it, and do everything in your power to advance its reputation." And then, like the recruiting sergeant he had always been, he added, "I hope the Battalion will soon be up to full strength . . ."

His elder son and heir died later that year, and he had already lost his only daughter in a hunting accident. His younger son, who would not long outlive him, spent the Second World War mostly in Churchill's coalition Government, with a brief spell in the Army first. The ageing Derby and his wife therefore only had their grand-daughter Priscilla with them at Knowsley and in 1941 she received the papers calling her up for some form of national service, like every other young woman of her age. Derby's response was exactly the same as that of thousands in the Great War, who had wondered how best to keep their men from serving at the front. He wrote to his son-in-law, Captain Bullock, in guarded but unmistakable terms: "I should like to have talked over things with regard to Priscilla's calling-up notice, but I am sure you will do everything that is necessary with regard to that. I hope they won't take her away from here, as she is such a stand-by to Alice, but of course if she has got to go she has to, but I daresay you could put in the necessary plea to allow her to remain here. It would be very lonely for us here without her, and more especially perhaps for me, as Alice now generally goes to bed before Dinner and Priscilla does so much for me in many ways and keeps me in touch with the outside world. I shall do nothing, but if there is anything you want me to do, you have only got to let me know." So the strings were pulled once more and, although Priscilla joined the Women's Royal Naval Service, she was posted to Liverpool until the end of the war, which allowed her to spend all her free time with her grandparents.

Lord Derby was not only ageing, his life saddened by family tragedies, but by then his health was failing, on top of which he was damaged in a motor accident. He was still able to get about during the war years and for some time after, but he was slowing down, no longer a big man who moved vigorously, but a huge man who was ponderous. In 1945 and 1946 he did not fail to make his annual visitation to the Mayor of Bury, but he remained in his Rolls-Royce outside the Mayor's Parlour, and His Worship came down to sit with and talk to Derby in the car. He still came to Gallipoli Sunday, where it had been the custom to reserve a stall for him near the Rector in the choir. But now he spent most of his time in a wheelchair, which meant that in the days before the service, Corporation workmen had to build a wooden ramp up the flight of steps from the Market Place to the churchyard, so that Lord Derby could be trundled into the church. The wheelchair then took him to the front pew on the south side of the aisle, just below the choir, so that the choristers were able to look down at him sitting there. The first time this happened, some of the boys realised with a sense of shock that at the offertory, as the words of "O Valiant Hearts" rolled round the church to the accompaniment of the regimental band, Lord Derby was weeping silently. The following years they watched for it, and surreptitiously nudged one another at the first sign. But no one was ever quite sure what was making Lord Derby cry; whether it was his family tragedies, the loss of all those young men a generation before, or a sense of guilt at his own contribution to their fate.

Bury's last sight of its patron was at Gallipoli Sunday in 1947, when he was eighty-two, with only a few more months to live. Again the tears ran unchecked down that bull sealion's head and into the white walrus moustache. When the bugle notes had died away, there was a long, long silence as Lord Derby's attendant wheeled him back to the west door and down the ramp, where people cheered him across the Market Place. He was conveyed to the saluting base, where his vehicle stood: and there, presently, to the thump and pomp of "The British Grenadiers", his slumped figure acknowledged through the open door the tramp of men who had known full well the horrors of Gallipoli and the Somme, and the young Lancashire Fusiliers in uniform who were still marching as to war.

# PART THREE

# 9

# In Spite of Myth

There was never any chance that memories of the Great War would be allowed to fade quietly from the public consciousness, that a natural healing process would be encouraged to begin as soon as possible without indecent haste. The very words Remembrance Day – another synonym for the commemoration of the Armistice – implied a summons, a requirement to dwell on what had happened to this nation between 1914 and 1918. That annual imperative was so great that, eight full years after the war was over, no fewer than 80,000 poppies were prepared for sale in Bury before November 11, which was many, many more than one for every man, woman and child in the borough; and few, indeed, of the adults in the twenties and thirties would have dared to be seen in public without an artificial flower pinned to the buttonhole or coat. Among the duties of every schoolteacher as the second week of November began, was that of persuading each pupil in the class to part with a penny at least for one of the cheapest productions from the workshops of disabled ex-servicemen.

Figuring much more prominently in the systematic preservation of the wartime mythology were the memorials that began to appear once the population had settled down to the peace. These went somewhat beyond the normal human impulse to recollect and make icons to the dead, which were traditionally confined to graveyards and to the inner walls of religious shrines. The war memorials sprang up everywhere, most of all and most prominently on secular ground. They were almost entirely symbolic, with no useful purpose except to remind; unlike the poppies, whose manufacture provided steady employment for otherwise unemployable men. In Bury there was a single exception to this pattern of monumental insistence on recalling the horrors of war, and it was an ambitious one.

In the spring of 1920 the civic war memorial committee launched an appeal whose object was to build a children's department as an adjunct to the local Infirmary. The estimated cost was £53,000, which amounted to about £1 per head of the population. Donations came slowly, and nearly three years later the fund was still short of £9,000. Building nevertheless went ahead and, when it was finished towards the end of 1924, the balance still required to pay all the bills was raised from the proceeds of a carnival organised by the local Trades Council. The largest single donation was one of £5,000 from Lord Derby, who laid the foundation stone and later performed the official opening of the new ward. This wasn't the only occasion when a subscription from Knowsley was necessary to make sure that a memorial would be completed, after a less than wholehearted response from the community whose grief and concern it was supposed to represent. But monuments tended to capture the local mood more surely than imaginative attempts to sublimate the memory of the war in high and positive hopes for the future.

Some eight months before the hospital appeal, there had been an altogether different call for £30,000, which was conspicuously more successful in touching the consciences and the pockets of the citizenry. It was for a second memorial to the Lancashire Fusiliers, and this fund was fully subscribed by Gallipoli Sunday 1922, when the appeal for the children's ward was still less than half-way to its target figure. The monument which already acknowledged the regiment's prowess (and lack of it) in the Boer War, had by this time been moved from its original position near Sir Robert Peel in the Market Place – because the Corporation needed to build a tram terminus on the site – and its buoyant bronze Fusilier now hailed people approaching the town centre along the road from Manchester. The new memorial was to stand at the entrance to the Barracks up the Bolton Road, and its designer was to be Sir Edwin Lutyens, the most glittering star in the British architectural firmament, busy with his grandiose plans for the new imperial capital of India in Delhi. Lutyens did not come cheap on any of his commissions, but he gave his services free to the Bury project, out of filial devotion and sentimental regard for the regiment: he was one of fourteen children who had been sired by a captain of the old XXth Foot, in which several generations of the family had served. When completed, the work was seen to resemble the national Cenotaph in London, which was scarcely surprising, for Lutyens had designed that, too. The Bury obelisk was on an appropriately smaller scale than that of its illustrious predecessor in Whitehall; of Portland stone on a base of Cornish granite, with delicately carved and painted flags draped on either side of the white column, representing the Regimental Colour and the King's Colour of the Fusiliers. The monument was unveiled on the seventh anniversary of the landing at Gallipoli, in the presence of three generals, a brace of local mayors, and Captain Willis vc. The unveiling was the occasion of new silver drums and bugles – bought as a result of over-subscription to the memorial – being presented to the regiment, and on these massed bugles the Last Post was sounded after prayers from the Rector of Bury. "Then followed a surcharged minute of silence, after which the beautiful strains to which Rudyard Kipling's noble 'Recessional' has been set were played by the band, and the company joined in with 'God of our fathers, known of old'; a hymn which would surely have prevented the war if Europe could but have grasped its spirit before July 1914."

By the time the monument at the Barracks was finished, Bury was replete with war memorials, in every parish and in all its surrounding districts. At Walshaw, for example, a runic cross had risen above a graven list of men who had not returned to the village from the war. This was typical of many scattered around the town, so numerously that there was virtually no church or chapel without some monument to the heroic dead by its gate or in its yard. The garrison church of the Lancashire Fusiliers, St Mary the Virgin in the Market Place, inevitably became more richly endowed with these testimonies than any other. The most conspicuous corner of its churchyard was cut away in 1924 in order to accommodate the town's Central War Memorial, a curving wall of granite and bronze, surmounted by a cross thirty-four feet high (the provision of a children's ward was thought to be an insufficient acknowledgement of 1914–18). Some eight years later, Lord Derby unveiled a plaque inside the church, which commemorated the 1,662 Fusiliers of the 1st/5th, 2nd/5th and 3rd/5th Battalions who had died in the war. Later still there was to be a memorial near the pulpit, cherishing the link between the regiment and HMS *Euryalus*. The day would come, after another generation had passed, when 800 tombs would be removed from the graveyard behind the Parish Church, in order to accommodate a Garden of Remembrance to the dead of two world wars.

Nor were memorials to 1914–18 found only beside or within places of worship, or on open-air sites chosen by secular authorities. Most of the cotton mills and other factories around Bury bore a wall plaque by 1920, listing the men who would never again clock-on for work. The year that saw Lord Derby laying the foundation stone for the memorial children's ward, also saw the unveiling of a tablet in the assembly hall of Bury Grammar School, which had sent over six hundred of its old boys to the war, of whom ninety-seven were killed. Eight families had each lost two sons from that school. The senior master, Mr J. L. Norton, who had taught French and German there for thirty-two years and knew every one of those lost, performed the ceremony of unveiling and somehow, without breaking down, managed to read out the names of the dead to the assembled school: Douglas Askew, Percy Barker, Harold Barlow, Henry Ernest Belchamber ... Richard Norris Wild, James Marmaduke Willis, William Clarence Yapp; and Richard Arthur Hopkinson, who had emigrated to Canada after leaving school but, at the age of forty, had returned to the Old Country to do his bit, and vanished one night during a German bombardment of the trenches on the Somme.

Nowhere in Bury, except in the Wellington Barracks and the Drill Hall, was an awareness of military tradition more carefully nurtured than in the Grammar School. The mythology of local soldiering was especially strong there because the school cadets – which became a unit of the Officers' Training Corps in 1908, during Haldane's Army reforms – had been originally raised in a deliberate association with the 5th Battalion of the Fusiliers. The inspiration for this bond had come in 1892 from the school's headmaster, the Rev. W. H. Howlett, who typified the ordained scholar in charge of most Victorian public schools. Bury Grammar was not, strictly speaking, one of these establishments though it came quite close in the educational pecking order, and Howlett was at one with the headmasters of Eton, Winchester, Rugby and the like in advocating muscular Christianity and the surpassing excellence of a good grounding in Latin and Greek. He most cogently expounded another part of his philosophy when he preached his last sermon at the school's Founder's Day, just before retiring in 1919. He mentioned one of his old boys, a lieutenant who had won the MC with the Fusiliers, and who found himself charged with guarding some high ground on the Western Front. "Around him were Portuguese,

Italians, French, mixed confusedly with his own men. Each had the traits of his nation, but as he gazed around he thanked God he was an Englishman. Why? Because Englishmen had learned to love fair play, to uphold justice, to honour women and children, to do and dare, to detest oppression and wrong. And where did he learn those high ideals, but in the schools of Old England . . .''

It was not coincidence, therefore, that at the school's annual prizegiving four months after the Great War began, the prizes should be presented by the commanding officer at the Barracks, Colonel R. W. Deane of the Lancashire Fusiliers. Nor was it a fluke that an officer who commanded the 1st/5th Battalion at Gallipoli, Lieutenant-Colonel F. A. Woodcock, a Bury solicitor when he wasn't a Territorial officer, should have been an old boy of the Grammar School; his earliest military training, indeed, had been in the school armoury, as a fourth-form cadet.* It was only to be expected that, even when prizegivings were not dominated by Army officers they should begin with full choral versions of the "Marseillaise", or other sympathetically bellicose airs, rendered fortissimo by hundreds of boys. The school was prepared for war almost as thoroughly as the regiment, it paid the same price in miniature, and it honoured its dead with the same determination to extract some glorious encouragement from the carnage. At regular intervals the pupils went in procession to the Parish Church and there held a memorial service for the latest batch of old boys who had fallen in a foreign field. On one such occasion, during the Gallipoli campaign, the Rector, Charles Hill, ventured to suggest that "the British soldier is largely the product of the public school spirit, which has become the prized possession of our land."

A more realistic voice – and a curiously waspish one – offered an assessment of wartime activities at the school that neither the headmaster nor the Rector could have found very comfortable. "Old members of the Bury Grammar School OTC, used to leisurely programmes in the days which went before the war, would be greatly surprised if they could have a week's experience of the work of the corps under present conditions . . . In pre-war times they went through many useful manoeuvres and exercises – lessons in every way as educational as the things which count in examinations –

---

* Woodcock took command of the Battalion in August 1915 after its original CO, Lieut.-Col. J. Isherwood, was invalided home from the Dardanelles.

but these exercises were sandwiched between weekend jaunts, socials, hotpots and what-not which detract somewhat from their seriousness if not from their usefulness and value. But today it is otherwise. Like it or like it not as we may, these sturdy, well-knit lads have no delusions as to why they are being taught this thing or that. Everything that they are being taught is calculated to make them more efficient in the grim work of killing. Killing whom or what? Their country's enemies; and at the present time the country has only enemies of one type. That is the German or the Hun type. Ergo the whole business is to make these lads understand that they are to become efficient, both as individuals and as parts of the military machine, in the work of killing Germans. This would be a very horrible thing if we did not know that the Germans, under present conditions, stand for the negation of honour and humanity, and everything that is lovely and wholesome in civilised life . . . Yes, Kaiser William's decoction of ambition, egotism and frightfulness is proving a sovereign tonic for Captain Spivey's little OTC."

In spite of the terrible litany of its dead that Mr Norton intoned, and its other casualties, the school maintained an unswerving allegiance to the military tradition of the town after the war. The OTC wasn't suddenly shunned by parents who preferred their children to be educated in more civilised arts than those practised on the school firing range. Membership was not compulsory for boys who reached the minimum age of fourteen and those who declined to don khaki for a couple of afternoons every week simply had extra lessons or were obliged to spend their time in private study. No sanctions were invoked against these non-combatants, no bullying by the boy soldiers was allowed. And yet the lads who did not join the OTC were made to feel that their abstinence from martial exercise had, implicitly and just a little, let the side down. This small and discreet moral pressure was probably enough to keep the OTC more or less up to strength; and where it alone might not have sufficed, a residual glamour attaching to the corps even after the horrors of 1914–18 would in all likelihood have done the trick. There was, quite simply, something attractive to most schoolboys in using firearms, in wearing military uniform, and in time acquiring stripes on the sleeve, and other manifestations of rank: this was an area in which a boy without hope of achieving academic excellence might visibly command those who were his superiors in the class. And on one day of the year he would not only be visible to any contemporary who looked out of the window and watched him drilling others in the school yard; he would be on show, in all the distinction of his rank, to the whole community.

Each May the school celebrated its foundation in 1625 with a morning service in the Parish Church, followed by a half-holiday. The boys and the masters, however, did not go straight to the church from their homes, individually. Founder's Day began with everyone assembling at the school and then forming up in a long column to move in procession for half a mile to the centre of the town. At the head of the column marched the OTC behind its drum and bugle band, taking precedence over the headmaster and his staff, over the prefects and other sixth-formers of pacific tendencies, over the descending age-groups of this not-quite-a-public school. Had there been no boys marching in uniform up front to the rattle of the kettle drums and the strident noise of the brass, this would have been a very haphazard procession, a rag tag and bobtail of pupils walking out of step behind a group of gentlemen in academic gowns, all of them slightly embarrassed to be on such public display. The corps, however, set a pace, it turned the matter of getting from the school to the church into a spectacle which the town stopped to watch: not so many people as Gallipoli Sunday attracted to the Market Place, to be sure, but quite enough to satisfy adolescent vanity. The OTC paid particular attention to its spit and polish for Founder's Day. Its boy sergeants and corporals, and many of its cadets who aspired to these ranks, were very conscious indeed of a precedent that had been set the month before by the Lancashire Fusiliers.

The Fusiliers, of course, held the copyright to all such local spectacles, and not only in the April Gallipoli parade. In 1919 the regiment resumed its old tradition of publicly celebrating the Battle of Inkerman at which, it was always emphasised, the XXth Foot had sustained greater casualties than any other British troops apart from the Guards. Every November 5 thereafter, the people of Bury were invited to be present at the Barracks to witness a torchlight tattoo which artfully complemented the Bonfire Night that the whole country always celebrated on that date. Visitors entering the Barracks from the Bolton Road did so under an arch which on this evening bore an illuminated XX. They found awaiting them in the darkness of the huge square beyond, the massed bands of the 5th Battalion and the Regimental Depot; and when all were settled in their places, troops with flaming torches marched on to the square and began to perform the most intricate evolutions in sixteen ranks of eight men apiece. The culmination of the first sequence was the formation of a star in the middle of the square. This dissolved and was re-formed into a cartwheel with eight spokes which revolved before disintegrating so that the torchbearers could form up anew in the pattern XX, while the bands played the "Minden March". "The torchbearers then led into a revolving maze consisting of several circles, each revolving in an opposite direction to its neighbour. From this the whole wound into a watch spring, winding tighter and tighter till the leader could go no further, when he led out between the ranks of those still leading in. After this, the band and torchbearers marched up the square *en masse*, the band remaining at one end while the torchbearers returned to the other. As they arrived at the end of the square they formed the word Inkerman, while the band again played the regimental march." Finally the soldiers formed up and sang two verses of "Recessional", massed bugles sounded the Last Post, and the Fusiliers marched off the square. There followed a twenty-minute fireworks display, which topped anything civilians might have put on elsewhere in Bury that night in pyrotechnic mockery of Guy Fawkes's attempt to blow up Parliament.

Yet the Fusiliers did not only offer spectacular models of drill movements for the aspiring young cadets in the Grammar School corps. The Army was happy to assist in other ways: by sending trained men to demonstrate a piece of new equipment, by providing observers when the lads undertook manoeuvres on field days, by supplying officers to examine boy soldiers for the certificates on which promotion depended. In much the same spirit, the regiment lent itself to the men who had fought with it in the war before returning to civilian life. Early in 1919 a Bury branch of the Comrades of the Great War was formed and, before the year was out, its members had themselves assumed the role of patron when they gave a party for 400 children whose fathers had been killed on active service.* The original intention had been for a jollification in the open air, but bad weather forced them to use the Drill Hall instead. As this was Army property, the Old Comrades had to ask for

---

* Already in existence since 1911 was a Lancashire Fusiliers Old Comrades Association, with which the specifically Great War Old Comrades eventually merged.

permission to use it, which was gladly given; asking was a mere formality, but a necessary one nonetheless.

The Drill Hall became headquarters for the Great War Comrades who, in their first year of existence, held no fewer than twenty-eight meetings there. Their objectives were very often charitable, and not only in having a whip-round to give orphans a party now and then: they also pressed the authorities for improved pensions, for gratuities to deserving cases, even for the award of decorations to those they thought unjustly ignored.* But what they mostly represented was a deep psychological need by some men not to let go of each other, of the regiment in which they had served, of the wartime memories they shared. For most of these old sweats, the war would be the biggest thing that happened to them between birth and death: nothing else in their lives would remotely excite them so much, give them such a sense of their own potential, such a pride in the extraordinary things they had found themselves capable of. They were never more than a minority of the ex-servicemen who lived in and around Bury in the post-war period.† Twelve months after the branch was formed there were 400 members, and by 1928 this had risen to 552. They were an élite, publicly acknowledged as such on Gallipoli Sunday; and so strong was the compulsion among some of them to be identified as a chosen band of brothers, that an even more select society of ex-servicemen was formed some fourteen years after the Great War finished. This was the Old Contemptibles Association, which had a Bury branch of seventy men by 1936, and was restricted to those who had served with the British Expeditionary Force in France between August and November 1914; in other words, to those who had been with the 2nd Battalion of the Fusiliers, and other Regular units, before the Territorial troops joined in the European campaign. The members of this association adopted their title in irony, to ridicule the Kaiser's jibe in 1914 about Lord Kitchener's contemptible little army. At their very first meeting in Bury, the commanding officer at the Barracks told them that "yours is the most exclusive of ex-servicemen's clubs."

* At their first annual general meeting they claimed success in the award of a couple of DCMs, a Belgian Croix de Guerre and a pair of 1914 Stars.
† No assessment has ever been made of the Great War veterans in the town; but the three 5th battalions of the Fusiliers, raised there in the early days, alone amounted to some 3,000 men before the casualties began.

The Army never failed to encourage the Old Comrades in their somewhat broader devices and desires. At their second annual meeting the members of the Bury branch received a message from the 1st Battalion of the regiment, then on garrison duty in Dublin, offering best wishes. It continued: "The young soldiers of today are doing their best to maintain the high standard which you created, and the old spirit of the XX lives for ever. Every officer, warrant and non-commissioned officer and man joins in sending a Minden greeting to each one of you." The Old Comrades always held their AGM on Minden Day. It emphasised the bond they felt with serving Fusiliers; and the regiment was itself anxious to maintain that relationship. Invariably, the CO at the Barracks was the chief guest at the annual meeting, and at the 1921 reunion he had this to say: "The spirit of comradeship that has existed between all ranks is responsible to a great extent for the building up of the high reputation which the regiment has always held. It is that feeling that brings out the best qualities in a man. He knows that those above him are with him in any enterprise and he knows he has their support. A man with that feeling is always cheerful. A certain General said to me in France that it was noticeable how, in every battalion of the regiment he had come across, the spirit of cheerfulness showed itself. No matter what the weather or conditions of life at the moment, everyone was always in high spirits, and the best was always made of everything. That feeling is bound to carry a man far, and I hope it will always exist, and that it will always be a distinguishing feature of the regiment we are so proud to call our own."

Minden Day 1920 had been the occasion of a ceremony held partly in private, with a public display in the Parish Church afterwards. There, the colours of three wartime battalions of the Fusiliers (the 9th, 12th and 3rd/5th) were laid up in the presence of many ex-servicemen who had laid wreaths beforehand on the Fusiliers' Memorial, all with poignant messages attached: "To our fallen comrades", "Till the barrage lifts" and other solemnities. The private ceremony had taken place in the Barracks, when the General commanding the 42nd (East Lancashire Division, Major-General H. T. Shoubridge, presented new colours to the local Territorials. In doing so, he had referred to an engagement involving the Fusiliers in France as "that marvellous fight at Messines, which captured the Messines ridge, and which was one of the best-fought and best battles of the war." His final words were aimed at a much wider audience, and referred to the banners shortly to be consecrated in the garrison church. "Don't let Bury people forget these colours," he said, "because they are the emblems of all that the gallant men of those battalions did for them. When people go to the church where the colours are, I would like them, their children and their grandchildren, to have the colours pointed out to them as a sign of all that the gallant battalions did for them in the Great War."

There was a very good practical reason for this advice, just as there was sound logic in the benevolent patronage the Fusiliers extended towards the Grammar School cadets, the Old Comrades Association and any other ex-servicemen's organisation which looked to the regiment for leadership and support. The regiment very badly needed to maintain its popularity in the town and to be regarded by the citizens as some sort of ideal. If it lost the reputation won at such cost in the Great War, it might easily wither and die; or, like the old XXth Foot in the nineteenth century, it might be obliged to move off to some other part of the country in order to be sure of replenishing itself. It was, in the nature of things, always in need of new blood.

The recruiting had begun again in earnest within a few months of the war's end. By the summer of 1919, the 2nd Battalion of the Fusiliers was scheduled to resume imperial duties in India, but was under strength after the demobilisations following the war. The Army invited demobilised members of the battalion to re-enlist on advantageous terms, provided they had earlier served with the regiment for at least six months: any such man between the ages of eighteen and thirty-seven would be welcome for a two, three or four-year engagement with the colours, and he wouldn't have to put in the customary time afterwards with the Reserve. The advertisement setting out these terms was crudely beguiling. "This is a glorious opportunity to see other parts of the world under Peace conditions. Think – are you settled in civil life? What are your prospects? Are they good? Then why not join again until things settle down? *Do it now*. The 2nd Battalion is here waiting for you." With 2,665 men unemployed in Bury at the time and strikes bringing the local cotton mills, paper and brick works to a standstill, this was an intelligent piece of emotional blackmail. And enough men responded to restore the 2nd Battalion to its full vitality, so that it was able to sail for Bombay as planned. But within a few months the recruiters were advertising again: "Opportunities in His Majesty's Army. Experience counts. A few years in the Army fits a man to go anywhere or do anything."

A much greater worry for the military authorities than the need to canvass for Regular soldiers, was the fact that the local Territorial battalions had become seriously undermanned, and that the unemployed of Bury and surrounding district seemed unwilling to relieve their financial hardship in return for a little part-time soldiering which obliged them to leave home for only a couple of weeks or so each year. The Territorial force in East Lancashire as a whole at the beginning of 1921 was short of 265 officers and 6,079 soldiers, and even the Liberal *Bury Times* found that a cause for alarm. In casting round for reasons why there should be such reluctance to follow the local tradition, it suggested that "There is no antagonism between active recruiting for the Territorial Force and the varied peace movements that are afoot in our midst. The youth who signs his attestation form may wish the League of Nations Union every success and will be guilty of no inconsistency if he pays his half-crown to that organisation, too. We all hope that the manliness of the Territorial Army may never again be tested as it was in 1914 and after but . . . recalling how bitterly we were all deceived seven short years ago . . . it will always be a source of satisfaction and comfort to know that this firm rampart remains to us." The 5th Battalion of the Fusiliers, Bury's own Territorial unit, reckoned on a peacetime establishment of 700 men; in fact, it could muster no more than 303 when those words were penned. The especially galling thing to those who mixed their civic and their military pride in equal parts, was that a local tradition had been most distinctly reversed. Bury had always been more ardent than any other town in south-east Lancashire in responding to the patriotic call, but now it was the community lagging farthest behind. Other Fusilier battalions were also under strength, but not by as much as the 5th. The 6th Battalion, of Rochdale men, stood at 530, and the two Salford Battalions, the 7th and 8th, were also doing better than the regimental depot town, with 500 and 415 men respectively.

The military went on the offensive to try to improve matters without delay. Throughout 1921, having clearly decided that advertisement alone would not pay off, senior officers and returned heroes lobbied the Mayor's Parlour and other points of influence, with great determination. The commanding officer of the 5th Battalion was an early caller on the Mayor, and told His Worship that he felt more help should be forthcoming from leading members of the community. Next man up was Major G. E. Tallents, who had been at the Lancashire Landing with the 1st Battalion and was now stationed at the Barracks. He wrote an open letter to the Mayor and Corporation, urging them to attend the forthcoming Gallipoli Sunday commemoration in the Parish Church and promising that several very senior officers had agreed to be at the service. One of these, Lieutenant-General Sir Beauvoir de Lisle, the officer in charge of Western Command, but not obviously a Lancastrian, secured himself an invitation to address the congregation in place of a sermon by the Rector, and offered a rousing panegyric on the regiment. Later that day, Major Tallents himself performed before the rump of Territorial officers in the Drill Hall, a lecture to which the press was cordially invited. The topic of his lecture was the Landing at Gallipoli, and his description of it was both vivid and detailed. Each man, he said, carried about ninety-seven pounds of equipment on his back. The barbed wire they had to cross was about three times thicker than British wire and couldn't be cut. And so on . . . Colonel Lockwood, commander of what passed for the 5th Battalion in 1921, thanked the Major and said that six years earlier the Lancashire Fusiliers had performed the greatest feat of arms ever performed by any regiment in any war.

These sallies made no appreciable difference to the figures either that year or during the rest of that decade. Nor did the appearance in Bury from time to time of one or other of the regiment's VCs, who were good for publicity but evidently for very little else. Sergeant Richards had been enticed north in 1920 for the presentation of new colours, and Captain Willis served his turn for the unveiling of the new Fusiliers memorial in 1922. A few years later, Richards returned, together with another of The Six, John Grimshaw, and Sergeant-Major Smith, who'd won his VC with the 1st/5th Battalion in France in 1918. All to no avail; the Territorial battalions of the Lancashire Fusiliers remained well under strength, and the 5th Battalion was in the worst plight of all. In almost every year of the 1920s, more men left the battalion than the number of new recruits. The regimental lifeblood was dribbling away.

Early in 1930, the Gallipoli hero Charles Ainsworth MP, who was by then also the commanding officer of the 5th, chaired a meeting in the Drill Hall at which Army officers met prominent citizens yet again to devise some strategy that would improve the position. The battalion was then 230 men under strength. A representative of the Chamber of Trade promised that shopkeepers in Bury would put advertisements for recruits in their windows, though the authorities must not expect these to be excessively large. "If we could have parades," he said, "it would be a good thing. A lot of lads always join after a parade." That spring, Bury held a good many parades, one after the other, from start to finish of a Recruiting Week. On the first day, the full battalion with regimental band, led by Colonel Ainsworth himself, marched round the town and out towards Heywood before heavy rain forced them to abandon the rest of the exercise; but they were more successful when they turned out later in the week. The Chamber of Trade did its bit for the cause by mounting a display along the front of two shops in The Rock, which were illuminated with fairy lights. Behind the windows a large Union Jack had been stretched and in front of it stood a model clad in the scarlet and blue full dress of a Fusilier, surrounded by every kind of sports equipment, to make the point that the Territorial Army had other attractions besides those of musketry and forming fours. There were photographs of Terriers in camp and on parade, and the display was festooned with a variety of slogans: "Boys of the Old Brigade – What about the Young Brigade? . . . Young Fellow, Can you say Yes I served with him in the 5th Battalion Lancashire Fusiliers? . . . Comradeship is essential to a happy life . . . All handsome men are sunburnt. Go to camp and get that bronze tint . . . Girls do your bit. Make him enlist."

Recruiting Week also saw special events which, like the sporting paraphernalia, were intended to lighten the military atmosphere. One evening there was a big gymnastic display, and on another there was community singing in the Drill Hall. These events culminated on the Saturday night with a Grand Recruiting Ball in the same building. Members of the 5th Battalion were allowed in free of charge, together with their ladies, as were young men who enlisted before the ball began; while those who signed on during the ball were able to obtain a refund afterwards at the door. The highlight of the evening was the appearance of Miss Clara Birnie, of the Pilot Mill, Bury's Cotton Queen for that year, who made her entrance half-way through the ball, wearing regalia worth £2,000 which had been lent for the occasion, a little nervously, by the local jeweller's,

Lepp's. She was accompanied by her two maids of honour and escorted to the platform by six buck sergeants of the Fusiliers: and there, after she had been greeted by Colonel Ainsworth and his fellow officers, she made a graceful little speech, whereupon the band struck up "She's a Lassie from Lancashire", which everyone in the Drill Hall sang most heartily. And whether it was the parades, or the shop-window display, the gymnastics, the community singing or the sparkling Miss Birnie's contribution to the ball, no one could tell; but the fact was that, during the week, 110 new recruits signed on with the 5th Battalion. It was also a fact, alas, that about this time, four young soldiers committed various felonies in the town – bricks through windows, petty theft and the like – in the hope of obtaining their Army discharge.

The authorities continued to persevere. Later in the year there was another meeting in the Territorial HQ, whose topic was "the drawing closer together of the Town Hall and the Drill Hall". A Major-General W. N. Beach, commanding the 42nd Division, said "A man need be none the less peaceably inclined a citizen by reason of his being prepared to defend his country in time of emergency." This may have been an innocent remark, or it was possibly very pointed: certainly it was unfortunate when the General was standing beside Bury's chief citizen for that year, Councillor W. E. Turner, who notoriously had managed to miss military service in the Great War. So much did the Mayor feel his honour had been impugned, that when his turn came to address the meeting he launched into a writhing defence of his absence from the front. "He said he felt it was their duty to do all they could to strengthen the 5th Battalion, which had its home in Bury. He had a little to do with the campaign last year, and any calls made upon him this year would be answered 'Yes' every time. He would be very pleased to help a recruiting campaign. He should have been a soldier himself but he was rejected. When he was eighteen he wanted to join up with two other men who were about six inches taller than he was. The other two were put in the Guards and he was asked what he would like to join. He replied 'the same as them' but they told him 'in very military language' that he was too short in the legs. That was why he did not become a soldier. He had always had that patriotic feeling for the Army which he thought every citizen ought to hold, especially as the Army of today was on a higher plane than at any other time."

The pressure to conform in these matters was very great, for anyone entering Bury's public life: Charles Ainsworth, whose venomous antipathy to conscientious objection had been a major theme of his first election campaign, was not the man to forgive or forget. Yet it was some sign of the times in Bury that the town council had elected a wartime non-combatant to the position of chief citizen. Another Mayor, a few years later, felt constrained, however, to let the townspeople know that "If he were a young man and the recruiting sergeant accepted him, he would willingly be a soldier, because everything was provided for him: his health was catered for, he was kept clean, he was taught manners – and manners helped people to travel through the world – and he was taught to be obedient, and to be prompt and civil; he was well clothed, well fed, and was never without a shilling in his pocket." Lord Derby could have put it no better. His Worship had just heard another visiting general, Major-General E. A. MacNamara, assure the townsfolk that the Army was theirs, not for aggressive purposes, but to police the Empire and to safeguard its interests. "It would seem," he continued, "that the community at large is not in very close touch with the way things go in the Army, and does not realise the advantages and the prospects the Army offers those who join it. Considering the state of things and the number of men out of work, one feels that they can't quite realise the prospects, the advantages and the happiness of life in the Army." Did they realise, the general wondered, that the average recruit put on between ten and thirteen pounds in his first few weeks of service? These were desperate blandishments; yet the point about unemployment was well made, with 30.9 per cent of the town's work force on the dole, and as many as 48 per cent without jobs a few miles up Rossendale.

The 5th Battalion was not only short of private soldiers and NCOs; it was not often up to its full complement of officers, who came from the town's professional and business classes. That was how George Horridge came to be back in uniform again by 1932, at the invitation of Colonel Ainsworth's second-in-command, Major R. M. Barlow, a local solicitor. Horridge had served on the Western Front with the 1st/5th after returning to the Dardanelles when his wounds had healed, but he finished the war in England, training new recruits at a camp in Scarborough. It was there that he broke open the bottle of champagne he'd brought from France and carried in his valise for months, in anticipation of the Armistice. His elder brother Walter came through the four years of fighting, too; but the youngest Horridge boy, Leslie, was killed shortly after the ceasefire in a flying accident over Croydon. For George Horridge the peace became a steady rise to prosperity in the family textile business, in spite of the slump, and there were other satisfactions in his life. He married and embarked with his wife on a honeymoon that took them round Africa and the Mediterranean, and lasted for months; and on his return he not only resumed his business life vigorously, but indulged his old obsession with sport. He was getting too old to be an effective soccer player any more, but he became involved in the administration of the town's professional football club as one of its directors, and in time became chairman of the board. Cricket was another matter, and Horridge was still a batsman not only good enough to punish most bowling in the local league, but even to play for his county as an amateur from time to time and to win his Lancashire Second XI cap. He was in many ways the archetype of a certain kind of northerner; inherently wealthy and privileged, but interested in things which bridged the gap that would otherwise have separated him totally from those he employed. He was not quite the same animal as the fox-hunting Charles Ainsworth, though he shared some of the MP's reflexes, including the one accepting certain obligations of patriotism, and with it grasping opportunities for advancement. He, too, had been bred to say yes when he was invited once more to become a Territorial officer. At his previous admission, not much more than a schoolboy before the war, there had been a waiting list of gentlemen anxious to get in. Now there was none. Yet in spite of the 5th Battalion's recruiting predicament, no one could obtain a commission except by personal invitation from its hierarchy. At this level it was quite a bit like joining an exclusive club. Its members preferred to suffer from a form of anaemia rather than let just anybody in.

George Horridge's return to part-time soldiering coincided with the rise of Fascism, not only in continental Europe but in Great Britain, too. In the summer of 1934 Sir Oswald Mosley opened a Bury headquarters of his British Union of Fascists, which was still respectable enough to be regarded by many Tories as an acceptable Right-wing ginger group, but which within a few weeks became discredited forever by starting to preach overt anti-Semitism. At his appearance in Bury, Mosley was given the stiff-armed salute by forty supporters as he entered his new office in Parsons Lane, while

a crowd outside greeted this display with derisive laughter. But a
year later, hundreds were unable to get into a packed Athenaeum
in the centre of the town to hear Mosley speak, and although he
was heckled throughout the meeting, there was no other trouble
from the Bury Communists. They, too, were flexing their muscles
locally, holding open-air rallies on "Hitlerism and the crisis" and
similar topics, sometimes to the sound of a military band marching
a few streets away in the hope of attracting recruits to the Lancashire Fusiliers. Mosley wasn't the only visitor to the town with
propaganda to make. As the clouds gathered across Europe again,
Eduard Beneš's nephew came to speak at a Peace Rally in the Co-
operative Hall, and a by-product of his appearance was an official
letter from Bury to the Czechoslovak city of Hradec Králové, assur-
ing those Bohemians that hearts in Lancashire were full of friend-
ship and sympathy. This was, unintentionally, deceptive. The week
in which a British Prime Minister, Neville Chamberlain, left
Czechoslovakia in the lurch at the conference with Herr Hitler in
Munich, also saw 60,000 gas masks arrive in the Lancashire cotton
town, just in case they were needed later on. Air Raid Precautions
had been taken seriously since 1936, when the local police were
first shown how to ward off the effects of mustard gas and other
poisonous substances liable to be dropped as bombs in a war.

And yet, even as it became increasingly obvious that 1914–18
had not, after all, seen the war that was going to end all wars,
enlistment in the depot town of the Fusiliers was still behind that
of anywhere else. The desperate measures taken to rectify this position now included offering a bounty to any serving member of the
5th who managed to bring in a new recruit, and the reward had been
more than doubled from 2s 6d to six shillings without achieving the
desired result. In 1934 the Battalion was four officers and 171 men
short; in 1936 it was 145 under strength; on October 12, 1938, the
week after Chamberlain was in Munich, it was announced that 115
men were still required before the unit had its numbers right. In
the previous twelve months, 97 recruits had joined up, but 112 had
decided that the Territorial Army was no longer for them. The 5th
required more recruits than any other two battalions in the East
Lancashire Territorial Division.

What, by then, made these figures particularly humiliating from
the regiment's point of view, was the fact that in some other
respects the people of Bury were conspicuously ready to be of ser-

vice to the community if war broke out. By the beginning of 1939 they had four hundred volunteers training to be auxiliary firemen, who were to become vital to national survival when the war began and the Blitz occurred. There wasn't a community in Britain with a better record than that. Bury, in fact, was the only borough in Lancashire and Cheshire which had more volunteers for duty in the Auxiliary Fire Service, Air Raid Precautions, and the Ambulance Service than it actually required. And yet, in March that year, less than six months before Great Britain went to war again with Germany, the 5th Battalion of its Territorials was 191 men short, and the Regular soldiers of the regiment were 105 under strength. Well might the chairman of the East Lancashire Territorial Association say, as Colonel Sir William Coates had said two years earlier, that "It is difficult to understand why we should have this everlasting trouble in a town of this size . . ."

With the nation on the verge of war, a Military Correspondent of the *Bury Times* – almost certainly a serving or retired Army officer – put matters more bluntly. "What are the young men of Bury and Radcliffe doing in the present time of international tension?" he asked. "Loath as one must be to belittle the patriotism of one's fellow townspeople, it seems astounding that under the shadow of the present international crisis, Bury and District, which has a great tradition, and is the home of the Lancashire Fusiliers, a regiment with a long and glorious record, should not be supported by her young men in this hour of danger . . . Why is it that other National Service organisations, such as ARP and Auxiliary Fire Service, can get the men they want, while the Territorial Army in this district is neglected by the men whose duty it is to join? Is it because the young men wish to ensure that should the calamity of war come upon us, they will not be called upon to fight in defence of their homes and liberty? If this were the case throughout the country, we would tremble for the safety of the nation. Yet the young men of the district do nothing. Is it not realised that the predatory instincts of the Dictator States can only be held in check by every man showing his willingness to serve this country? Deeds not words are what count at this time to prove our united strength and will to preserve peace with honour." The last was not so much a thrust at Neville Chamberlain, who claimed that his signature at Munich had brought "peace in our time": it was aimed at the very local lobby which throughout the thirties had passed one resolution after another in favour of platitudes formulated by the League of Nations. A Peace Ballot organised by the Bury National Declaration Committee in 1934 had been typical of these activities. It had canvassed all adults in the town over the age of eighteen with a simple question: should Britain remain a member of the League and implicitly continue to back the peacemakers? Officials of the committee claimed that 28,277 answered in the affirmative, and only 912 said No.

It is possible that in the spring of 1938 Bury twice supplied at least part of the answer to the question that baffled all the recruiting officers and their superiors. A couple of girls were sitting one day beside Whitehead's Lodge, a reservoir for a local bleachworks above the village of Walshaw, when they noticed a man loitering on the bridge that crossed the middle of the water. He looked over one side and then the other before he took off his coat and jumped in. He surfaced once and cried out before he sank again and was gone for good. A few hours later, police with grappling irons dragged his body out, its jacket and trouser pockets weighted down with stones and a piece of metal. He was Albert Forrest and, before drowning himself, he had left a letter under the coat and cap which he had rolled up and tied into a bundle with a dog lead. This is what it said: "Dear Wife and Darling Son. Whatever I have thought about you and said, I know now that I have made the greatest mistake of my life, as the song says. To show you I meant every word I said when I told you I could believe you, I will try to repay you by forfeiting my life, which is the most precious thing to anyone, as I can never undo anything I have done in any other way. The sooner I am dead the sooner you will get the peace I have denied you. I am waiting for a chance to get the job done properly in Whitehead's top lodge. You have nothing to forgive, so try to forget. God bless you and Billy. I have gone off the bridge not insane, but broken-hearted through my bad thoughts."

Mrs Forrest interpreted this sad and incoherent farewell to the Bury Coroner, who was now Colonel R. M. Barlow and the officer commanding the 5th Battalion. Her husband, she said, had come back from the Great War after service with the regiment, a changed man. He used to get pains in his head that sometimes hurt so much they made him cry; but at other times he would just sit and stare into the fire for hours on end. He had never managed to hold a job for long, though he had been in a Ministry of Labour training camp, which was supposed to prepare him for employment after a twelve-week course. But he'd left after three weeks, saying he couldn't stand the camp, which was too much like the Army and a wilderness. He had never threatened to take his life, but on the day of his death he had apologised for the trouble he had caused her, and asked the boy to be good to her.

Colonel Barlow heard of another death by drowning that week. The second inquest was on Henry Martin, a contemporary of Forrest who, with his body likewise weighted, jumped into a reservoir on the other side of town. Martin, too, had fought with the Fusiliers and had been wounded severely enough to spend six months in hospital before his discharge at the end of the war. He had been attended by the doctor until 1921, but continued to suffer from his nerves, was forever "jumpy", and his hair had started to come out. He had spent time in the Jericho Institution and in a mental hospital across the county which specialised in broken warriors; and on emerging from these he had managed to hold down a job in his trade as a joiner's labourer. His depressions and his loss of hair tended to come and go, and usually depended on what was happening in his life. When his daughter got diphtheria he was very down, according to his wife, and this time he did not revive again after she stopped being ill. He seemed to lose interest in everything. At the usual time one morning he had set off to work as usual. "I had a feeling something was wrong. He kissed my daughter and said to me 'It's a bad job you ever knew me.' I replied 'Don't be silly.'" Those were the last words they exchanged before he left the house. The attendant who hauled Henry Martin's body from the reservoir weighed the stone that had been so carefully selected to make sure he drowned. It was only 3 lb 2 oz, but that was quite enough.

The recruiting officers underestimated the depths of despair that lurked in Bury long after the Great War; or perhaps they never even understood the nature of it. They were so baffled by the disappointing figures because these seemed to run contrary to the evidence of their own eyes. For the people of Bury had never turned their backs on the regimental mythology that was intended to maintain recruitment at the desired level. The number of spectators watching the Gallipoli Sunday parade appeared to grow year after year. When the old colours of the 1st Battalion were laid up in the Parish Church in 1934, the building was not only overflowing with congregation, but a crowd estimated at between five and six

thousand people awaited the end of the service in the streets outside. When the Fusiliers celebrated their 250th anniversary in 1938
and the 2nd Battalion performed the ceremony of Trooping the
Colour, it was decided that the only place big enough to accommodate all those who would want to be there was the ground belonging
to George Horridge's football club; and eight thousand people duly
filled Gigg Lane to witness the spectacle.

What no one in authority seemed to appreciate was that it was
possible to be proud of the regiment and to enjoy its gorgeous displays as a form of theatre, while at the same time taking care not
to be more closely involved. The Great War, the Lancashire
Fusiliers, had left too much human wreckage behind in Bury for it
to be otherwise. Some of this was liable to be washed up before the
coroner even now. Others who had, after a fashion, survived the
regiment's part in the war still struggled with life, but without
much hope of ever being whole again. And all were known to their
fellow citizens. This was a community still small enough for everyone to be aware of what was going on.

# 10

# "We are quietly disappearing"

The Second World War left few scars to rival those inflicted on the regimental depot town by the First. The potential injury had in many ways been greater, for the threat of aerial bombardment was ominous in 1939, when Lancashire's people braced themselves for suffering like that endured in the Spanish Civil War two years earlier by the citizens of Guernica. And there was, indeed, heavy bombing of Manchester and Liverpool, with consequent damage and civilian casualties comparable to the regular experience of London and other cities in the Midlands and South. Bury, however, got off lightly, as did most towns of its size in the North. Air raid warnings occurred at frequent intervals in the first years of the war, and schoolchildren were occasionally thrilled by the sight of vapour trails overhead, which meant that Spitfires or Hurricanes were battling with Dorniers and other German planes. But death and destruction on the ground was mercifully small at the foot of Rossendale: the worst domestic moment of the war came on the penultimate day of 1944, when a rocket landed on an outlying village, where six people were killed. Once the very real threat of invasion had receded, the conflict in this corner of Lancashire, so far as most of its inhabitants were concerned, resolved itself above all into frustration caused by shortages and restrictions of one sort and another; and anxiety for kith and kin who might be imperilled in a dozen different theatres of the war. This was a conflict which embodied military conscription from the start, so that the exhortations of the Second World War were directed entirely at the civilian populace: who were ceaselessly invited to Dig for Victory in the vegetable patch, to Help Build Me a Ship (or a Plane, or a Tank) by finding cash, or sternly warned off potentially dangerous gossip because Walls Have Ears. And Bury, by and large, was extremely dutiful. In 1941, during War Weapons Week, no less than £18 per head of the population was raised as a contribution to restocking the national arsenal.

Something else was markedly different from the First World War, and that was the scale of military casualties, which were nowhere near as large as before. For example, Bury Grammar School, which had ninety-seven old boys killed in 1914–18, lost only forty-six in 1939–45. The columns of newsprint listing Local Heroes who had died for their Country, which were such an anguished feature of every paper a quarter of a century earlier, were much less common now, and much, much shorter when they did appear. There were various reasons for this and the principal one was that warfare had changed from the strategies of Flanders and the Somme, where the crude solution to most problems had been to throw a few more thousand men at the enemy's guns. But an important local allegiance had changed, too, which meant that if Bury's own regiment had been badly mauled in any one battle or campaign of the Second World War, there would not have been so many people in the town bereft of husbands, sons and brothers as happened after Gallipoli and other catastrophes of the First. Most of Bury's young men did not go to war the second time as Lancashire Fusiliers.

As Christmas 1940 approached, two thousand of the town's servicemen were sent seasonal greetings by the Mayor, on behalf of the whole town, together with a woollen garment and a postal order for a few shillings as a Christmas box. Only one tenth of the recipients were Fusiliers. The rest belonged to other regiments or were serving in the Royal Navy or the Royal Air Force. One family became locally celebrated for having nine people in uniform by 1943, seven of whom were in the Army; but not a single Petch had joined the Fusiliers. Tom Perkins had come home from Gallipoli, where he was wounded by a bayonet thrust, to a wife and three small sons, and when the call to arms again rang round the town the boys joined up, but not in their father's old regiment. One became a sailor, one an airman, and the solitary soldier did his time in the distinctly unglamorous Pioneer Corps. The Rector of Bury had two sons in the Second World War, but one of the Hornby boys was commissioned in the King's Royal Rifle Corps, the other in the Navy. Other ranks as well as officers had a certain amount of choice in deciding where they would spend their conscripted war, and in Bury the Navy and the RAF were consistently more popular than

the Army, partly because they seemed so much more exciting tech-
nologically, with high-performance machinery under their control,
compared with – at best – lumbering tanks and static artillery. But
the reasons why a majority of local Army recruits preferred to soldier with regiments and corps other than the unit they were most
familiar with can only be surmised. It seems unlikely that a blood
descendant of the Gallipoli tradition would go to the Pioneer Corps
– whose badge was symbolically a pick and shovel – unless he
had been discouraged from following his father by the older man's
experience in the First World War; and perhaps in its aftermath.

Nothing that befell the Lancashire Fusiliers in the war was
remotely comparable to their experience at Gallipoli. Four battalions were involved in the epic retreat to Dunkirk and one of
them, the 1st/8th, was almost destroyed in covering the withdrawal
of the British Expeditionary Force and the French from the beaches.
Other units of the regiment fought throughout the campaign in
Burma, some of them in Wingate's irregular Chindit force which
became famous for its activities in the jungle behind the Japanese
lines. The most sustained active service was undertaken by the 2nd
Battalion, which was at Dunkirk and then fought its way across
North Africa and up the length of Italy, to finish the war as part of
the British army of occupation in Austria. It claimed to be the most
highly decorated battalion in the Army by 1945, with one VC, four
DCMs, twenty-three MCs, thirty-eight MMs, one MBE, fifteen
Mentions in Despatches, two American Bronze Stars and one
American DSC; the only Victoria Cross awarded to the regiment
was won by Fusilier Frank Jefferson in the assault on Monte Cassino
in 1944. If the regiment now failed to match the collective renown
of the earlier generation, it was more than compensated by sustain-
ing only a fraction of the Great War casualties. The Fusiliers lost
13,642 men then. This time, no more than 1,285 of its soldiers
didn't come home.

Nor was there the same note of triumphalism in the depot town
at the end of this war, as had marked the Armistice in 1918. There
was public rejoicing when the war in Europe ended in May 1945,
and again when the Japanese surrendered three months later. Bonfires were lit and flags were waved, as before; but no one called for
the humiliation of the enemy, as had happened in 1918. Instead,
Hugh Hornby invited his congregation in the Parish Church to
consider the damage done to Germany by Hitlerism, before

anything else. "Germany was once a country of great scholars, philosophers, poets and theologians," he said. "It has produced none of these lately, nor is it likely to do for a generation or more to come, for every scrap of spontaneity and originality has been crushed and ground into the pulp of uniformity by the weight of a ruthless and soul-destroying machine." German prisoners of war were quartered in an old mill not far from where the Rector spoke, and they were to remain there for another eighteen months or so, before being allowed to return home. But soon after VE Day, a process of rehabilitation was begun, as they were gradually and very carefully allowed to become acquainted with the English community. They were invited to a service in a church near the camp, and on the first Sunday of their attendance, the vicar addressed them as soldiers of the German army, the second as fellow Christians. Eventually, they were allowed to accept invitations from local families for Christmas dinner, and they could travel up to five miles from the camp without escort. Some English found this regime intolerable, among them a Mr James Kenyon, a millowner who had been educated at Eton and Cambridge and had been an Army captain until 1945, and who declared that the German prisoners "are not little heroes . . . They do not deserve the attention of English girls who go and hang round their prison camps." To the end of their stay in Lancashire, the POWs were forbidden to enter pubs, cinemas or restaurants, or to use public transport, or to watch football matches. But most people in Bury, judging by the mail received by the vicar who invited the prisoners into his church, were in favour of treating the Germans decently. A Victory Parade through the town was abandoned after only one third of the ex-servicemen's and youth organisations bothered to answer the civic invitations to take part.

Yet the Fusiliers were still exalted locally. Some months before the war ended, the town council decided to award the Freedom of the borough to the regiment; a distinction made only fourteen times earlier in Bury's history, and never before except to an individual. In this case, it was solemnly declared, "the Council do confer by Deed upon the Lancashire Fusiliers in perpetuity, the right, title, privilege, honour and distinction of marching through the streets of Bury on all ceremonial occasions with drums beating, bands playing, colours flying and bayonets fixed . . ." On August 3, 1946, the ceremony took place at the Gigg Lane football ground, where thousands watched the Mayor – a woman that year, Alderman Mrs Goodall – hand the scroll establishing the new regimental rights to the Colonel Commandant of the Fusiliers, Major-General Surtees. The failing Lord Derby was there, the last person to be granted the Freedom. And so were five of the regiment's eight living VCs. The three absentees were the survivors of The Six who had won their crosses at Gallipoli. When the ceremony on the football ground was over, the troops marched in all the aforementioned panoply up the Manchester Road and through the centre of the town, then out again on the other side to the Wellington Barracks. Almost every yard of the way saw crowds standing two and three deep on the pavements, to cheer the soldiers on as they swung past. The old mystique still held, and not only on occasions of ritual and celebration. In 1950, the Bury magistrates fined an old soldier £100 for receiving a quantity of stolen cloth from George Horridge's print works, and told him that only his record in the First World War had saved him from imprisonment. He'd been awarded the DCM after attacking a machine-gun singlehanded on the Somme, and at the time his commanding officer had said that he ought to have been given the VC.

The tradition which bound Bury to the Lancashire Fusiliers was safe, in spite of changed recruitments, as long as the regiment continued to make its home in the town and was perpetually visible there. The public displays that commemorated Minden, Inkerman and Gallipoli were the best insurance against local forgetfulness, but even without these there were reminders throughout every year. There was the familiar starkness of the Barracks, for example, which busload after busload of people passed each day; and the sentry who was always on duty beside Lutyens's little cenotaph; and the periodic sound of small-arms fire from the range somewhere within, which reverberated briskly round the adjacent council housing estate and produced a syncopated echo from its grimy red-brick walls. There were young men in khaki, wearing the familiar badge and hackle in their caps, moving about the town off duty, glimpsed at a bus stop, in a cinema queue, across a market stall, courting Bury girls.

The ties might be looser than before, but they would not be broken as long as there were people alive who still remembered the Great War, even if they hadn't served in it, and these would be numerous until three full decades after the Second World War had passed. This wasn't merely a matter of elderly men meeting formally, though it certainly included that. "There was a grand spirit then," said one of the Old Contemptibles at their annual dinner in 1950, of the time when the Kaiser had patronised them, "and we lived together as brothers. We have been told we are getting too old and should enlist members of other associations to keep us young. We came into being in a burst and, like old soldiers should do, will slowly fade away. Good luck to the last man." The ties were also in the safekeeping of old men who joined no organisation, preferring to spend their time trundling their woods on the bowling greens of the town; or who played a quiet game of dominoes over no more than two pints in the Wellington, the pub alongside the Barracks, on the one night of the week they were allowed, and could afford, to call their own. Their middle-aged children knew all about Gallipoli, for they too had lived through that time, vicariously. The grandchildren were also aware, introduced to the tradition by the old men in infancy, in apostolic succession, by an informal yet very deliberate laying on of hands.

Some few of these young people, the last generation to be born into the traditions of British imperialism which the Lancashire Fusiliers in part represented and had always upheld, would also hand on the tablets. The ones most conscious of such a responsibility were the Grammar School boys, whose corps had never been more flourishingly successful than in the years after the Second World War. It had undergone certain nominal and decorative changes since 1939, having first been translated from the OTC to the Junior Training Corps, and then to the Cadet Corps, which is how it had begun back in 1892; and the outbreak of war had also seen it abandoning its traditional peaked cap and puttees for the modern soldier's dress of forage cap, then beret, on the head, and webbing anklets which had to be blancoed the statutory shade known as Khaki Green No 3. When they subsequently received permission to wear the famous hackle of the local regiment, the boy soldiers of the Grammar School were indistinguishable, except for their age, from mature Lancashire Fusiliers. At their annual inspection in 1954, 180 of them turned out, which was the biggest muster in the history of the corps. Twelve months later there were 208, which was eighty-three per cent of the boys in the school who were eligible to join: only thirty preferred to spend the weekly corps time in extra study of their academic subjects. Colonel C. G.

Howarth of the Adjutant-General's staff subsequently told the cadets precisely what was the point of all the smartness and drill movements they learned to execute when on parade. "It is vital," he said, "that each soldier has an instinctive reaction to an order. The trained soldier doesn't have to think." This was a strange thing to hear at a school which prided itself on the Classical scholarships and exhibitions it annually secured for its pupils in the universities of Oxford and Cambridge, many of these places going to lads who were sergeants in the corps.

The tradition was secure, the mystique still held, the mythology was assured of continuity . . . even though Bury in these years was at the start of a transformation more complete than at any other time in its history; except once. What began to happen to the old milltown shortly after the Second World War was over, was an upheaval as dramatic as the Industrial Revolution had been; and in many ways it was a reversal of those dynamic processes and their residual effect on everything that touched the community. It was inseparable from the end of Empire, which was presaged by the war, though at least one element in the transformation originated in events that occurred half a world away and a long time before. For a few years after 1945 the local cotton industry prospered so much that there was actually a shortage of trained operatives to sustain the demand for fabrics at home and overseas, which led to another slogan directed at the civilian populace – Britain's Bread Hangs by Lancashire's Thread. But the boom was short-lived and by 1952 the industry was again in a recession from which, this time, it never recovered. The textile mills of Bombay, which had been built by Indians in the nineteenth century to take advantage of a cotton glut that had been encouraged to assist Lancashire, had prospered exceedingly and had multiplied. They could produce cotton goods much more cheaply than any mill in Lancashire; and so could other mills elsewhere in the East. Ironically, this cheap labour in the Orient was greatly assisted by having at its disposal the most up-to-date textile machinery, which some Lancashire factories were busily turning out for export within a few miles of weaving sheds that were, one after the other, paying off their workers and closing down. The final rite of the old cotton industry in the North of England was delayed until the very end of 1968, when the Royal Exchange in Manchester closed its doors for the last time, its Cotton Prices indicator high above the cavernous room bearing the latest figures from Khartoum, Alexandria, New Orleans that no longered mattered in Lancashire. The board, with those same figures, is still there for anyone to see. With a fine touch of imagination it was left in place when the Royal Exchange was adapted a few years later for use as a theatre, which now houses one of the finest repertory companies in the land.

One consequence of cotton's decline and ultimate demise was a change in the appearance of Bury and its surroundings. Some of the mills were able to adapt to the manufacture of synthetic fibres and cloths, but the majority either had no future at all or could only survive by changing their purposes completely. They became warehouses for factories newly built from scratch on the most modern lines; or their functions changed from a form of heavy to the lightest of industries; or they occasionally found a new life style as distribution centres for mail-order businesses, full of people sealing envelopes and despatching catalogues. What scarcely any old cotton mill needed in its new lease of life, if it had one, was the original chimney poking high into the sky. There was a great demolition of these as the cotton industry collapsed; sometimes accompanied by the destruction of an entire mill. The town and its immediate surroundings looked significantly different within a very few years. Where there had been thickets of mill chimneys visible in a great arc of perhaps 200 degrees, there were now only sporadic gestures to what had once been there, slender pillars in isolation, with much space in between.

As if to compensate for the loss of these totems, tower blocks housing people began to thrust upwards in some directions and affected the view from Bury, though they were never built inside its boundaries. But many of the old slum properties were bulldozed to make way for something new and more popular, and much less likely to last. Other changes were made to the appearance of the town. The trams disappeared very quickly after the war, and eventually the tramlines were removed, as was almost every vestige of the old cobblestones. Union Square was eradicated as if by some form of pest control, which meant the destruction of the famous herbalist's shop and the even more celebrated premises where the original Bury black puddings were made. These officially authorised acts of vandalism were done in the name of progress, but what the town acquired in exchange for an area where much distinctive character was displayed, where annually its spirit was renewed at the Whit

Walks, was a shopping precinct that might have been located anywhere between Land's End and John o' Groats, or even further
afield, for it was totally devoid of local character, an apotheosis of
the municipally null and void. Other landmarks that were deemed
to have outlasted their time included the Derby Hotel, where the
Dutch lovers consummated their suicide pact in 1899. Arterial
roads were flung this way and that, usually after thick segments of
the borough had been flattened to make way for them, and always
to the consternation of natives who returned to Bury after an
absence of some years and could no longer find their way about its
central thoroughfares.

The one unquestionable improvement that these years of
revamping and renovation conferred hereabouts was in the atmosphere. The collapse of cotton in Lancashire coincided with a Clean
Air Act, which produced the country's first smokeless zone in Manchester, gradually extended to the towns and the countryside
around. By degrees the citizens of Bury became aware not only that
the sulphurous winter fogs which produced darkness at noon were
a thing of the past, but that local visibility all the year round was
now extravagantly increased. The Pennines emerged from man-
made mists like a coastal clifftop revealed to the mariner when a
sea fret rolls back. From the loftiest ground in the borough it was
now possible to see the uplands as far away as Derbyshire for the
first time in a century and a half, and the nearer heights such as
Holcombe Hill seemed in the finest weather to be close enough to
touch. The dramatic reduction in smoke affected the urban attitude
to buildings which were covered with the soot of a hundred years
and more. There was a large-scale cleaning of stonework, which
lightened the general aspect of the town, and the Parish Church
was only one of many prominent structures which were revealed
to be pleasantly tawny beneath their coating of black. Other forms
of pollution were steadily reduced, partly because many of the culprits no longer functioned in the new economy, but increasingly
because a powerful public lobby insisted on ridding the land of its
filth. The biggest gains of all in this part of the North were made
in the rivers and streams, which again ran with water sweet enough
for fish. At Bury Bridge, the Irwell flowed as it had not done for
many generations, without froth, without stains, without a sicken-
ing stench.

The people changed, too. Twenty years after the Cotton Prices board in the Manchester Royal Exchange became irrelevant, it was hard to find anyone in Bury with the exaggerated lip movements of the cotton operative, accustomed to mee-mawing amid the din of the looms. Clogs were just as rarely seen. And although the workers still had to endure the ups and downs of trade their forebears had always known, they had acquired certain material possessions that would have been thought far beyond the reach of their immediate predecessors: by 1967, when the population of the town had risen to 62,750, one third of the families there owned cars. Their political choices were no longer what they had been, either. Three years earlier the always peculiar Tory hegemony in this workaday place had been broken when Bury returned a Labour candidate for the first time in 132 years of general elections; so that after the long sequence of mill-owning squires and businessmen who had enjoyed an easy ride to Westminister, as a foregone conclusion since the First World War, the voters suddenly found themselves represented by someone who described himself as "actor and television personality" – which said as much about the era the town had entered as did the new MP's party allegiance. Other and less tolerable social preferences became noticeable in these times. Swastikas and the old Nazi slogan *Juden Raus* were daubed on the back of the market hall one night, were obliterated by council employees a few hours later, and were not seen again. At the anniversary of the Armistice in 1970, a wooden cross with poppies attached to it at the Central War Memorial was defaced with the words "I Love Drugs". The acknowledgement of Armistice Day had, by then, become perfunctory. The town no longer stopped in its tracks on the stroke of eleven o'clock.

The biggest social change of all was racial. During the last brief boom of the cotton industry immediately after the war, a number of what were then known as displaced persons arrived in Bury from camps in southern England, attracted to the North because there weren't enough local millworkers. The first of them were Ukrainians, Estonians, Latvians, who had been deported from the Soviet Union to Germany in 1942, and who had been further displaced when the Allied armies overran the continent in 1944 and 1945. They were followed by Poles and other refugees from Eastern Europe, who had preferred to start a new life in Great Britain rather than face the rigours of communism. They brought their rivalries as well as their own forms of community life to Bury, and one of

Major General Surtees receives from the Mayor the freedom scroll by which the Fusiliers have "the right, title, privilege and distinction" of marching through the town on ceremonial occasions with drums beating, bands playing, colours flying and bayonets

In 1946, the Lancashire Fusiliers were granted the Freedom of Bury, an honour which had been offered to only a few individuals before. The ceremony was conducted at Gigg Lane, home of the local football club, the only place big enough to accommodate the crowds wishing to be there. Here, in front of the grandstand, the Mayor (Alderman Mrs E. Goodall) and Town Clerk present the ceremonial scroll to the Colonel Commandant of the regiment, Major-General G. Surtees.

The Lancashire Landing Cemetery, just above W Beach, Cape Helles, Gallipoli. Many of the Fusiliers killed on April 25, 1915 are buried here, together with others who lost their lives during the rest of the ill-fated campaign.

BELOW "Wipe away your tears . . . Your sons have become our sons now." Kemal Ataturk's magnanimous message to the grieving mothers of the British Empire, carved in sandstone near Anzac Cove on Gallipoli. The monument is illuminated by the sun each evening, as it goes down across the Aegean Sea.

March-past, Gallipoli Sunday 1987, by men who fought as Lancashire Fusiliers in the Second World War. The three bemedalled figures watching on the left are George Cook, Bob Spencer and George Peake, who fought in the Dardanelles in 1915. On the saluting base itself, in his wheelchair, is Major George Horridge, last surviving Fusilier officer who was at Gallipoli. He died a few months after this photograph was taken.

BELOW Bury Grammar School Founder's Day, 1990. The school cadets, traditionally associated with the Lancashire Fusiliers, on parade at the town's War Memorial outside the Parish Church. Their commanding officer (left), Lieutenant-Colonel G. Bennett, was otherwise Classics master at the school, of which he had himself been a pupil and cadet.

The last of the Gallipoli Fusiliers . . . Gallipoli Sunday 1990. Bob Spencer of Bury (left) on the annual parade. With him is Benny Adams, who also served in the Dardanelles, but with the Manchester Regiment.

these produced a sensational trial which began in the local magistrates' court and ended with a hanging in Strangeways Prison, Manchester: one Yugoslav had murdered another on the railway line up Rossendale, after a quarrel which originated in the war, when they had been on opposite sides during the fighting in the Balkans. By the time this case was over, hundreds of such refugees were no longer displaced persons in Bury, but had become assimilated into the life of its Catholic parishes. The Poles and the Ukrainians especially added a touch of the exotic at the Whit Sunday walks, and here and there throughout the town maintained their own traditions in small but important ways by setting up clubs where they spoke only in their native tongues. Their children, though, grew up with the accents of Lancashire superimposed upon the sibilants and the sharper vowels of the Slav.

It was cotton, and a last turn of the imperial wheel, that brought another immigrant people to the town in the post-war years. In a despairing attempt to beat Bombay and the Chinese at their own game, the Lancashire millowners before finally conceding defeat sought to make what they could from relatively cheap labour recruited in the East, which meant the old British Indian Empire; which, in Bury's case, specifically meant Muslims from what, since 1947, had been Pakistan. Twenty years later, there were about 600 of these people in Bury, who sought permission for the building of the town's first mosque, which would save them having to travel to Rochdale or to Manchester for worship every Friday. Permission was given: with it Bury licensed the most exotic growth of all in its entire history, and one that was laden with the most delicately complicated possibilities for the future, involving greater birthrates than the local norm, more adamant religious zeal, less eagerness to be subsumed in the prevailing culture. In 1967, Ramadan was celebrated for the first time beside the Irwell and the former television personality was sufficiently conscious of his most colourful constituents to visit Karachi and its hinterland as a guest of Pakistan's Government. Yet while Bury's Muslims were at one with Bury's Slavs in wishing simply to live peaceably with their native neighbours, there was one striking difference in the relationship that each enjoyed with the host people. Those of Pakistani origin had settled in a town whose local regiment was once vilified as an invader by some of their ancestors; and whose soldiers for almost a century had belonged, it might be said, to an army of occupation;

in a land that the forefathers of the Muslims, too, had once seized by conquest.

Otherwise, the traditions of the Lancashire Fusiliers, and certainly the mythology of Gallipoli, meant nothing to any of these immigrants, whether they came from Eastern Europe or from the great sub-continent. They meant little enough to many native Lancastrians who had matured in the years after the Second World War, were educated and articulate, resented whatever they identified as high-handed authority, and were eventually in open rebellion against the Army. Their quarrel with the military was over a large tract of moorland, including Holcombe Hill, where the Pennines came nearest to Bury and other communities to the west and south-west of the so-called backbone of England. It was bleak hill country on which sheep had been run for hundreds of years, and it was also very suitable for training soldiers in some of the skills of their profession. The Army had, in fact, used 800 acres of it – one and a quarter square miles – for target practice and other purposes ever since the early years of the twentieth century. In modern times, it had been used in 1940 for the battle training of the Army's first parachutists, who were Lancashire Fusiliers from Bury Barracks. Even more recently, the 1st Battalion of the Fusiliers, together with a unit of the SAS, had blown up some derelict farm buildings which dated from the beginning of the eighteenth century, and were destroyed because they represented an imaginary terrorist hideout. Holcombe Moor and its immediate surroundings could be quite a dangerous place when the Army was letting fly with its ammunition and explosives, and even when it had packed up and gone home. The military were at great pains to warn civilians against picking up strange objects they might come across in their wanderings, in case these were lethal devices that had failed to detonate.

What made the area attractive to the military was partly what appealed to many civilians, too; its wildness and its remoteness from urban life. It was land on which you could sometimes walk for hours without seeing another soul. But there were other things up there that were important to those with a taste for local and natural history. There were at least forty species of bird and other wildlife inhabiting the moor, there was an oak woodland that had been growing and regenerating since prehistoric times, and there was much interesting geology. There was also the stone which marked a resting place in the Middle Ages of pilgrims who were crossing the moors on their way to the Cistercian abbey at Whalley in North Lancashire; and the nineteenth-century tower commemorating Sir Robert Peel. Holcombe Hill figured considerably in the folklore of Bury, because of its Peel connection and because of the celebrations that took place there every Good Friday, when thousands would enjoy themselves if the weather was fine. And for three quarters of a century the military and the civilians had co-existed amicably, side by side. The soldiers hauled up their red flags on training days and the civilians gave them a wide berth: the Army, for its part, respected the public rights of way that had been established by ancient usage across this invaluable wilderness.

The trouble began when the Ministry of Defence announced new by-laws designed to restrict public access near the firing range. At a public meeting called by protesting civilians in 1972, this was denounced as a scandal, and some quite intemperate things were said about the military. One man suggested that if a public walk of protest were held across the disputed land, it was likely that demonstrators would be shot like demonstrators in Ireland: he went on to inveigh against peaceful surroundings "shattered by the rattle of rifle fire and the barbaric shouting of officers' amplified voices." The protests subsided as people recognised the *fait accompli*, and a truce was observed for some years until the Ministry suddenly acquired another 167 acres of land on the edge of the existing training area in 1984. This had the protesters up in arms again, very angry indeed when they discovered that training exercises were being conducted across certain public rights of way. On more than one occasion after this, walkers crossing the moors on public footpaths were turned back by officers, who threatened them with arrest. The civilians now began to organise themselves into an effective pressure group, drawing in support from all parts of Lancashire and even further afield, in their efforts to thwart what increasingly began to look like a mixture of military arrogance and bureaucratic complaisance. Their worst fears were confirmed when the Ministry of Defence dropped its biggest bombshell yet, in the autumn of 1986; it required planning consent to use a further 916 acres of common land on Holcombe Moor for training purposes.

This proved to be one demand too many for the local authorities, who thereupon ranged themselves on the side of the civilian pressure group against their historic partners in the preservation of social stability and the status quo. A public inquiry by the Department of the Environment was arranged as a result of this alliance, and the department's inspector began to hear evidence from all the interested parties in the spring of 1988. Part of this was given on behalf of Bury Council which, for more than a hundred years, had gladly played host to, and had conferred its highest honour upon, a regiment whose heirs stood as adversaries in this matter.* This was, in some respects, the most remarkable and the most unlikely transformation among the many that had overtaken the town in the generation that followed the Second World War. Nor was the old relationship forgotten in the thrust and counter-thrust of argument that went on intermittently for the best part of a year. The Army did not hesitate to use the mythology to assist its case. A Colonel John Rice made the point one day that he was the officer in charge of local Territorial units which "carry on the proud traditions of the Lancashire Fusiliers".

But the regiment had been extinct for twenty years by then. The first rumours of its mortality were heard during the decade after the Second World War, when a reorganisation of the entire Army, comparable to the rearrangements ordered by Cardwell and Haldane, were foretold. Once again there were to be amalgamations, disbandments, and a renaming of parts in order to produce a renewed and reinvigorated fighting force better fitted to meet the menace of the Cold War in a nuclear age. The Colonel of the Lancashire Fusiliers, Brigadier P. G. Bamford, assured his soldiers that the regiment would not be destroyed by the reorganisation, that it would retain its identity, but this sounded like wishful thinking, as indeed it was. At the beginning of 1959, the Wellington Barracks staged one of those ceremonies that the armed forces of the British have always handled perfectly, with a fine instinct for symbolism married to an exhibition of controlled pomp and circumstance that

---

* The inquiry was concluded at the end of October 1988 but the inspector's report was not published until July 1991, eighteen months after the Army announced that it had gone ahead with purchasing the moor from its owner, Lord Clitheroe. With one small qualification, the report supported the military position against the civilian opposition, but by then the military position had changed; the Army now declared its intention of using the land more often than it had stated at the inquiry. On publication of the report, objectors were given just three weeks in which to make their own fresh representations before the matter was finally closed by the Secretary of State for the Environment.

is never allowed to stray in the direction of pantomime. The event on this occasion was modelled on the most famous of all British military rituals, Trooping the Colour, but on this cold and snow-bound day it was a trooping of the badges through the drawn-up ranks of men.

A sergeant of the Lancashire Fusiliers carried the regiment's traditional badge – the flaming grenade with the superimposed sphinx and the suspended scroll – on a silk cushion. On his left was a sergeant of the Royal Northumberland Fusiliers, on his right a sergeant of the Royal Fusiliers (City of London Regiment) similarly burdened with badges of their own. Solemnly and with cushions held before them, like magi bearing gifts, the three NCOs slow-marched along the files to the strains of "Auld Lang Syne", while the troops presented arms, officers flourished their swords in salute, and Old Comrades of the Fusiliers removed their hats in respect. John Grimshaw VC had come to Bury for this ceremony, which marked the amalgamation of the three Fusilier regiments, whose shared cap badge in future was to be a flaming grenade with St George and the Dragon surrounded by a laurel wreath: the Lancastrians among them, however, would still be allowed to wear the primrose hackle awarded by Edward VII after the disaster at Spion Kop in 1900. It was said at the time that the amalgamation would not be completed for another two years, when the three units would at last be quartered as one in a new depot – formerly a wartime base used by the RAF for its barrage balloons – at Sutton Coldfield in the Midlands. Some eighteen months later it was stated that the local element in the new organism would continue to recruit in Lancashire, which was at present supplying the regiment with a dozen new men a month, though the authorities were looking for about fifteen, in order to keep numbers up to strength. At the beginning of November 1960, sixty recruits passed out of the Barracks before being posted to the 1st Battalion, serving with the British Army of the Rhine in Osnabruck. They were the last young men in history to be trained for service with the Lancashire Fusiliers. Five months later the regiment marched through the town before large crowds in an official farewell that ended with a civic luncheon in the Drill Hall, the only building in the borough that could accommodate everyone wanting to be there.

The forecasts were not completely accurate. The new Royal Regiment of Fusiliers did not, in fact, officially exist until St George's

Day 1968; and when its advent was signalled it consisted of four, and not three, traditional regiments parcelled into one. To the original trio who had been reconciled to losing their separate identities for several years, was added the Royal Warwickshire Fusiliers, which seemed no more than common sense, when Sutton Coldfield lay in Warwickshire. For some reason never explained publicly, the indulgence granted the Lancastrians in the matter of a distinctive flourish was withdrawn. Everyone would wear a hackle in his cap in future, but it would be the red and white favour which had always been characteristic of the senior regiment of the four, the Royal Northumberland Fusiliers, which was raised in 1674 as the Irish Regiment, becoming the 5th Regiment of Foot in 1751. Yet even the birth day of the new amalgamation did not draw together all the loose ends left by those varied histories and parallel traditions.

The spring of 1967 had seen the end of Bury's very own battalion of the Lancashire Fusiliers, the 5th, which had come into existence as a result of Haldane's reforms and had shared the glory of Gallipoli. On a sharp sunny day in March that year, the Territorials proudly marched through the town as the Freemen they collectively were, with their bands playing, their drums beating, their bayonets fixed, their colours flying, with four Pioneer sergeants going before in white buckskin aprons and with silver axes carried on the shoulder, four mounted policemen riding ahead of them. Again the crowds turned out to choke the centre of the town, and the Mayor took the salute. The battalion had already given a farewell supper to their civilian staff at the Drill Hall, presenting each with an engraved silver pencil as a remembrancer of times past. Later, their officers held a farewell dinner of their own. "You could say," said one of them to an enquirer, "that we are quietly disappearing. It is a little bit ghost-like." But the disappearing took some time yet. There was one more ceremony to perform, and its turn did not come until two full years after the Royal Regiment of Fusiliers was born. Then, at Gallipoli Sunday in 1970, the colours of the 5th Battalion of the old regiment, together with those of the also disbanded 1st, were paraded through the streets of Bury for the last time and laid up in their final resting place at the Parish Church.

There remained the matter of the Barracks and the Drill Hall, very specialised buildings that were evidently no longer required for their original purposes. Ever since the first rumours about the future of the Fusiliers had circulated, there had been talk about ways and means of adapting them for civilian utility. The first suggestion was that the Barracks might become an adjunct of Strangeways Prison, Manchester, but this was quickly discounted. Then rumour said it might become an old folks' home, or be turned into a factory, though no one had any idea what this might produce. Later still there were said to be plans to auction the whole rambling structure, together with the fifteen acres of land it enclosed. Eventually, the Corporation paid £20,000 for the land, on which it built some houses, the rest being turned into playing fields. The old nineteenth-century buildings, which had been so austerely familiar to several generations of people, were demolished; apart from one small block. This was retained in order to house the secretariat that in the foreseeable future would be necessary to attend to the ongoing business of the Fusiliers' Compassionate Fund, and to other military affairs in the locality. The block also sheltered the regimental museum, and the precious possessions that had been accumulated since William of Orange's time. One other thing remained at the famous outpost along the Bolton road, and that was Edwin Lutyens's white memorial, which was shifted a few yards from its original position to stand within the small emplacement that was left to posterity as a token of what had earlier been there. Just over a mile away, where the town's medieval castle had once stood, the Drill Hall was untouched by the new dispositions of the military. For the Army had not finished with Bury yet.

# 11

# A Distant Trumpet

Nor was Bury inclined to let go of the military. In spite of the transformations that had overtaken both in the post-war years, and in spite of the differences that were to arise over Holcombe Moor, there remained an identity of interest that each was reluctant to dissolve. Just over six years after the Royal Regiment of Fusiliers was born, the town repeated the gesture it had made once before to a body of troops, and offered their successors the Freedom of the borough. To coincide with this, the municipal art gallery mounted an exhibition which portrayed three centuries of history that – in Northumberland, in Warwickshire, in the City of London and (not least) in Lancashire – had preceded the fusion in Sutton Coldfield. As in 1946, large crowds gathered to watch the colourful display in and around the Town Hall and the Parish Church; for the new Freedom was astutely linked by someone in authority to Gallipoli Sunday. At an appropriate moment in the proceedings, the Colonel of the Regiment, General Sir Kenneth Darling, thought it necessary to remark that "In these days the British soldier and all he stands for is taken for granted by far too many people in this country. Whatever duties he is called upon to discharge, he does so with good humour, tolerance and professionalism that no other army in the world can match." He was thinking, as much as anything, of the Army's role in Ulster, where the 2nd Battalion of Sir Kenneth's regiment had already put in four tours of duty. As it had done periodically ever since the days of Sir Robert Peyton's Regiment of Foot, and through the times of the Lancashire Fusiliers, Ireland again haunted the English. There was strict security throughout that weekend of the Freedom and Gallipoli Sunday in 1974, and checks were made in the church, the Town Hall and the Drill Hall, for any bombs the IRA might have planted there.

The most treasured talismans of those three centuries remained for safekeeping permanently in the town, in what was left of the Barracks, where a notice defiantly announced that here still was the last stamping ground of XX The Lancashire Fusiliers. Lovingly tended and carefully displayed in its museum were the tangible mementoes of, as Alexander Kinglake once wrote, the sacred historic tradition of that regiment. Here was the sash that James Wolfe bequeathed to his fellow officers of the XXth Foot, and the strands of grey hair – there were scarcely enough to be called a lock – that had been snipped from Napoleon's head on St Helena; and a report of the autopsy performed on the Emperor by the regiment's Dr Arnott and four other surgeons – "On a superficial view the body appeared very fat . . . upwards of one inch thick over the Sternum and one inch and a half over the Abdomen . . ." Here was a portrait of Lady Harriet Acland, pregnant wife of a wounded major in the XXth at Saratoga in 1781: she was treated gallantly by the American General Gates, who remarked of her that "She is the most amiable, delicate piece of quality you ever beheld"; and she looked just so in her picture, all winsome and demure, like a china doll from Dresden. Here, too, were the fragments of colours, too fragile to hang with the others in the Parish Church, presented by the Duke of Wellington and carried by the regiment through the Crimean War and the Indian Mutiny. The elaborate silver cask containing the document conferring the Freedom of the borough on the Lancashire Fusiliers lay in the museum. So did many mementoes of Gallipoli, among them a bugle belonging to a Fusilier, which some Anzacs found beside his body in no man's land and kindly handed back to the "bloody Poms" instead of souveniring it, as they might have been expected to. There were also a few medals which had been issued to Turkish troops for their gallantry in the Dardanelles.

A whole room was full of medals won down the years by soldiers from Lancashire – row after row of silver and bronze, tin and brass shapes attached to ribbons which gaudily and discreetly ran through every colour in the spectrum, together with many shades in between. Here were decorations which meant preposterous bravery by individuals in some of the most dreadful encounters human beings have ever inflicted on each other, and here were baubles which were handed out with the rations to every man who had slogged his way through yet another godforsaken campaign in some distant and deeply unappreciated part of the globe. Pre-eminent among the former were three Victoria Crosses, all awarded in the Great War for Civilisation (as one of the most common 1914–18 campaign medals styled it). One was won by Private J. Lynn, of the 2nd Battalion, at Ypres in 1915, after holding up the German advance in the middle of a gas attack, from the effects of which he died the following day. Another had belonged to Sergeant J. Clarke, of the 15th Battalion, who attacked machine-guns at Happergarbe in northern France in 1918, took prisoners and survived the war. The third was one of the Six VCs from Gallipoli, earned by Sergeant Stubbs before he was killed on the day of the Lancashire Landing. His sister, a Miss Stubbs, had approached the Fusiliers in 1964, saying that she wanted to sell the cross to the sergeant's old regiment. The Fusiliers pointed out that, while they'd gladly buy it, she might get more than twice the amount they could offer from one of the big London dealers. She insisted that she wanted the regiment to have it; so the Fusiliers increased the amount they had mentioned and bought it for £300.

Of the other five Gallipoli Victoria Crosses, only two – those won by Grimshaw and Keneally – were never put up for sale. Willis's VC appeared in an auctioneer's catalogue in January 1967, within a year of his death, when it was listed at £950. Sergeant Richards's cross was sold for £10,000 at a London auction in February 1984. Bromley's decoration was the one which attracted the speculators most of all, though it was not valued as highly as the Richards VC. It was first sold in 1984 for £1,500 and was listed at £1,700 in another auction just over a year later. In November 1985, Christie's offered it for £7,500, but it failed to attract a buyer at that price.

The rarest keepsakes of all were locked in the memories of ageing people who had known the time of Gallipoli. They were a declining number who sometimes did not live in the town any more. Fifty miles away on the coast, where many rivers flow out of the hills into the moody shoalwaters of Morecambe Bay, a white-haired old lady could picture as clearly as if it had just happened, the terrifying moment when her mother collapsed at the news that her father would not be coming home from the Dardanelles. Alice Scowcroft then, she was Alice Mitchell now, with grown-up children of her own, contented, secure, but marked for life by the tragedy that had overtaken her family when she was only six. The thrift that her mother Sarah had needed to practise on a widow's pension and what little else she could earn, had stood Alice in good stead when she herself was married and running a boarding house for holidaymakers from the inland towns of Lancashire: she instinctively knew about value for money, and how not to let anything go to waste, and how to plan a domestic economy that never broke down. But there was pain, still, when she recalled her mother's suffering and devotion to the memory of James Scowcroft. The little family never could face the idea of watching the soldiers march at Gallipoli Sunday. Instead, when Alice got married, Sarah took her bouquet after the couple had left on their honeymoon, and laid it on the War Memorial outside the Parish Church. Alice's own grief had been increasingly focused on her mother's because that did not end until the day Sarah died; and because Alice's memories of James had been so relatively short.

Her last image of him was when she came home from school and saw him walking towards her with his uniform over his arm. He was on his way back from the Drill Hall, where he'd just reported for duty with the 1st/5th, and he picked her up and gave her a big hug. After that, everything was blank. In her later years, retired and able to savour the tranquil loveliness of the estuary beside her home, Alice would occasionally remember that parting wistfully – it was now no worse than that – and wonder where her mother had got the strength to carry on. Sometimes she would go to the drawer where small things had been kept carefully, so that they could always be found; some Cairo tram tickets, a Christmas menu from the Grand Continental Hotel, and a birthday card for February 1915, with "6 lugs" beneath a big kiss in her father's hand. She would run her fingers over these fragile slips of paper and feel comforted by their touch before putting them away again. Then she would clear her throat and go to the front window, and look out to see whether the tide was running yet, and if anyone was up to his bare knees in the water, treading for flukes.

As Bob Spencer got older, his memories of being recruited into the 1st/7th because the 1st/5th was full up, began to fade, and so did almost everything that happened to him at Gallipoli. He could recall being wounded in the left leg, but not what it felt like or just where he was when it happened; and he remembered nothing of his last few months in the Dardanelles, after returning from hospital in Egypt. Likewise, his recollection of the remainder of the war was dim. He spent a lot of it in Italy, he seemed to remember, but he wasn't all that sure. He never did have much taste for foreign parts. He had been glad to be home, to be treated as good old Bob because he'd been with the Fusiliers at Gallipoli, but especially to resume civilian life and eventually to win those prizes in London for the bread he baked. In his middle years he became diabetic, so he had to get a "sit-down job" as a clerk, which was how he spent the Second World War. Until he was an old man he had only once been to Gallipoli Sunday. That had been many years earlier, and because his brother – a sailor in the Great War – had given it a miss, Bob had felt a bit out of place and decided not to repeat the experience. For much the same reason, he never became involved in the Old Comrades Association of the Fusiliers. His brother had never been inclined to join ex-servicemen's organisations, so Bob had left them alone, too. He was essentially a reticent man, never the sort to be one of the boys. Poor Billy Schofield, who died under the walls of Krithia, was the only best friend Bob ever had. It may have been loneliness that tempted him to try Gallipoli Sunday again. His sisters and his brother were dead, and he was living by himself in the house from which, so long ago, he had gone forth innocently and nervously to war. In the mid-eighties, when he himself was approaching his ninetieth year, he suddenly felt like taking part in Gallipoli Sunday again. At once he found himself surrounded by the warmth he had known when he returned from the war; but that hadn't lasted long. This time the warmth continued, was palpable every year in the cheering of the crowds and in the fellowship offered by and to the other old sweats. Moreover, the warmth could be felt at times in between the anniversaries, because the regiment kept in touch with him now that it had found him again; had, very deliberately, re-recruited him. It also sent him invitations to the buffet luncheon in the Drill Hall that always followed the big parade. Bob Spencer had waited long for this sensation of being sought and wanted ardently. It was nothing less than a consummation of his life.

George Horridge had almost total recall of everything that had happened to him, even when he was otherwise so frail that he had to be carried up the stairs to the officers' mess at the Drill Hall lunch. He could recall things that had happened at Uppingham, where a much older boy called Tomlin had befriended him on his first day at the school, inviting Horridge minor to walk up to the football field with him to watch the game: "perhaps the kindest act ever done to me." Tomlin was captain of football and cricket, and remained Horridge's idol for the rest of the Bury man's life. He was killed in the carnage of the Western Front, which caused his protégé to say, nearly three quarters of a century later, that "men like Tomlin are too good to escape death in a world war". George Horridge had not so many more years to look forward to himself when he said that, an elegantly tall and thin man, become a little bent with age, who would sit, sometimes with his Lancashire County Cricket Club cap (Second XI) on his balding white pate, and remember things about Gallipoli with the utmost clarity.

He was haunted especially by the day he and young Parks went to bring in the wounded soldier of the Manchester Regiment from no man's land; and by a consequence of this decency. At the time, Horridge had clearly recognised his responsibility to rescue the man, at peril to his own life, and had acted on that instinct without hesitating much. But "as soon as I was hit I stopped thinking about the Manchester soldier, so I hadn't really been thinking about him; I'd merely satisfied my own conscience. And I'm afraid that was what mattered most." He had wrestled with this moral dilemma ever since; also with the part that Providence played in his life at that time. He had never been able to rid himself of the certainty that, had he not risked his life on that errand of mercy and been wounded as a result, he would have died a couple of days later. On June 6, 1915, when George Horridge was bound for medical treatment in Egypt, his platoon was enfiladed in a trench by machine-gun fire and many men, including Alice Mitchell's father James, were killed. "Being an officer and unusually tall, my chances of survival would have been small." More than seven decades of his life, he was convinced, had been spent in extra time; but they had condemned him for ever to stand apart from and below the heroic wraith of Tomlin. That also haunted him.

There was a continuity, represented in part by such old people who could tell of Gallipoli and the rest of the Great War, that many others in the town were reluctant to break. These, military and civilians alike, clung to whatever could be invoked or created to conjure up the mythology and renew its vitality in each generation.

This was something other than, as well as, the military need for icons to attract recruits, or the need that some veterans of all wars have to relive their most intensely exhilarating hours. It was as if some people believed that this community at the foot of Rossendale would lose all sense of its old identity if it let the matter of Gallipoli drop. One of the casualties of the reorganisation that produced the amalgamated regiment was the band of the old 5th Battalion of the Lancashire Fusiliers, Bury's own. Its military connection was severed in 1967, but its members continued to play privately as civilian musicians without Territorial obligations. Four years after the disbandment they rearranged themselves yet again as the official band of the Fusiliers Association (until 1960 the Old Comrades) and held a practice every Wednesday night throughout the year in the Drill Hall, the traditional Territorial HQ. Both they and the Army wished to be related again.

The need for such continuity was not confined to Bury, as the history of the Gallipoli Association demonstrated. From time to time since 1915, there had been suggestions that some such body should be founded, but they had all come to naught. George Horridge tried to start one after he had revisited the Dardanelles with his wife in 1934, but it was stillborn. There had been associations of various units that had fought at Gallipoli and elsewhere, such as the Twenty-Ninth Division's and the Royal Naval Division's; and these in due course had been wound up as their members died or withdrew. In 1969, however, Major E. H. W. Banner, who was a man of Kent, not Lancashire, decided that there ought to be a body whose aim was to preserve the memory of that campaign alone. "In these days when even some second-war associations are fading away," he wrote, "history is being made by the foundation of this association fifty-four years after the campaign, a sign that the Dardanelles-Gallipoli saga, that epic campaign with its naval action followed by successful landings, but with indeterminate results, is an everlasting nostalgic memory to those who took part in it over half a century ago." The modest hope of its founder was for one hundred members to subscribe, but it soon attracted many more than that, including sixty-two men who had actually fought on the peninsula. They were not all British ex-servicemen. The Gallipoli Association in 1969 opened its fellowship to, among others, anyone who had been there in 1915, in any capacity. Its membership, therefore, included from the start a number of old Anzacs and even a sprinkling of Turks, who were evidently as nostalgic for this episode as any militarised Englishman.*

But the feeling for Gallipoli and for continuity was particularly strong in Bury, where the anniversary was kept as it was kept nowhere else in Britain outside Westminster Abbey; and there the occasion honoured the Anzacs above all. As always, the focal point in the North of England remained Bury Parish Church, even when this had ceased to be a garrison church because there had ceased to be a regiment known as the Lancashire Fusiliers. In other ways, too, the principal Anglican place of worship in the town had changed over the years. Its musical tradition had declined until its choir was no more distinguished than a dozen others in the neighbourhood. Its priests could no longer expect preferment, the last of them to achieve it having left in 1966 to become Dean of Peterborough. His successor was a man of patently robust faith, with a high reputation as a fund-raiser and a knack of making his congregations laugh at jokes delivered with gusto from the pulpit; which were not among the talents that Charles Hill or Hugh Hornby had ever cultivated. But this Rector of Bury, J. Reginald Smith, also had a fine feeling for the military tradition he had inherited. Within five years of his induction yet another memorial was unveiled in his church, to all who had served in the Lancashire Fusiliers throughout its history, lately terminated. In 1982, with the Falklands War in full swing, Canon Smith was minded to mount his pulpit on Gallipoli Sunday and to declare in ringing tones; "Here we are, sixty-seven glorious years later, and once again our forces are going forward to protect those we care for against the oppressor. We pray for peace, but our duty is to protect our responsibilities . . ." The old regimental banners of the Lancashire Fusiliers no longer hung high above the congregation from the clere-story of the nave, having been more discreetly deployed from the lower ceiling of the side aisles; but the spirit was still in place.

The thrust of the anniversary service subtly shifted over the years. What had once been a memorial to the part the Lancashire

* In due course the Gallipoli Association devised a tie for its members, maybe in compensation for the campaign medal and ribbon that George V forbade. It had wide green bands to represent the land of Gallipoli and blue-grey ones for the waters of the Dardanelles. There were also thin stripes of navy blue and scarlet for the services.

Fusiliers played at Gallipoli, and to nothing else, was already more widely focused even before 1968. At some point after the Second World War, although Gallipoli remained the excuse for this sanctifying act, the wording of some prayers was altered to take account of the regiment's more recent activities. After the amalgamation, this process continued until eventually there was no mention at all of Gallipoli on the service sheets printed for the congregations each year on the nearest Sunday to April 25. The occasion had become the "Annual Commemoration Service. XX The Lancashire Fusiliers", but the Regimental Collect which Hugh Hornby composed shortly after coming to Bury had been modified to invoke divine guidance for the Royal Regiment of Fusiliers instead. Otherwise, the form of the service remained more or less intact, beginning with a colour party bringing banners to be laid on the altar, and ending with that same Last Post and Reveille which had made the flesh creep in the building each year for most of the twentieth century. For years, the two climactic calls had been sounded on a silver bugle which was presented to the Lancashire Fusiliers by the fifth HMS *Euryalus*, to commemorate the renewed relationship between the regiment and cruisers bearing that name, during the Siege of Malta in 1941–43. There was some variation in the hymns from time to time, but all the old stalwarts remained unchanged. "Onward, Christian Soldiers" continued to make the walls vibrate as the band of the Fusiliers Association encouraged both choir and congregation to open their lungs, whether they were tone deaf or not. "O Valiant Hearts" still brought a lump to many a throat, but there was now no Lord Derby to weep at the offertory. The 18th Earl, never having owned property in this part of Lancashire, lacked the ties that had always bound his grandfather closely to this place and he did not often visit the town, even less frequently attending the annual homage to its heroic past.

For all the liturgical and other adjustments, however, this remained Gallipoli Sunday in the local imagination, rather than some convenient neologism. That is how it was still referred to in the public prints and in the speech of south-east Lancashire. This was in spite of the fact that, as the years wore on, the local newspaper felt it necessary to explain its significance to readers who had not received the tablets from the generation before (". . . This epic display of courage happened seventy-two years ago and every year a crowd gathers in the Bury town centre to witness an emotional parade which ensures that the dead of the past are never for-gotten . . .") An incalculable number of citizens were in no need of such explanations, even unto the third generation after the cam-paign in the Dardanelles. As for civic leaders, they aided and abetted the military resolve to keep the mythology in good repair by their unfailing presence year after year. The Mayor of Bury would have been disgraced had he not turned out in his chain of office, and local Members of Parliament would have been thought seriously lacking in political acumen had they not ensured that they were on show, too, on this day. But these were not the only public figures who, as the years advanced, regarded it as a duty to attend the ceremony. The year before the Lancashire Fusiliers disbanded, no fewer than seventeen mayors and other council heads were at the service and the march-past afterwards; and although that figure was never repeated, the number scarcely ever fell below half a dozen.

The church was always packed with scores of the virile young, and the march-past afterwards never failed to include its quota of Army, Sea and Air Cadets: yet this became pre-eminently a salute to the bravery and comradeship of creaking and dwindling veterans. For weeks before April 25, old men for miles around removed a row of beribboned medals from the ancient Gold Flake tin, or wherever they kept it wrapped in tissue paper, and began to rub away the traces of tarnish that had appeared since the previous year. Closer to the event there would be a deal of pernickety clothes-brushing, as if for a kit inspection, in addition to the now daily chore of polishing. These were men who, whatever life had or had not given them in the decades since 1915, never failed to respond to this trumpet call as best they could, out of a recollected discipline, and out of self-respect. They were going on parade again, and they wanted to look as good as they could, in spite of an inability now to get that arm up to shoulder height, or a slight unsteadiness at the quick march. There was a tune the band played every year after the Second World War, and it was meant for these old men alone, who could recite the words by heart, as fewer and fewer of the people watching them were able to:

> Where are the boys of the old brigade
> Who fought with us side by side?
> Shoulder to shoulder and blade by blade,
> Fought till they fell and died.

Who so ready and undismayed?
Who so merry and true?
Where are the boys of the old brigade,
Where are the lads we knew?
Steadily, shoulder to shoulder,
Steadily, blade by blade,
Ready and strong,
Marching along,
The boys of the old brigade.*

A full decade after the Second World War, there were fifty members of the 1st Battalion who had been at the Lancashire Landing and had survived to attend Gallipoli Sunday that year. One of them had become Alderman William Elliott and was to be Mayor of Bury in 1957, when his official valet was Peter Rowley, who had also been at Gallipoli, but as a Territorial. There were then eighty-four members of the 1st/5th Battalion still able to attend the annual parade; and at a Drill Hall luncheon later that year, Elliott told these men, who had gone ashore a few days after the Regular Fusiliers had taken such punishment on W Beach, "We were glad to see you when you arrived." As well as a warm expression of gratitude, this was a gentle reminder of precedence. For as the survivors became old men, the pecking order in the regiment, as reflected in the parade, began to matter to them more and more. Always it had been acknowledged that pride of place should go to the survivors of the 1st Battalion, that they should march at the head of the column, to receive a tribute from the crowd that they, more than anyone else, deserved. But the old soldiers of the 1st/5th and other Territorials who had also fought with distinction on the peninsula, were originally mixed up with Old Comrades who had never been near the Dardanelles. This irked George Horridge, for one; so much so that eventually he wrote to the commanding officer of the Fusiliers and asked that a separation of the 1st/5th and other Gallipoli Terriers should be made from those who had fought only on the Western Front or in Macedonia, so that the Gallipoli men might march where honour demanded, immediately in the wake of the 1st Battalion; and this was done.

By 1978, only one member of the 1st Battalion was left in the parade, eighty-eight-year-old William Walker, whose home was at

* *The Old Brigade* by Frederic Edward Weatherly (1848–1929).

Gatley, on the Cheshire side of Manchester. He lived for two more years, but that was his last Gallipoli Sunday. John Grimshaw VC also died in 1980, but he hadn't been well enough to attend since 1971. A page of history was turned, the most renowned part of the continuity had come to an end. There was still a gallant rearguard of Territorials, though, and these now took precedence in the special pews at the church service, and afterwards when marching past the saluting base. In 1981 they were slightly outnumbered by the civic leaders who turned out, but by 1984 they had recovered somewhat and five of them were there, led by George Horridge, the only remaining officer who had served with the Lancashire Fusiliers at Gallipoli. That same year saw the appearance of Bobby, an Indian black buck with corkscrew horns, mascot of the Royal Regiment of Fusiliers, who was flanked by two corporals in full dress, each holding a tether firmly in both hands. This gave the parade a touch of the exotic it had not known before, something extra to delight all the animal-lovers in the crowd, a thoughtful move by the military.

Two more anniversaries passed with the men of Gallipoli still holding their own but ageing visibly, slowing down a bit more each year. In 1987 there were only four of them, and for the first time Major Horridge did not march past. He was now confined to a wheelchair, as Lord Derby had been, and after the service this was positioned on the saluting base beside the Mayor and the General taking the salute. But it was the sagging figure in a heavy blue overcoat, wearing his regimental tie, who held the attention of bystanders as the ceremony began. After the music struck up and as his three comrades from those long-ago days began to step off, he raised a gloved hand to his head, and took off his hat to them. As they drew level with the dais they seemed to stiffen slightly, to draw themselves more nearly upright again; but it was quite impossible to tell whether they were doing so out of good manners to the visiting brasshat, or from some deeper loyalty and respect for one of their own. George Horridge never appeared in public again. He died just before Christmas at the age of ninety-three.

Gallipoli Sunday in 1988 held a double significance: not only was it the anniversary of the Landing, but it took place in the tercentenary of the Lancashire Fusiliers. This was celebrated with quite remarkable persistence throughout the county, considering that the regiment had not, in fact, survived for three hundred years.

There were dances and Rugby matches and concerts and parties and reunions and dinners in a dozen towns, spread across nine months. There was even a cocktail party in the Tower of London, which had become the Regimental Headquarters of the Royal Regiment of Fusiliers. Most of the events, however, took place in and around the old depot town. Bury was where they again hailed Minden Day and Inkerman Day with all the enthusiasm of the past, where the Royal Regiment exercised the privilege that the town had first given its predecessors there, of marching in full panoply, as if going ostentatiously to war. At Gallipoli Sunday a medley of dignitaries was on show, including seven Mayors, two High Sheriffs, a Lord Lieutenant, two Members of Parliament and the Australian Consul in Manchester. The survivors of 1915 were now down to three, all of them ninety-one years old. They had served together in the Dardanelles with the 1st/7th Battalion, and two of them, George Cooke and George Peake, came from Manchester way. The other was the fellow who had never in his life known such a fuss as was being made of him in his extreme old age; Bob Spencer, the only Bury man who had been to Gallipoli and was still alive.

Two years later he was the last of these Lancashire Fusiliers to be on parade. Gallipoli Sunday 1990 was another signal moment in the saga, being the 75th anniversary of that first and resounding April 25. Two thousand miles away at the Dardanelles, there occurred during that week a great acknowledgement of what had happened there, with the Prime Ministers of Turkey, Great Britain, Australia and New Zealand attending memorial events on the peninsula, together with a number of Anzac and other veterans, and the usual turnout of their military heirs. In Bury, the civic leaders again mustered in force and the soldiers acknowledged that this was an extra-special occasion by extending the route of their marching to a couple more streets than usual. There was a great tribal display of bowler hats by ex-officers of the Lancashire Fusiliers dressed in mufti, and Gallipoli Sunday had become virtually the only time in any year when this archaic form of headgear was to be seen in the town. Among the watching crowds were a number of people, darker than most, wearing the skullcap of Muslim orthodoxy or the shalwar kameez appropriate to Islamic modesty, who studied the convolutions of the marching men with a solemn and completely undemonstrative curiosity. The Army had reinforced the solitary hero of the hour by discovering a man whose credentials were almost as good as his. This was Benny Adams, who had been at Gallipoli not as a Fusilier but as a private in the Manchester Regiment, a boy who had faked his age when he joined up and celebrated his fifteenth birthday on the peninsula.

These two, then, awaited the order to march a good fifty yards ahead of anyone else in the parade, but with a couple of young soldiers standing close by just in case either of the veterans faltered and needed a helping hand. The big drum boomed thrice and the instruments of brass launched into "The boys of the old brigade". Two thin and bespectacled figures stepped forth, the younger of them quite briskly, ninety years old though he was, as the crowds filling the Market Place and the adjacent streets began to cheer, and the din grew, and people produced cameras to record this moment in the local history for citizens of Bury yet unborn. Bob Spencer moved more gingerly than his companion, prodding the ground with a thick stick as he walked, and the Fusilier beside him looked as if at any minute he was going to do what a concerned grandson might do in such circumstances; take the old man by the arm. But he held off and Bob Spencer made it all the way past the saluting base without aid; whereupon he and Mr Adams fell out and took a breather in the chairs that were awaiting them. The music changed to the "Grenadiers", then switched again to the "Minden March", and now it was the turn of merely ageing men with grey hair to swing past to the thump of the tunes, veterans of Dunkirk and Monte Cassino, of Medjez-al-Bab, and the infested jungle between Mogaung and Imphal. Then came the ranks of khaki, with the red and white hackles in their caps, bayonets gleaming from the rifles on their shoulders at the slope; and God alone knew what campaign medals they might be wearing before they were through, or even how many of them would survive their Army time to become nonagenarians in some annual parade. After them marched even younger things in uniform, children still, whose horizons and ambitions should have been limitless, but who probably did not even contemplate the second half of the twenty-first century, which most of them had a right to believe they could reach with only moderate luck.

Earlier, before that day began, someone had put it to the Rector of Bury that Gallipoli Sunday would have lost its point when no one who was there in 1915 was left alive. The priest replied: "If there are no survivors left there will always be something to remember. I am proud to remember them as long as the regiment wants us to. The Gunpowder Plot was even longer ago, but we still remember that." On being asked the same question, Major John Hallam, officer in charge of the Lancashire rearguard at what was left of the old Wellington Barracks, pointed out that although Gallipoli remained the focal point of the Sunday bearing its name, the service that day had become a memorial to all Fusiliers who had fallen in battle. He added: "We shall certainly continue as long as we are able."

There is no question of ignoring the ghosts of 1915 at Gallipoli itself, where they are almost tangible. And you can see, the moment you reach Cape Helles, where the Lancashire Landing cemetery is, just why Churchill thought it necessary to fight for the Dardanelles, and why the Turks did not dare let it go. Control those straits and you command all traffic between three seas and beyond. Today there is not a moment in any day or night when at least one vessel is not within sight of the memorials that stand sentinel at the Aegean end. Ceaselessly the tankers and the container ships, the dull grey warships and the rusty tramps, follow each other in procession towards Istanbul or to Odessa or Batum; or, having come out of the Black Sea and down the Bosphorus, across the Sea of Marmara and through these straits, they sail out into the Aegean, which is rarely an end in itself, but a means of reaching the Mediterranean and Gibraltar and the great wide world that comes after it. Like the Bosphorus, this narrow length of blue water is not only a thoroughfare of priceless worth to the merchant and the strategist; it is also a boundary between the West and the East, a place where different cultures might merge or always eye each other uneasily, with Europe on the northern side and Asia Minor facing it. The shores of the Dardanelles were fated to know the tramp of armies from the beginning of time; occasionally, as when Agamemnon marched on Troy, and again in 1915, to echo to the sound of their agonies.

The peninsula running down the European side is now one of the most peaceful places on earth: everyone who goes to Gallipoli remarks on its profound silences. In summer only breezes off the sea and the sweetness of birdsong can be heard at the southern end, where cornfields ripen everywhere in the heat of Cape Helles, and clusters of fruit hang drowsily in the olive groves. The stillness is even greater up the outer edge of the peninsula, where nothing stirs in the gullies and on the ridges above Anzac, where no fields of grain seethe gently in bowing to the wind. The silence of Gallipoli is so powerful that it intimidates some visitors. Young Australians, boisterously loud elsewhere, speak in low voices here, deeply conscious that they are exploring, as was promised them from birth, a national shrine. The occasional hum of their battered transit vans only points up the primeval quietness that descends on the coves and the sandy defiles and the bush-covered slopes the moment they are gone. The silence is most powerful of all in the cemeteries, where the ghosts defy intruders to disturb their long possession of this ground.

The Allied cemeteries are superficially much alike, apart from the one occupied by the French on a slope above the Dardanelles, where every grave is marked by a large iron cross made from the stakes of barbed-wire entanglements, each tip fashioned into the shape of a fleur-de-lys. The Commonwealth commissioners have gone in for masonry, with a small sandstone slab tilted a few inches above each grave, separated by plants and low shrubs and Judas trees.* Without exception they are immaculate, usually within a surrounding wall, though this is not always obvious. Beach Cemetery, just south of Anzac, seems to slip from its grassy bank straight into the sea. Most of the British are buried at the end of the peninsula, though the great obelisk which counterpoints the Cape Helles lighthouse half a mile away, marks the memorial to 20,763 men who have no known graves. Their names – from all the old imperial lands – are inscribed on marble panels inset in the walls which form the sides of this Helles Memorial to the Missing. The most numerous names are those of Lancashire Fusiliers. After that, men of the Manchester Regiment.

Within sight of that obelisk is the Lancashire Landing Cemetery, on the eastern slope of Hill 114, where Sergeant Stubbs was killed. It lies beside a gravel track, with corn growing on the other three sides, and it is only a few hundred yards from the top of the gully that Captain Willis and his men climbed to get at the Turks who were sweeping W Beach below with their fire. Even today, the Turkish Army is encamped on those heights, keeping an eye open

---

* *Cercis siliquastrum* is commonly found in the cemeteries of the Near East. Its popular name in English stems from the belief that Judas hanged himself from this tree in his remorse at having betrayed Christ.

for uninvited persons who might approach this coast, especially uninvited Greeks. The guards do not trouble visitors to the cemetery, so long as these do not stray beyond it, to the gully and the beach. What the visitor sees of the Lancashire Landing place, therefore, beyond the field of corn, is high ground covered with a belt of scrub, the top of a sandhill which drops steeply to the sea. Some shelter is afforded the cemetery by tamarisks and evergreen oaks, but these do not grow thickly enough to obscure the view for miles across the countryside to the long incline of Achi Baba, and out to sea, where the shipping trudges to and fro. Inside the cemetery, the purple seed pods of the Judas trees rub together drily when a branch barely stirs, and low bushes of rosemary make the air fragrant between the tilted stone slabs. There are row after row of these, not all belonging to men of the 1st Battalion of the Fusiliers, though enough of them are; quite enough. Among them is the tablet for one of The Six. "1809 Lance Serjt W. S. Kenealy vc. Lancashire Fusiliers. 29 June 1915. Age 29" is what it says, *
then follows the line "Lord Have Mercy on His Soul RIP". A few of the slabs have no superscription other than that identifying the soldier; but where the masons did add something in memoriam it is almost always something familiar, like that chosen for Keneally, or "Greater Love Hath No Man", or another conventional phrase from the Christian necrology.

Where New Zealanders lie, at Hill 60, at Lone Pine, at Chunuk Bair, and especially amid the manukas that were sent from Wellington to be planted around the National Memorial on the crest of Conkbayiri, there is a curious absence of sentiment. These are all lofty places, for most New Zealanders died at Gallipoli when assaulting the ridges and other high ground and were buried where they lay, instead of being brought lower, like many Australians and Englishmen. At Chunuk Bair, where the dead lay so thickly in one trench that another had to be dug, you can see the Dardanelles miles away in one direction, the Aegean directly below in another, and distantly to the north-east the white pan of the salt lake just inside Suvla Bay. The majority of New Zealanders are remembered *en masse*, like the soldiers whose names are carved on the Helles

---

* Apart from misspelling the name, this also gets the rank wrong. The mason's instructions may have confused Private Keneally with Lance-Serjeant Stubbs, the VC who has no known grave on Gallipoli.

memorial. But where individual stone tablets are set into the ground, they invariably give information and nothing more – "12/136 Private P. E. Tonkin. NZ Otago Regt. 7 August 1915 Age 22." That is typical of the men who came "From the Uttermost Ends of the Earth", a line inscribed on the column which honours the unknown dead at Chunuk Bair. It is the nearest thing to an expression of feeling about their tragedy that the New Zealanders seem to have allowed themselves.

The Australian graves are the most moving of all in their unaffected eloquence, which neither the British nor the New Zealanders approach. This is true of all their cemeteries; at Beach and Ari Burnu, which are both close to the sea; on Plugge's Plateau, from which the ghosts overlook the cove where the Anzacs landed on April 25; in Shrapnel Valley, where the dead lie in orderly lines amid a clearing cut out of the bush; and in any of the other places where Diggers were buried on the peninsula. Here is the grave of Trooper E. W. Lowndes, of the 3rd Australian Light Horse, who was thirty when he was killed on May 23. "Well done Ted" it says on his stone. Here is Private W. Turton, 9th Battalion Australian Infantry, twenty-four years old, died on May 20: "The Best of Lads None Better May He Rest in Peace." Here is Private J. J. R. Carroll, 6th Battalion Australian Infantry, died on August 7 when he was twenty-five: "My Jim Gave His Life For Freedom. Loved & Remembered By His Dad." The grave of Private G. R. Grimwade catches the eye in Shrapnel Valley because something has been propped alongside the normal tablet marking it. The tablet records Grimwade's rank, name and number, the fact that he was in the Australian Army Medical Corps when he was killed on September 23 and only twenty years old; and there follow the words "Dearly Beloved Second Son of Mr and Mrs Norton Grimwade, Melbourne." Leaning against the back of this white tablet is a darker piece of masonry, irregularly shaped. It, too, bears an inscription, but one carved by another hand: "This stone from the home of George R. Grimwade, Melbourne, Australia, was brought and placed here in ever loving remembrance by his parents, April 1922." Everywhere you look in the Australian cemeteries are the marks made by broken-hearted people reaching out from ten thousand miles away.

Not far from where Jim Carroll lies – at a distance a good outfielder might just manage to throw a cricket ball – is the most remarkable inscription of all on Gallipoli. Standing prominently

above the sea in that rippling coastline, on a ledge at the northern
end of Anzac Cove, is a memorial which the Turks have erected,
a heavy piece of masonry, an abstract sculpture that is supposed to
represent hands held open, in the Islamic manner, at prayer. On it
is something that Kemal Ataturk said in 1934, not so very long
after he had thrown the invading armies off his land:

> THOSE HEROES THAT SHED THEIR BLOOD
> AND LOST THEIR LIVES . . .
> YOU ARE NOW LYING IN THE SOIL OF A FRIENDLY COUNTRY.
> THEREFORE REST IN PEACE.
> THERE IS NO DIFFERENCE BETWEEN THE JOHNNIES
> AND THE MEHMETS TO US, WHERE THEY LIE SIDE BY SIDE
> HERE IN THIS COUNTRY OF OURS . . .
> YOU, THE MOTHERS
> WHO SENT THEIR SONS FROM FAR AWAY COUNTRIES,
> WIPE AWAY YOUR TEARS.
> YOUR SONS ARE NOW LYING IN OUR BOSOM
> AND ARE IN PEACE.
> AFTER HAVING LOST THEIR LIVES IN THIS LAND THEY HAVE
> BECOME OUR SONS AS WELL.

The sun sets each evening behind Imbroz and Samothrace, far out
to sea, its last rays warming that inscription with their light just
above the Aegean shore. Next morning the sun will rise once more
over Troy, on the other side of the Dardanelles, and the cycle of
renewal will begin again, always including this peninsula and its
well-remembered dead; and this monument to a generosity in the
human spirit that can and must transcend the obscenity of war.

# Select Bibliography

Ashmore, O. *The Industrial Archaeology of Lancashire*. Manchester, 1969

Aspin, C. *Lancashire; the first industrial society*. Helmshore, 1969

Aspinall-Oglander, C. F. *Official History of the Great War; Military Operations, Gallipoli*. 2 vols, London, 1929, 1932

Bagley, J. J. *A History of Lancashire*. Chichester, 1982

Barnett, Correlli. *Britain and Her Army 1509–1970*. London, 1970

Barrett, Helen. *Bury As It Was*. Nelson, 1976

Barton, B. T. *History of the Borough of Bury and Neighbourhood*. Bury, 1874

Bean, C. E. W. *Gallipoli Correspondent; the Frontline Diaries of*. Edited by Kevin Fewster, Sydney, 1983

Beckett, Ian F. W. and Simpson, Keith. *A Nation in Arms*. Manchester, 1985

Birdwood, Field-Marshal Lord. *Khaki and Gown*. London, 1941

Blythe, Ronald. *Akenfield*. London, 1972

Bond, Brian. *War and Society in Europe 1870–1970*. Leicester, 1983

Bush, Eric. *Bless Our Ship*. London, 1958

*Gallipoli*. London, 1975

Butterworth, J. *An Historical and Topographical Description of the Town and Parish of Bury in the County of Lancaster*. Bury, 1829

Campbell, Fred. *Bury's Two Rivers*. Swinton, 1988

*Five Till Nine*. Bury, 1984

*The Staff of Life*. Swinton, 1987

Churchill, Randolph. *Lord Derby, King of Lancashire*. London, 1959

Dangerfield, George. *The Damnable Question*. Boston, 1976

*Dardanelles Commission: Two Reports, a Supplement and Appendices*. London, 1917, 1919

Dawson, R. M. *Winston Churchill at the Admiralty*. Oxford, 1940

# Select Bibliography

Denham, H. M. *Dardanelles: A Midshipman's Diary*. London, 1981

Farnie, D. A. *The English Cotton Industry and the World Market 1815–1896*. Oxford, 1979

Foote, Shelby. *The Civil War; a narrative*. New York, 1958

Forster, E. M. *Abinger Harvest*. London, 1936

Fussell, Paul. *The Great War and Modern Memory*. Oxford, 1975

Garratt, S. R. and others. *Customs and Practices of XX The Lancashire Fusiliers*. Bury, 1962

Gibbon, Frederick P. *The 42nd (East Lancashire) Division 1914–1918*. London, 1920

Gray, Margaret. *The History of Bury, Lancashire, from 1660 to 1876*. Bury, 1970

Halley, R. *Lancashire—its Puritanism and Nonconformity*. Manchester, 1869

Hallows, Ian S. *Regiments and Corps of the British Army*. London, 1991

Hamilton, Sir Ian. *Gallipoli Despatches*. London, 1915 and 1916 *Gallipoli Diary*. 2 vols, London, 1920

Harnetty, Peter. *Imperialism and Free Trade; Lancashire and India in the mid-nineteenth century*. Vancouver, 1972

Henderson, William O. *The Lancashire Cotton Famine 1861–1865*. Manchester, 1934

Higgins, Trumbull. *Winston Churchill and the Dardanelles*. London, 1964

Hopwood, E. *A History of the Lancashire Cotton Industry and the Amalgamated Weavers' Association*. Manchester, 1969

Howe, A. C. *The Cotton Masters*. Oxford, 1984

Jordan, W. K. *The Social Institutions of Lancashire*. Manchester, 1962

Keegan, John. *The Face of Battle*. London, 1976

Kemal, Mustafa. *Diaries and Gallipoli Memories*. Translated typescript at Imperial War Museum, London

Laffin, John. *Damn the Dardanelles! The Story of Gallipoli*. London, 1980

Latter, J. C. *The History of the Lancashire Fusiliers 1914–1918*. 2 vols, Aldershot, 1949

Lewis, Bernard. *The Emergence of Modern Turkey*. London, 1968

Liddle, Peter H. *Gallipoli 1915*. London, 1985 *Men of Gallipoli*. London, 1976

Longmate, Norman. *The Hungry Mills; the story of the Lancashire cotton famine 1861–65*. London, 1978

Mackenzie, Compton. *Gallipoli Memories*. London, 1929

McPherson, Bimbashi. *A Life in Egypt*. London, 1983

Masefield, John. *Gallipoli*. London, 1916

Mills, David. *The Place Names of Lancashire*. London, 1976
Millward, R. *Lancashire and the History of the Landscape*. Manchester, 1955
Moorehead, Alan. *Gallipoli*. London, 1956
Nicholls, W. *History and Traditions of Radcliffe*. Bury, 1920
Orr, Philip. *The Road to the Somme*. Belfast, 1987
Pakenham, Thomas. *The Boer War*. London, 1982
Pevsner, Nikolaus. *The Buildings of England; South Lancashire*. London, 1969
Pugsley, Christopher. *Gallipoli; the New Zealand Story*. Auckland, 1984
Ray, Cyril. *Regiment of the Line*. London, 1963
Rhodes James, Robert. *Gallipoli*. London, 1984
Robertson, John. *Anzac and Empire*. London, 1990
Salvesen, Paul. *The People's Monuments*. Manchester, 1987
Sandberg, L. G. *Lancashire in Decline*. Columbus, Ohio, 1974
Scott, R. D. H. *The Biggest Room in the World; a short history of the Manchester Royal Exchange*. Manchester, 1973
Shadbolt, Maurice. *Voices of Gallipoli*. Auckland, 1988
Simkins, Peter. *Kitchener's Army; the raising of the new armies of 1914–16*. Manchester, 1988
Smyth, B. *A History of the Lancashire Fusiliers*. 2 vols, Dublin, 1903
Smyth, Sir John. *The Story of the Victoria Cross*. London, 1963
Steel, Nigel. *The Battlefields of Gallipoli, now and then*. London, 1990
Sunderland, Frank. *Bury a Century Ago*. Blackpool, 1990
Swallow, Charles. *The Sick Man of Europe; Ottoman Empire to Turkish Republic 1789–1923*. London, 1973
Swinson, Arthur H. *A Register of the regiments and corps of the British Army*. London, 1972
Taylor, Phil and Cupper, Pam. *Gallipoli; a Battlefield Guide*. Kenthurst, NSW, 1989
Terraine, John. *Impacts of War*. London, 1970
Tippett, L. H. C. *A Portrait of the Lancashire Textile Industry*. Manchester, 1969
Tuchman, Barbara W. *August 1914*. London, 1980
*Victoria County History, Lancashire Volume 5: Bolton, Bury, Oldham, Rochdale*. London, 1910
Walton, John K. *Lancashire; a Social History 1558–1939*. Manchester, 1987
Ward, Geoffrey C. *The Civil War*. London and New York, 1991

# Acknowledgements

The book could not have been written without help from a great number of people, including many survivors of Gallipoli and their relatives, who talked to me about their experiences during the Great War and after. My tape-recorded conversations with Major G. B. Horridge, Mr Bob Spencer and Mrs Alice Mitchell were particularly valuable, as will be obvious from my text. I'm also deeply in debt to Major John McQ. Hallam, Regimental Secretary (Lancashire), Royal Regiment of Fusiliers, for making the archives of the Lancashire Fusiliers available to me, and for other unstinting assistance over the years of my research. Without the cheerful help over a long period of Rita Hirst and her colleagues in the Bury Reference Library there would have been no book; and I'm also grateful for the material willingly provided by Janet Allan from the resources of the Portico Library in Manchester. Others I have to thank include Christopher Dowling and Nigel Steel of the Imperial War Museum, Brigadier P. D. Johnson of the Officers' Association, Bill Allen and Roy Bolton of the *Bury Times*, John Terraine, Canon R. B. McFadden, Mrs E. Smith and Mrs B. Knott, David Swithenbank, Frank Sunderland, Jim Roberts, Bill Westall, T. Fleming, J. P. Barlow, W. Greenhalgh, Dr Michael Pegg, George Franki and M. E. Occleshaw.

# Sources

# Sources

23 cotton figures, Walton, p. 198; Bagley, p. 87

23 "Sir; I am living in the centre", Scott, p. 32

26 "A beautiful queen", *BT*, October 1, 1924

26 footnote; origin of Bury's name, Mills, pp. 43, 69

27 "After that, what happened", Walton, p. 311

31 "My commission is at your Highness's . . .", Ray, p. 24

32 "I never thought to see", *ibid.*, p. 37

32 "So unexpected was our entry", B. Smyth, Vol. I, p. 325

33 Kinglake quotation, Ray, p. 79

36 "one of the worst", *ibid.*, p. 98

37 "on the right of ", Garratt, p. 29

38 Size of Territorial Force, Beckett/Simpson, p. 130

39 1900 recruiting figures, LFA Nominal Roll, 1881–1902

## 2 "The Natives Here Are Very Funny"

43 Ulster arms from Hamburg, Dangerfield, p. 111

43 footnote; "possessed of a genial", Latter, Vol. I, p. 5

44 "the rule of England", *BT*, July 25, 1914

44 "another sad day", *BT*, July 29, 1914

44 Michael Davitt, Salvesen, p. 53

44 Billeting parties to Limerick, Latter, Vol. I, p. 7

45 "A week ago", *BT*, August 1, 1914

46 19,000 looms, *BT*, Sept. 14, 1914

46 "of slightly foreign", *BT*, Sept. 9, 1914

47 25,000 OTC, *The Times History of the Great War*, Vol. I (London 1919), p. 132

47 Bury OTC in camp, *BT*, August 1 and 8, 1914

48 "4,000 khaki-clad warriors", *BT*, June 10, 1914

49 "not necessarily . . . Army pattern", *BT*, August 5, 1914

49 "The general feeling", *BT*, August 8, 1914

50 "When not engaged in drilling", *BT*, August 29, 1914

51 Sarah Scowcroft, AM tapes

51 George Horridge, GH tapes

52 "Wake up Bury", *BT*, Sept. 5, 1914

53 Origins of 2nd line battalions, Latter, Vol. I, Chapter 8

53 Bob Spencer and Billy Schofield, BS tapes

54 Entraining 42nd Div. in Bury, *BT*, Sept. 12, 1914

56 "Homeland, homeland", GH tapes

57 "It's like a palace", *BT*, October 17, 1914

57 "We try and talk to the Indians", *ibid.*

57 "The people are mostly coloured", *BT*, October 24, 1914

58 "The natives here are very funny", *BT*, October 17, 1914

58 "An expert swindler", *BT*, April 3, 1915

59 Corporal Evans, GH tapes

59 "The men looked at each other", Latter, Vol. I, p. 47

59 "All the boys are looking", *BT*, April 24, 1915

## 3 Lancashire Landing

60 "Nature was so peaceful", Rhodes James, p. 95

62 order of the day, Latter, Vol. I, p. 49

63 "Not a sign of life", Rhodes James, p. 117

63 "About 100 yards", *ibid.*

64 "I got up to my waist", Rhodes James, p. 118

65 "One hundred corpses", *ibid.*, p. 119

65 1st Battalion figures, Latter, Vol. I, p. 46 and p. 55

65 Footnote figures, Rhodes James, p. 119

66 "Confidently expecting", *ibid.*, p. 141
66 "It was difficult to select", McPherson, p. 139
66 6,000 Turks, 20,000 British, Rhodes James, p. 138
66 Krithia casualties, *ibid.*, p. 141
67 "All the lads seem", *BT*, June 2, 1915
68 "We landed here last Wednesday", *BT*, June 5, 1915
69 "For quite an hour", Rhodes James, p. 159
70 Corporal Evans, GH tapes
70 Privates Scotson, *BT*, June 26, 1915
70 Tennant brothers, *BT*, June 5, 1915
71 Horridge's experience, GH tapes
72 Billy Schofield's death, BS tapes
73 Eighty per cent with dysentery, Rhodes James, p. 222
73 "It is impossible to describe", *ibid.*, p. 263
73 Fusilier casualties, Latter, Vol. I, pp. 69, 76
74 "splashed their way ashore", *ibid.*, p. 72
75 1st/5th casualties, GH tapes
76 Private Dawber's song, GH tapes
76 "I have been three weeks in hospital", *BT*, July 31, 1915
77 Drowned and frozen Fusiliers, Latter, Vol. I, p. 80
78 "I hope *they* won't hear", Birdwood, p. 288
79 Fusilier casualties, Latter, Vol. II, p. 181

## 4 Profit, Suicide, Jealousy

83 Flour price rise, *BT*, August 5, 1914
84 Dayfield Body-Shield, *BT*, March 11, 1916
84 "Come now ye sons", *BT*, August 15, 1914
85 "To some of our most eminent", *BT*, October 17, 1914
85 League of Honour, *BT*, April 28, 1915
86 Captain Stonestreet's poster etc., *BT*, May 22, 1915, June 2, 1915
86 Private Sales's death, *BT*, June 5, 1915
87 7,000 Bury men to war, *BT*, May 1, 1915
87 St Mark's parish recruits, *BT*, October 17, 1914
87 "Are we to do it all?", *BT*, November 11, 1914
87 First news of Gallipoli, *BT*, April 28, 1915
87 "The news . . . is good", *BT*, May 1, 1915
88 "our casualties are heavy", *BT*, May 5, 1915
88 "Many baseless rumours", *BT*, May 19, 1915
89 "he died a soldier's death", *BT*, April 3, 1915
89 "I have the sad news", *BT*, July 3, 1915
90 "I am awfully sorry", *BT*, July 10, 1915
90 First Local Heroes, *BT*, May 22, 1915
91 Obituary verses, *BT*, July 10, 1915
92 "two buglers in attendance", *BT*, July 21, 1915
93 "it was one of those sad", *BT*, August 18, 1917
94 footnotes; 264 shot for desertion, Hansard, March 20, 1930
94 Amelia Hallam's trial, *BT*, June 13, 1917
95 "Perhaps the query I am asking", *BT*, April 24, 1915
96 "The Shirker's Soliloquy", *BT*, July 17, 1915
96 miners strike, *BT*, July 3, 1918
96 tribunals, *BT*, March 11, 1916 and Sept. 16, 1916
99 millgirls prosecuted, *BT*, Dec. 8, 1917

# Sources

117 Stone through Mayor's window, *ibid.*

118 three gaoled, *BT*, March 29, 1922

118 William Townsend, *BT*, January 15, 1919

118 Stephen Johnson, *BT*, August 20, 1919

118 Albert Hoyle, *BT*, November 15, 1919

118 James Wrigley, *BT*, November 24, 1920

119 Norman Howarth, *BT*, February 17, 1917

119 Bob Spencer, BS tapes

120 Will Hoyle, personal knowledge

121 Charles Ainsworth taking Stonestreet's place, GH tapes

121 1918 election campaign, *BT*, December 1918, *passim*

122 Prince of Wales, *BT*, July 4, 9, 1921

## 6  Six VCs Before Breakfast

124 Testimonials to 1st Battalion, Latter, Vol. I, pp. 52/53

125 Gallipoli decorations, Latter, Vol. II, pp. 7–88, *passim*

125 Great War VCs and footnote, Latter, Vol. II, p. 6

126 First investiture, Sir J. Smyth, pp. 41/42

126 VCs at Rorke's Drift, *ibid.*, 123/124

127 Interview with Willis, *BT*, August 28, 1915

128 "I saw him stand up", *BT*, April 24, 1965

128 "Drawn by S. Begg", *Illustrated London News*, September 4, 1915

128 Willis presented with original picture, Lancs Fusiliers *Annual 1914–15*

129 Regimental historian's assurance, Ray, p. 135

129 Hunter-Weston directive, Latter, Vol. II, p. 2

130 Major Bishop's nomination, *ibid.*

130 Lieutenant Nightingale, Steel, p. 39

130 Hunter-Weston endorsement, PRO, WO/32/4994

130 Hamilton endorsement, *ibid.*

130 Robb rebuttal, PRO, WO/32/4995

131 13th clause, PRO, WO/32/4995

131 Hunter-Weston, July 14, 1915, *ibid.*

131 Wolley-Dod, July 25, 1915, *ibid.*

132 "gross injustice", Latter, Vol. II, p. 2

132 Footnote on Grimshaw's DCM, Steel, p. 39

133 Renaming W Beach, Latter, Vol. I, p. 53

133 Prince's speech, *BT*, November 13, 1929

134 Grimshaw, IWM, G65 (VC Box 22)

134 Keneally, IWM, K11 (VC Box 28)

134 Richards, IWM, R20 (VC Box 39)

134 Stubbs, IWM, S92 (VC Box 44)

134 Bromley, IWM, B87 (VC Box 6)

134 Willis, IWM, W63 (VC Box 49)

135 Bromley's address, Latter, Vol. I, p. 67

136 Grimshaw's coolness, *ibid.*, p. 52

136 Willis's sons emigrate, *BT*, February 19, 1966

136 Willis's grants from funds, LFCF, case number 14195

137 Willis advertisement for £100, *Daily Telegraph*, February 11, 1966

137 Question in House, Oral Answers, November 14, 1957 (Hansard, Vol. 577, p. 1142)

137 Willis at Palace, Sir J. Smyth, p. 472

137 "I am so nearly blind", IWM, W63 (VC Box 49): letter to Canon W. M. Lummiss

138 Peachment's VC, *BT*,

|   | November 20/December 1, 1915, August 11, 1956 |   | November 5, 1938 |
|---|---|---|---|
| 138 | Hutchinson's homecoming, *BT*, September 13/16, 1916, December 6/13/16, 1916 | 153 | dangers of conscription, *BT*, May 3, 1939 |
| 140 | The forbidden medal, Dr John Laffin, *Independent*, April 25, 1990 | 154 | "memories are subtle things", *BT*, April 27, 1938 |
|   |   | 155 | "an atmosphere ... at variance", *BT*, November 11, 1925 |

## 7 Church Militant

| 141 | 1851 census figures, Walton, p. 184 |
|---|---|
| 145 | Sermon at outbreak, *BT*, August 14, 1914 |
| 146 | Hill on Sir Galahad, *BT*, August 19, 1914 |
| 146 | on St George, *BT*, April 28, 1915 |
| 146 | "we must provide MORE MEN", *BT*, November 7, 1914 |
| 147 | "I know the Fusiliers", *BT*, December 9, 1914 |
| 147 | Charles Hill missing, *BT*, April 29, 1916 |
| 147 | Mrs Hill grieves alone, personal knowledge |
| 147 | "But, men of Lancashire", *BT*, May 10, 1916 |
| 149 | "right and fitting", *BT*, April 29, 1925 |
| 149 | "The scars it has made", *BT*, November 13, 1918 |
| 149 | "what of our own dear land", *BT*, November 20, 1918 |
| 150 | Dardanelles report buried, *BT*, November 19, 1919 |
| 150 | "I felt something of pain", *BT*, May 1, 1920 |
| 151 | £2,000 for new Rector, *BT*, August 2, 1930 |
| 151 | "No one, unless he is a fool", *BT*, April 29, 1931 |
| 152 | "some who, mistakenly", *BT*, April 20, 1932 |
| 152 | "We cannot separate", *BT*, May 1, 1935 |
| 153 | "All these emblems and memorials", *BT*, May 1, 1940 |
| 153 | "unsanctified patriotism", *BT*, July 22, 1942 |
| 153 | "Is it really worth while", *BT*, |

## 8 King of Lancashire

| 160 | George V as bully, Churchill, p. 159 |
|---|---|
| 162 | Derby's income, *ibid.*, p. 95 |
| 163 | His Bury estate, *BT*, May 30, 1925, February 7, 1948 |
| 163 | "To the people of Bury", *BT*, May 30, 1925 |
| 164 | brass band to Knowsley, *BT*, April 16, 1924 |
| 164 | Freeman of Bury, *BT*, September 11, 1926 |
| 165 | raised five battalions, *Dictionary of National Biography* |
| 165 | "I have two sons", Churchill, p. 184 |
| 165 | Knowsley staff, *ibid.*, p. 104 |
| 166 | "I receive applications", *BT*, June 30, 1915 |
| 166 | Joe Tinker, Beckett/Simpson, p. 17 |
| 167 | recruiting "murdered", Churchill, p. 186 |
| 167 | Bury demonstration, *BT*, October 6, 1915 |
| 169 | "most efficient recruiting sergeant", Churchill, p. 187 |
| 170 | "to prove to Labour", *ibid.*, p. 191 |
| 171 | "I would do anything", *ibid.*, p. 212 |
| 172 | "I quite agree with you", LRO, 920 DER (17) 26/1 |
| 172 | "With Your Majesty's permission", Churchill, p. 215 |
| 172 | £200 for POW relatives, *BT*, September 6, 1916 |
| 173 | cigarettes for Old Comrades, *BT*, February 25, 1933 |
| 173 | Derby and Hornby cousins, LRO, 920 DER (17) 15 |

173 "members of a great regiment", *BT*, April 27, 1938
174 granddaughter's call-up, Churchill, p. 614
174 enfeebled at Mayor's Parlour, LRO, 920 DER (17) 15
175 tears at Gallipoli Sunday, personal knowledge

## 8 In Spite of Myth

179 80,000 poppies, *BT*, November 13, 1926
180 Derby subscription to memorial, *BT*, July 18, 1923
180 Fusiliers memorial, *BT*, April 26, 1922
181 "a surcharged minute", *BT*, April 29, 1922
182 Grammar School tablet, *BT*, May 7, 1924
182 Howlett's sermon, *BT*, May 10, 1919
188 Marseillaise at prizegiving, *BT*, December 22, 1915
183 "the British soldier is largely", *BT*, October 6, 1915
183 "Old members of the OTC", *BT*, October 28, 1916
185 Founder's Day march, personal knowledge
186 torchlight tattoo, *BT*, November 1, 1919
186 Old Comrades formed, *BT*, March 1, 1919
187 twenty-eight meetings in first year, *BT*, August 4, 1920
187 552 members, *BT*, February 29, 1928
187 Old Contemptibles formed, *BT*, February 2, 1935
188 "spirit of comradeship", *BT*, August 13, 1921
188 "that marvellous fight at Messines", *BT*, August 4, 1920
189 recruiting advertisement, *BT*, January 24, 1920
190 Terriers 6,079 short, *BT*, February 9, 1921

190 "no antagonism", *BT*, February 5, 1921
190 comparative strengths, *BT*, March 9, 1921
192 "if we could have parades", *BT*, March 26, 1930
192 Recruiting Week, *BT*, May 7, 1930
193 soldiers' felonies, *BT*, May 10, 1930
193 Mayor's confession, *BT*, November 29, 1930
194 "if he were a young man", *BT*, February 25, 1933
194 dole figures, *BT*, June 8, 1932
195 Horridge rejoins Territorials, GH tapes
196 Bounty for recruiters, *BT*, April 29, 1933
196 Recruiting figures, *BT*, October 10, 1934, April 11, 1936, October 12, 1938
197 "difficult to understand", *BT*, December 11, 1937
197 "What are the young men doing", *BT*, April 3, 1939
198 Peace Ballot figures, *BT*, December 13, 1934
198 Albert Forrest and Henry
199 Martin, *BT*, April 30, 1938

## 10 "We are quietly disappearing"

202 £18 per person raised, *BT*, March 26, 1941
202 Grammar School casualties, *BT*, February 7, 1951
202 Petch family's nine, *BT*, June 5, 1943
202 Perkins boys, *BT*, August 22, 1942
202 Rector's sons at war, personal knowledge
203 2nd Battalion decorations, *BT*, September 22, 1945
203 1,285 lost in war, Ray, p. 129
204 Hornby sermon, *BT*, May 16, 1945

204 German POWS, *BT*, May 18/
22, 1946

204 Kenyon rebuke, *BT*, June 1,
1946

204 Freedom to Fusiliers, *BT*,
March 3, 1945, August 7,
1946

205 old soldier avoids prison, *BT*,
May 17, 1950

206 "There was a grand spirit", *BT*,
April 8, 1950

206 Biggest cadet musters, *BT*,
May 22, 1954, November 9,
1955

207 "doesn't have to think", *BT*,
June 2, 1962

210 families with cars, *BT*,
September 2, 1967

210 first Labour MP, *BT*, October
17, 1964

210 swastikas daubed, *BT*, January
6, 1960

210 "I love drugs", *BT*, November
11, 1970

211 Yugoslav murder, *BT*,
November 11, 1950

211 Muslims seek mosque, *BT*,
July 8, 1967

213 "shattered by . . . barbarian
voices", *BT*, April 1, 1972

214 "carry on the proud traditions",
*BT*, March 18, 1988

214 Brigadier Bamford, *BT*, May 7,
1958

215 still to recruit in Lancashire,
*BT*, September 24, 1960

215 the last recruits, *BT*,
November 6, 1960

216 "quietly disappearing", *BT*,
April 5, 1967

## 11 A Distant Trumpet

218 "In these days the British
soldier", *BT*, April 30, 1974

220 the Stubbs VC, LFA
Regimental Council
minutes, RC/3/2

220 Alice Mitchell, AM tapes

221 Bob Spencer, BS tapes

222 George Horridge, GH tapes

224 Gallipoli Association, *The
Gallipolian* No. 60 (autumn
1988)

225 "sixty-seven glorious years
later", *BT*, April 30, 1982

226 "This epic display", *BT*, May 1,
1987

228 "glad to see you", *BT*, August
21, 1957

229 precedence of Gallipoli men,
GH tapes

231 Adams and Spencer, *BT*, April
27, 1990

231 the future of Gallipoli Sunday,
*BT*, April 20, 1990

233 most numerous names on
Helles memorial, Taylor/
Cupper p. 103

# Index

# Index